Human Rights in the Community

Rights as Agents for Change

Edited by
COLIN HARVEY
Queen's University Belfast

·HART·
PUBLISHING

OXFORD AND PORTLAND, OREGON
2005

The British Institute of
HUMAN RiGHTS

Hart Publishing
Oxford and Portland, Oregon

Published in North America (US and Canada) by
Hart Publishing c/o
International Specialized Book Services
5804 NE Hassalo Street
Portland, Oregon
97213-3644
USA

Hart Publishing is a specialist legal publisher based in Oxford, England.
To order further copies of this book or to request a list of other
publications please write to:

Hart Publishing, Salter's Boatyard, Folly Bridge,
Abingdon Road, Oxford OX1 4LB
Telephone: +44 (0)1865 245533 or Fax: +44 (0)1865 794882
e-mail: mail@hartpub.co.uk
WEBSITE: http//www.hartpub.co.uk

British Library Cataloguing in Publication Data
Data Available
ISBN 1–84113–446–5 (paperback)

Typeset by Hope Services (Abingdon) Ltd.
Printed and bound in Great Britain by
Page Bros Ltd, Norfolk

HUMAN RIGHTS IN THE COMMUNITY

There has been a considerable focus in the last few years on the meaning of the Human Rights Act 1998 and its real and potential impact on judges and lawyers. Much has been written on the implications of the new legislation for a variety of areas of law. With the rising level of case-law the emphasis is now turning to the impact of the legislation on specific areas of social life. In this volume the focus is on the practice of human rights and how they are enforced in reality. There is much discussion in the literature of a 'human rights culture' but how precisely is such a culture to be created, and how do we make sense of human rights? In order to address these questions this volume is in two parts. Part I examines general issues surrounding the full and effective implementation of human rights. Part II explores the implications of human rights standards in particular areas in order to test whether a 'human rights culture' has emerged.

Volume 5 in the series Human Rights Law in Perspective

Human Rights Law in Perspective

General Editor: Colin Harvey

The language of human rights figures prominently in legal and political debates at the national, regional and international levels. In the UK the Human Rights Act 1998 has generated considerable interest in the law of human rights. It will continue to provoke much debate in the legal community and the search for original insights and new materials will intensify.

The aim of this series is to provide a forum for scholarly reflection on all aspects of the law of human rights. The series will encourage work which engages with the theoretical, comparative and international dimensions of human rights law. The primary aim is to publish over time books which offer an insight into human rights law in its contextual setting. The objective is to promote an understanding of the nature and impact of human rights law. The series is inclusive, in the sense that all perspectives in legal scholarship are welcome. It will incorporate the work of new and established scholars.

Human Rights Law in Perspective is not confined to consideration of the UK. It will strive to reflect comparative, regional and international perspectives. Work which focuses on human rights law in other states will therefore be included in this series. The intention is to offer an inclusive intellectual home for significant scholarly contributions to human rights law.

Volume 1 Importing the Law in Post-Communist Transitions
Catherine Dupré

Volume 2 The Development of the Positive Obligations Under the European Convention on Human Rights by the European Court of Human Rights
Alastair Mowbray

Volume 3 Human Rights Brought Home: Socio-Legal Studies of Human Rights in the National Context
Edited by Simon Halliday and Patrick Schmidt

Volume 4 Corporations and Transnational Human Rights Litigation
Sarah Joseph

Contents

Acknowledgements

I would like to thank Candy Whittome, formerly of the British Institute of Human Rights, for her assistance with this project. Without her help it would never have started. Sarah Cooke, the Director of the Institute, provided encouragement from the beginning. Lisa King was, as ever, a constant source of inspiration and support.

List of Contributors

Mohammed Aziz is a commissioner on the Commission for Racial Equality.

Maggie Beirne is Director of the Committee on the Administration of Justice.

Frances Butler is a Visiting Research Fellow with the Institute for Public Policy Research and the Vice-President of the British Institute of Human Rights.

Tessa Harding is Head of Policy at Help the Aged.

Neville Harris is Professor of Law, Department of Law, University of Manchester.

Colin Harvey is Professor of Human Rights Law, School of Law, Queen's University Belfast and a member of the Advisory Board of the British Institute of Human Rights.

Anna Lawson is a lecturer in the School of Law, University of Leeds.

Christopher McCrudden is Professor of Human Rights Law and Fellow of Lincoln College, University of Oxford.

Camilla Parker is a solicitor and legal member of the Mental Health Act Commission. She was Legal and Parliamentary Officer at Mind and now works as a freelance consultant advising on mental health law and policy.

Sarah Spencer is Director of Policy Research at the Centre on Migration, Policy and Society at the University of Oxford and Deputy Chair of the Commission for Racial Equality.

Carolyne Willow is the National Co-ordinator of the Children's Rights Alliance for England.

Robert Wintemute is Professor of Human Rights Law, School of Law, King's College London.

Table of Cases

CANADA

EUROPEAN COMMISSION OF HUMAN RIGHTS

EUROPEAN COURT OF HUMAN RIGHTS

EUROPEAN COURT OF JUSTICE

SOUTH AFRICA

UNITED KINGDOM

UNITED STATES OF AMERICA

Table of Legislation

Directives

FRANCE

GERMANY

ICELAND

INTERNATIONAL

IRELAND

LUXEMBOURG

NETHERLANDS

NORWAY

SOUTH AFRICA

Statutory Instruments etc

UNITED STATES OF AMERICA

1

Creating a Culture of Respect for Human Rights

COLIN HARVEY

INTRODUCTION

THE IDEA FOR this edited collection evolved from discussions with Sarah Cooke and Candy Whittome of the British Institute of Human Rights on the impact of the Human Rights Act 1998 in practice. This book is intended as a contribution to the ongoing human rights debate in Britain and it reflects the commitment of the Institute to the promotion of a culture of respect for human rights. The objective is to provoke further discussion about how human rights might be more effectively protected in practice, and as a result advance legal and political reform.

The expectations surrounding the UK's new human rights legislation were high and it has generated a considerable amount of comment. It was always likely that the Act would be absorbed more easily than many expected within the existing legal system; not least because of the time spent preparing judges and others for its arrival. The principal concern of government appeared to be with the responsible and cautious practical implementation of the legislation. Some hopes have not been met and it is evident from the available research (from the British Institute of Human Rights and others) that more work is needed to ensure that rights are taken seriously in, for example, public administration. But what does this mean in precise terms? Are we talking about a culture of human rights litigation? Is there a pressing need in Britain for a new commission tasked with human rights protection? How can Parliament contribute? What benchmarks exist to measure progress? The UK Government has answered these questions, making it plain that a culture of human rights does not mean a culture of human rights litigation and that it now wishes to establish a new Commission for Equality and Human Rights. The Joint

Committee on Human Rights at Westminster is also there to assist Parliament in considering the human rights implications of legislation. The emphasis, which is also reflected in a number of contributions to this book, is on making human rights a normal part of political and public policy discussion and ensuring that public administration is aware of existing legal obligations and takes them fully into account at all stages. This approach views government as not only central to guaranteeing respect for rights but also to the positive promotion of human rights. Faith is therefore retained in public administration to rise to the challenge and the ability of Parliament to guarantee reasoned debate and hold the executive to account. This view also offers the possibility of creating regulatory regimes through legislation which will advance the cause of human rights without relying excessively on litigation. The argument might provoke understandable scepticism. Can we really place our trust in majoritarian processes to make the correct decisions on what rights we have? It is, however, simply a fact that many progressive legal measures have been the direct result of determined parliamentary action and not judicial activism. Judges, like politicians, have often been on the wrong side of the human rights argument. This 'mainstreaming' approach does not rule out litigation, it simply views it as a last resort and evidence that other mechanisms have failed.

There are limits to the utility of Parliament and legislation in promoting human rights. Those who make the argument above must, for example, confront the dominance of the executive in the Westminster system and the way that party allegiance distorts parliamentary democracy. Parliament is subject to pressures which can prove difficult to resist. As this collection indicates, some individuals and groups cannot rely exclusively on the legislative process to respect and promote their rights. Minority groups, particularly those which do not command significant political power, will often be forced to resort to litigation to ensure that their voices are heard. This suggests that individuals and groups must be able to rely on a range of political and legal mechanisms and that there must be a shared institutional responsibility for the promotion and protection of rights. It does not mean that litigation should necessarily be at the core of a culture of respect for human rights. It does mean that the legislature, executive and judiciary should all be engaged in the common progressive enterprise of making this cultural change a reality.

MAINSTREAMING HUMAN RIGHTS AND EQUALITY?

Part I of this collection concentrates on the legal and policy debates ongoing over the effective protection of human rights in Britain. The idea of human rights mainstreaming has proven attractive. Christopher McCrudden examines the concept of mainstreaming, explains what it means and argues that it is, in principle, desirable. His support is not unequivocal; he suggests that more discussion is required and that some ways of mainstreaming rights may not work or may be counter-productive. He includes an examination of the existing approaches to equality mainstreaming and how these might, or might not, be usefully applied to human rights. The references to the innovative arrangements in Northern Ireland are instructive, particularly the establishment there of a regulatory regime which does not rely exclusively on litigation. McCrudden's argument is anchored in his careful analysis of what the positive obligations of government are and a sound understanding of the potential and genuine limits of mainstreaming.

As the title of her chapter suggests, Sarah Spencer welcomes the connections now made between equality and human rights and constructs a case for why this is to be applauded. She has argued in support of such a development for some time. Her claim is that the most important factor in bringing the two together is the current strong focus within both agendas on systemic change in public services. She contends that this is integration for a progressive purpose. The specific purpose of this human rights and equality partnership, she suggests, is to deliver tangible outcomes for individuals. Maggie Beirne follows this general theme by stressing the importance of human rights in making a difference in practice. Her emphasis is on socio-economic rights. She believes that the majority of people can understand and relate to these rights precisely because they impact on everyday life. Beirne highlights the development of activism in Northern Ireland and the usefulness of coalitions (the Equality Coalition and the Human Rights Consortium) in bringing a diverse range of individuals and groups together. This contribution suggests that the emergence of a culture of human rights may depend on a strong and vibrant community and voluntary sector with the resources and general capacity to engage effectively with public administration. Beirne presents the case for the universality of human rights and stresses that they should not become hostages to political expediency.

Frances Butler explores further the meaning of 'human rights culture' and is persuaded by the formulation adopted by the Joint Committee on Human Rights. In her opinion the Government intended only minimum compliance by public authorities and was particularly concerned to constrain the legal system. She finds little evidence of the emergence of a human rights culture and demonstrates that serious misunderstandings about human rights remain in circulation. The challenge which she presents is to convince people that human rights belong to majorities as well as minorities.

USING HUMAN RIGHTS

Part II is thematic and concentrates on the effect of the Human Rights Act in particular areas. Neville Harris looks at the impact of the Act on education. One of the problems he notes (which is a general difficulty for any such assessment) is the lack of definitive benchmarks and the open-textured language of the European Convention on Human Rights. He examines human rights challenges on school admissions, discipline and organisation, as well as other matters such as the education rights of asylum applicants. From a purely legal perspective he suggests the impact has not been significant, with the courts generally holding education policy to be compliant with the Human Rights Act. He does, however, note a general culture shift, with the language of rights increasingly referred to in discussions of education policy.

Several contributors believe the Human Rights Act is of important symbolic as well as practical value. Tessa Harding argues that the Human Rights Act challenges ageism and age discrimination by asserting the equal dignity of each person. She discovers no real evidence of the hoped for culture shift. Her chapter provides useful information on the extent and impact of ageism. Anna Lawson argues that traditionally the treatment of disabled people was not viewed as a human rights issue. In the past, discussion of disability was often dominated by medical discourses. She welcomes the human rights focus, as it helps to highlight the significant barriers which prevent disabled people from participating fully in community life. She surveys the current legal position and the implications of Convention rights are explained clearly and fully. She shows that making use of the Human Rights Act is not easy and practical access to rights is particularly problematic in this area. Camilla Parker suggests that the proposed human rights culture is essential in the field of mental health law and policy due to, for example, the use of detention and the widespread prejudice and discrimination which exists. She outlines the key issues, identifies where the problems are and makes suggestions for further reform. Robert Wintemute claims that lesbian, gay and bisexual individuals and transsexual individuals are the two social minorities which have benefited the most from human rights. According to Wintemute they have used human rights law successfully to achieve what is described as dramatic progress in the last decade. He notes that change resulted both from legal challenges and, on some occasions, voluntary reform undertaken by government. He concludes with a clear statement of what remains to be done. Mohammed Aziz reflects on the right to freedom of religion and the right not be discriminated against on the basis of religion. He focuses on the Muslim community in the UK. He examines how a culture of rights might be advanced and notes the challenges which await the proposed Commission for Equality and Human Rights. In the final chapter Carolyne Willow argues that there has been a failure thus far to use the Human Rights Act effectively to protect the rights of children. She acknowledges the many positive developments (often not discussed in terms of 'rights'), but indicates that the concept of children's rights is still not taken sufficiently seriously.

CONCLUSION

This edited collection contains a diverse range of perspectives as well as strong views and arguments on the current state of human rights protection. It includes the work of academics and human rights and equality activists. While differences of emphasis exist, the contributors appear united in the belief that a culture of respect for human rights would be a 'good thing'. They would like to witness its emergence in practice. Those who highlight a lack of progress do so with regret for opportunities lost and view this as a problem to be solved. Positive trends are noted in this collection. However, the overall impression is that there is much more to be done. If the objective is to mainstream human rights, then it has not been achieved thus far.

The arguments presented in this book are surfacing in discussions of the proposed new Commission for Equality and Human Rights (many of the contributors to this collection are also engaged in the debate). Will this new Commission have the structures, functions, powers and resources to assist in the task of creating a meaningful culture of respect for human rights?

Part I: Making Human Rights Count in Practice

2

Mainstreaming Human Rights

CHRISTOPHER McCRUDDEN

INTRODUCTION

T HE ADVENT OF the Human Rights Act 1998 (HRA) has significantly
increased consideration of how best to ensure the effective delivery of
human rights in the UK. In this chapter I examine an additional mechanism, the 'mainstreaming' of human rights in governmental decision-making,
which may help to address some of the limits of existing approaches to human
rights compliance. By 'mainstreaming', I mean the reorganisation, improvement,
development and evaluation of policy processes, so that a human rights perspective is incorporated in all policies at all levels and at all stages, by the actors
normally involved in policymaking.[1] My discussion of the issue reaches the
conclusion that mainstreaming human rights is a desirable policy but
that there is a need for considerably more discussion as to the most effective practical means of achieving this and that some methods that have been suggested
might be counter-productive. I attempt to draw out some of the issues that need
to be considered in adopting mainstreaming. In particular, the applicability to
human rights of existing approaches to equality mainstreaming are examined.

CURRENT DISCUSSION OF HUMAN RIGHTS MAINSTREAMING

The need to mainstream human rights in government decision-making has
been identified as a priority by the United Nations High Commissioner for
Human Rights.[2] It has proven a popular argument in academic and human

---

[1] Drawing on the definition of mainstreaming in Council of Europe, Rapporteur Group on
Equality Between Women and Men, Gender Mainstreaming, GR-EG (98) 1, 26 March 1998, at 6.
[2] UN Office of the High Commissioner for Human Rights, *Mainstreaming Human Rights*, available at http://www.unhchr.ch/development/mainstreaming-01.html (last visited 3 March, 2004).

rights policy circles.[3] Of more relevance for our purposes, it was also identified as a necessary component in the initial implementation of the Human Rights Act in the UK.[4] This led to several initiatives within the British public service before and after the coming into effect of the HRA.[5] These included the establishment of a specialised unit within the Home Office (subsequently, the Lord Chancellor's Department) to oversee the implementation of the Act and to help departments and other public bodies to comply. It led to extensive training of judges. The HRA itself also included a mechanism whereby ministers would be required to identify whether or nor proposed legislation was in compliance with the Act when measures were presented to Parliament. Of particular importance, a Joint Parliamentary Committee on Human Rights was established.

The joint committee has played an important role in challenging the effectiveness of the mechanisms established by the Act and by the Government independently to ensure that a human rights culture is inculcated in British public authorities. It has carried out investigations into the extent to which human rights have been effectively 'mainstreamed'.[6] One of the measures it suggested to address apparent deficiencies in this regard was the establishment of a commission that would have the function, like existing commissions in the field of equality, of promoting compliance with human rights obligations more proactively.[7] The response of the current government has been to accept that 'mainstreaming' should be encouraged, to establish procedures within Whitehall to

---

[3] Cf C J Harvey, 'Review Essay: Gender, Refugee Law And the Politics of Interpretation' (2000) 12 *International Journal of Refugee Law* 680: 'As the human rights movement moves forward in this new century, we all must turn to effective enforcement and implementation of international standards. Mainstreaming human rights norms is the task for this century. Human rights lawyers should engage with other fields of knowledge in order to advance these ends. Human rights law must matter, not simply to individual litigants, but to the vast array of oppressed individuals and groups. Making human rights law matter in a concrete sense requires commitment and practical engagement. Human rights lawyers face the challenge of joining others engaged in connected struggles (those working on participatory models of development, for example) to achieve the practical realisation of the ideals of human rights law.' See also, T Clark and F Crepeau, 'Mainstreaming Refugee Rights: The 1951 Refugee Convention and International Human Rights Law' (1999) 17 *Netherlands Quarterly on Human Rights* 389–90.

[4] I Bynoe and S Spencer, *Mainstreaming Human Rights in Whitehall and Westminster* (London, IPPR, 1999).

[5] For a detailed consideration, see *Human Rights and Public Authorities:* A report prepared for the Joint Committee on Human Rights, researched and written by Jeremy Croft (January 2003), 6th Report, *The Case for a Human Rights Commission* (Report together with Proceedings of the Committee, Appendices, HL 67-II, HC 489-II 19 March 2003).

[6] See, eg, 6th Report, *The Case for a Human Rights Commission* (Report together with Proceedings of the Committee, HL 67-I 19 March 2003), HC 489-I; 2nd Special Report, *Implementation of the Human Rights Act 1998* (Report together with Proceedings of the Committee, HL 66-I, HC 332-I 10 April 2001).

[7] *Ibid.*

take this work forward,[8] and to accept the need for a commission to have a role in human rights promotional activities.[9]

In a report published in 2003, the joint committee had also considered whether it would be appropriate to impose a mainstreaming obligation on public authorities to promote human rights, comparable to the positive duty to promote race equality imposed on public authorities by the Race Relations (Amendment) Act 2000.[10] It had decided that, on the evidence then available to it, it was unlikely to be useful.

In its May 2004 report, however, the committee revisited the issue in the light of new evidence which showed both the limited extent to which public authorities have proactively engaged with human rights in their decision-making processes and the apparent success of the positive duty to promote race equality in improving the quality of decision-making and service delivery. The committee concluded:

> We are now persuaded by the evidence that imposing a 'positive' or 'general' duty on public authorities to promote human rights will be an effective way of advancing this. It would provide a firm statutory foundation for the framework within which the new commission would operate, giving it a very clear role in the articultion of guidance for the implementation of the duty. Requiring public authorities to assess all of their functions and policies for relevance to human rights and equality, and in the light of that assessment to draw up a strategy for placing human rights and equality at the heart of policy making, decision making and service delivery, would be an effective way of achieving the mainstreaming of human rights and equality which will be one of the commission's principal purposes.[10a]

The Government responded to this proposal in July 2004, and announced that it was 'not persuaded that positive statutory duties in relation to human rights, going beyond those contained in the Human Rights Act, are needed.'[10b] The joint committee clearly considers that the issue should be pursued. In August 2004, it noted that the Government's White Paper did not deal with the introduction of a public sector duty relating to human rights, but it recommended that the legislation should do so.[10c] That is the issue I explore in this chapter.

---

[8] Minutes of Evidence taken before the Joint Committee on Human Rights, 'The proposed commission for equality and human rights and the meaning of "public authority" under the Human Rights Act', Monday 8 December 2003, Lord Falconer of Thoroton QC.

[9] White paper, *Fairness for All: A New Commission for Equality and Human Rights*, May 2004, Cm 6185.

[10] Sixth Report, Session 2002–03, *The Case for a Human Rights Commission*, HL Paper 67-I and II, HC 489-I and II.

[10a] *Ibid*, para 32.

[10b] Government Response to Joint Committee on Human Rights, Eleventh Report of Session 2003–04: *Commission for Equality and Human Rights: Structure, Functions and Powers*, Cm 6295 (HMSO, London, 2004) p 3.

[10c] Joint Committee on Human Rights, Sixteenth Report of Session 2003–04: *Commission for Equality and Human Rights: The Government's White Paper*, HL 156; HC 998 (HMSO, London, 2004).

HUMAN RIGHTS AND THE POSITIVE OBLIGATIONS
OF GOVERNMENT

In order to examine this issue, it will be useful, following the typology articulated by Henry Shue, to distinguish three somewhat different obligations on the state that may arise in the human rights context: the duty to *respect* human rights; the duty to *protect* human rights; and the duty to *fulfil* human rights.[11] These obligations may be either legal, or moral, or both. Although often used in the context of discussions of social and economic rights,[12] the typology is as useful in identifying various state human rights obligations generally. The obligation to *respect* human rights requires that states refrain from infringing a human right directly through its own actions. Thus, it would be contrary to this obligation for the state to authorise the torture of individuals by its police or armed forces. The obligation to *protect* social rights places the state under a duty to prevent a right from being infringed by actors other than the state. This obligation requires a state to prohibit others, from torturing or murdering. The obligation on the state to *fulfil* human rights requires states to facilitate access to these rights, or to provide these rights directly through the use of state power.

The HRA itself, and interpretations both in the European Court of Human Rights (ECtHR) and in the domestic courts, can usefully be discussed using this typology. The obligation under section 6 of the 1998 Act on public authorities is an example of the duty on the state itself to *respect* human rights. Section 6 makes it unlawful for a public authority to act in a manner that is incompatible with the rights contained in the European Convention on Human Rights (ECHR). Public authorities are required to ensure that their own actions are in compliance with these rights.

However, it is clear that the obligations on public authorities under the HRA go beyond this limited obligation. Although not specifically incorporated in the HRA, Article 1 of the Convention binds the parties to the Convention, in international law, to 'secure to everyone within their jurisdiction' the convention rights. As the joint committee has explained: 'This means that the obligation of states goes beyond mere non-interference with the rights. In some circumstances, they are obliged to take active steps to protect people's rights against interference by others, or to enhance people's capacity to take advantage of the rights.'[13]

The legislation imposes an obligation on the courts to interpret legislation (and common law) so that non-state actors do not infringe human rights. This

---

[11] H Shue, *Basic Rights: Subsistence, Affluence, and US Foreign Policy* (2nd edn, Princeton, Princeton University Press, 1996). International Human Rights texts use similar language. For discussion of these terms by the UN High Commissioner for Human Rights, see http://www.unchr.ch/html/menu6/2/fs21.htm.

[12] C Scott and P Macklem, 'Constitutional Ropes of Sand or Justiciable Guarantees? Social Rights in a New South African Constitution' (1992) 141 *U Pa L Rev* 1.

[13] Para 26, 6th Report.

is seen as an example of the obligation to *protect* human rights, in the sense discussed above, being addressed. For example, the state is obliged to police demonstrations in such a way as to enable individuals to exercise their rights to freedom of expression and association, under Articles 10 and 11 respectively, without being unreasonably restricted by counter-demonstrations.[14] The right not to be intentionally deprived of life, provided in Article 2, has been interpreted as imposing an obligation on the state to protect people against threats in some circumstances and to take reasonable steps to ensure that those responsible can be made legally accountable.[15] In the UK context this obligation is often described as involving the 'horizontal' effect of the HRA.

The obligation on the state to *fulfil* human rights is seen in interpretations of the human rights guarantees that impose positive obligations on the state to actively promote certain rights, such as where a state is under a duty to promote diversity of ownership in the mass media in order to ensure that freedom of expression is actively facilitated.[16] An example also arises under Article 3, which prohibits the subjection of anyone to inhuman or degrading treatment or punishment. This has been interpreted as imposing duties to continue to permit an individual suffering from AIDS to reside in the UK and not be deported to a country that was unable to provide effective medical treatment.[17] Article 8 imposes certain obligations on the state regarding environmental protection.[18]

The institutional mechanisms in and around the HRA may also be usefully seen as addressing these three obligations. Enforcement is largely in the hands of the courts acting on complaints by victims of alleged violations of convention rights. In addition, however, the establishment of pre-legislative scrutiny in the shape of a requirement on the Government to consider the compatibility of proposed legislation with the Act, the role of the Joint Parliamentary Committee on Human Rights itself, and the role envisaged for the proposed equality and human rights commission, will all provide opportunities for government to be challenged, encouraged, and pressured to adopt policies that respect, protect and fulfil human rights. (Although the embarrassing performance of the Northern Ireland Human Rights Commission provides a stark warning that this may not be so.)

MAINSTREAMING AND THE LIMITATIONS OF EXISTING MECHANISMS

Given this plethora of overlapping obligations and institutional mechanisms, what could 'mainstreaming' approaches to human rights bring that might be

---

[14] *Plattform 'Ärzte für das Leben' v Austria* Series A, No 139 Application no 10126/82 (1988) 13 EHRR 204.

[15] *Osman v UK*, 5 BHRC 293, ECtHR (1998); *Z v UK* (2002) 34 EHRR 3.

[16] *Groppera Radio* (1990) 12 EHRR 321.

[17] *D v UK* (1997) 24 EHRR 423.

[18] *Lopez Ostra v Spain* (1994) 20 EHRR 394; *Guerra v Italy* 4 BHRC 63 (1999); *Hatton v UK* (2002) 34 EHRR 1.

useful? In general, the mechanisms currently in place are more successful in preventing direct abuses by the state than in ensuring the promotion and fulfilment of human rights by the state more broadly. In practice, the effect of these existing mechanisms is of considerably less significance in the context of protecting and fulfilling human rights than they are in ensuring that government respect human rights itself. So, although mainstreaming assists in ensuring that the state itself respects human rights, in my view the major added value of mainstreaming in the human rights context should be the better delivery of obligations to protect and fulfil human rights, particularly the latter. In other words, mainstreaming may help reach the obligations that the mechanisms currently in place do not reach successfully.

How, then, does mainstreaming differ from traditional human rights compliance approaches? Mainstreaming concentrates on government proactively taking human rights into account. Mainstreaming approaches are intended to be anticipatory, rather than essentially remedial, to be extensively participatory in the definition of the issue and how it might be addressed, and to be integrated into the activities of those primarily involved in policymaking. It aims to complement existing approaches to compliance, rather than replace them. It emphasises compliance rather than enforcement. It does not see litigation as central to achieving compliance.

ROLE OF MAINSTREAMING AND THE CONTROVERSIAL NATURE OF POSITIVE OBLIGATIONS

The role that mainstreaming may play, therefore, in the future implementation of human rights is partly dependent on the extent to which these promotion and fulfilment obligations are accepted. One major uncertainty involved in the utility of a mainstreaming approach applied to human rights lies in the extent to which these obligations to protect and promote are seen as sufficiently important to require a mechanism particularly suited to ensuring governmental compliance with them. The controversial nature of this triptych of obligations should not be underestimated. Many of the substantive rights adopted internationally and regionally, commonly called socio-economic rights, such as the right to healthcare, the right to an adequate standard of living, the right to housing, that can best be seen as requiring the protecting and promoting obligations, have not been specifically implemented in the UK. The debate over what legal status should be accorded in the proposed European Constitution to the 'solidarity' rights set out in the Charter of Fundamental Rights, and in particular the introduction of a distinction between enforceable rights and programmatic principles, reflects a continuing unease in UK government over such rights.[19]

---

[19] EU Charter of Fundamental Rights. For difference between 'rights' and 'principles', see final report of Working Group II CONV 354/02, para 6, Brussels, 22 October 2002.

In the context of those rights that have already been directly incorporated into UK law, essentially the narrower group of rights under the ECHR, the extent to which courts and public bodies in the UK will interpret the provisions of the HRA as imposing the 'positive' obligations on public bodies to protect and promote remains controversial and has yet to be fully clarified.

Why are the obligations relating to promotion and fulfilment regarded as problematic, even in the context of traditional civil and political rights? At the risk of oversimplification, there are at least three common objections to more extensive 'positive rights' interpretations. The first is philosophical: that human rights are primarily about liberty (particularly freedom from arbitrary or unjustified *state* action), and that a positive rights interpretation confuses this by smuggling in an approach that relies on the state to *intervene* more. The counter argument, that human rights are primarily about equality and distributive justice, and that positive rights are therefore uncontroversial since we expect government to be involved in such distributional issues, or that human rights are essentially about furthering human dignity and that restricting the state's role to one of avoiding harm caused by its own actions is too restrictive, cuts no ice with the libertarians.

A second objection to the positive rights enterprise is more pragmatic: that positive rights potentially have considerable resource implications, if taken seriously. Clearly, the extensive margin of appreciation given by the ECHR to Member States on the issue is intended to allow different approaches to this issue to be developed nationally. But when we come to the national courts, how should judges react to arguments against positive (or indeed negative) rights on the basis that they cost too much, or that the courts are just not the appropriate institutions to engage in these kinds of expenditure decisions?

This brings me to a third objection to the positive rights enterprise: the institutional objection. The gist of this objection is that, leaving aside issues of resources, courts are just not the right places to be making positive rights decisions. My guess, and I take this to be uncontroversial, even trite, is that UK courts will be particularly sensitive to questions of comparative institutional competence and legitimacy in the interpretation of the HRA. To fail to address the institutional consequences of adopting a 'positive rights' approach is, I think, a mistake also. Whatever might be said about the utility of any *theoretical* distinction between positive and negative rights, there are important *institutional* differences in the Court's involvement, in areas such as remedy, fact-finding and representation.

These arguments may or may not be convincing. I do not here seek to address the merits of these arguments. My point, rather, is that to the extent that these arguments against further developing the protecting and promoting obligations are accepted in the UK, the role of a mainstreaming approach is not likely to seem particularly attractive; if there are few extensive positive obligations, whether arising from the future incorporation of more socio-economic rights into domestic law, or from the Charter of Fundamental Rights, or from a broad interpretation of the HRA, then mainstreaming is unlikely to play a novel role.

But that is not the end of the story. So far, I have assumed that mainstreaming is likely to play a significant role only if *prior* agreement has been reached on the reach of positive obligations of the protect and promote type. Mainstreaming may, however, have a function of encouraging sceptics of such obligations to be more welcoming to them. If the sceptics' main source of concern arises from problems in the institutional competence of the courts to handle these obligations, then to the extent that mainstreaming provides a non-judicial mechanism for implementing such rights, the incorporation of these rights may seem less unmanageable. The role of mainstreaming, in this scenario, is to provide a mechanism for a more 'programmatic' approach to the implementing of these positive obligations. Herein lies a possible danger of mainstreaming. In a context where there is a debate about how far to incorporate 'positive obligations' and socio-economic rights more generally, there is a danger that the more programmatic compliance approach that mainstreaming offers may be seen as offering an *alternative* to the more traditional enforcement and recognition of human rights, rather than as an *additional* method of human rights protection. 'Mainstreaming' may become a soft option.

EPISTEMIC COMMUNITIES AND SOME POSSIBLE PROBLEMS WITH MAINSTREAMING

A set of objections to incorporating these positive obligations arising from institutional considerations comes from human rights advocates, rather than government. At this point, it is useful to introduce the concept of the 'epistemic community'.[20] An epistemic community consists of a network of professionals with recognised expertise in this particular domain and an authoritative claim to knowledge within that domain who have a shared set of normative beliefs, shared causal beliefs, shared notions of validity, and a common policy enterprise. The debates about the extent to which human rights should play a central role in government decision-making can be seen to involve a clash of two different epistemic communities: one involving primarily professional administrators, and one involving those primarily with a human rights perspective. The latter often regard including the former in human rights interpretation as dangerous.

A crucial way in which the legal system operates to mediate these competing expectations is through the process of legal interpretation. The inevitably compromised, often ambiguous, usually open-ended nature of the legal texts advancing human rights are the site of debates at the international, regional and national levels over their meaning and implications. Given this, some might see

---

[20]   P Haas, 'Introduction: Epistemic Communities and International Policy Co-ordination' (1992) 46 *International Organization* 1–35.

the involvement of public servants and politicians in the human rights interpretation that mainstreaming involves as problematic from a human rights perspective. The argument runs as follows: the epistemic community that consists
of public administration professionals with a predominant non-human rights
orientation will have a dominant position of interpretation of their functions. To
the extent that human rights values are exogenous to that epistemic community,
but are given to such administrators for their interpretation, such values may be
underestimated in importance in interpretation, or given an interpretation different from what a human rights body would give them. It is, therefore, better
not to try to integrate human rights into government decision-making in the way
that mainstreaming envisages, because the human rights dimension will lose out.
The interpretation of human rights instruments should be concentrated in bodies whose primary function is human rights interpretation, otherwise human
rights will become domesticated, stripped of their radical promise.

We see a similar debate currently taking place in discussions involving the
relationship between human rights and international trade issues.[21] Human
rights professionals perceive a risk of growing 'economisation' of human rights
interpretation and implementation by epistemic communities in the trade area,
and some argue that it is better to stick to tried and tested methods of implementation where interpretation of human rights is in the hands of an epistemic
community of human rights professionals. Is it worth running risks with linking
trade with human rights when there are alternative policy instruments available
with fewer problems? Is there a danger that the different conceptions of human
rights that are in play in the different spheres become homogenised into a 'trade
view' of human rights? We need, I suggest, to consider seriously the implications
of this argument surrounding the 'economisation' of human rights in the
integration of social and economic policy more generally.

MAINSTREAMING AND EQUALITY: AN ANALOGY?

Can an approach to mainstreaming be developed that successfully navigates
these problems? There have long been somewhat similar discussions on the
benefits and problems of mainstreaming in the context of equality and non-
discrimination requirements. Some have argued that human rights considerations be 'mainstreamed' in similar ways to those adopted for equality
mainstreaming. In this context, two rather different models are often examined.
The first is the approach to equality mainstreaming developed in Northern
Ireland, currently the paradigmatic example of equality mainstreaming in the
UK. The second, examined in less detail, is the system of mainstreaming estab-

[21] Ernst-Ulrich Petersmann, 'From "Negative" to "Positive" Integration in the WTO: Time for
"Mainstreaming Human Rights" into WTO Law' (2000) 37 *Common Market Law Review* 1363–82;
P Alston, 'Resisting the Merger and Acquisition of Human Rights by Trade Law: A Reply to
Petersmann' (2002) 13 *European Journal of International Law* 815.

lished under the Race Relations (Amendment) Act 2000. Can these approaches provide any assistance in determining whether, and if so how, mainstreaming might provide a useful additional mechanism for helping government to meet its human rights obligations? How far have these developments addressed the issues discussed above?

Equality and discrimination issues featured significantly in the Belfast (or Good Friday) Agreement.[22] Section 75 of the Northern Ireland Act implemented the Agreement's proposals with regard to a new statutory duty on public bodies. It would be a mistake, then, to see the development of the Northern Ireland equality-mainstreaming model divorced from either constitutional context, which places equality issues high on the political agenda, or the extensive statutory provisions dealing with anti-discrimination and equality, which preceded the Agreement. This distinguishes the equality agenda in Northern Ireland from many other areas of human rights in the rest of the UK, where no equivalent extensive statutory protections existed prior to the HRA. To that extent, mainstreaming human rights more broadly would not be able to rely on the already embedded domestic norms that equality mainstreaming did, nor on the political salience of the issue, thus placing much greater weight on any human rights mainstreaming approach.

That issue aside, we can turn to the details of the Northern Ireland equality mainstreaming approach. Section 75 provides that each 'public authority' is required, in carrying out its functions relating to Northern Ireland, to have 'due regard' to the need to promote equality of opportunity between certain different individuals and groups. The relevant categories between which equality of opportunity is to be promoted are between persons of different religious belief, political opinion, racial group, age, marital status, or sexual orientation; between men and women generally; between persons with a disability and persons without; and between persons with dependants and persons without. This equality duty represents an important shift away from relying on the operation of traditional anti-discrimination law to address structural inequalities. Without prejudice to these obligations, a public authority in Northern Ireland is also, in carrying out its functions, to have regard to the desirability of promoting good relations between persons of different religious belief, political opinion or racial group.

The Race Relations (Amendment) Act 2000 differs from this in several respects. First, the duty applies only to racial and ethnic equality, rather than covering a broad range of grounds. The Act requires that each of a specified list

---

[22] For detailed discussions, see C McCrudden, 'Mainstreaming Equality in the Governance of Northern Ireland' (1999) 22 *Fordham International Law Journal* 1696; C McCrudden, 'Equality' in C Harvey (ed) *Human Rights, Equality and Democratic Renewal in Northern Ireland* (Oxford, Hart Publishing, 2001); C McCrudden, 'Mainstreaming Equality in Northern Ireland 1998–2004: A Review of Issues Concerning the Operation of the Equality Duty in Section 75 of the 'Northern Ireland Act 1998', in E McLaughlin and N Faris, *The Section 75 Equality Duty—An Operational Review* (November 2004), vol 2. See also R D Osborne, 'Progressing the Equality Agenda in Northern Ireland' (2003) 32 *Journal of Social Policy* 339.

of public bodies must, in carrying out its functions, have due regard to the need to eliminate unlawful racial discrimination, and to promote equality of opportunity and good relations between persons of different racial groups.[23] The Secretary of State has made an order that imposes certain specific duties on a more limited group of public bodies and other persons who are also subject to the general duty.[24] The racial equality duty has provided the model for more recent initiatives. The Disability Discrimination Act 2005 includes an equivalent disability equality duty and the Government has committed itself to introduce a statutory gender equality duty.

We shall see that there are significant differences in practice between equality mainstreaming in Northern Ireland and Britain, and between equality mainstreaming and human rights mainstreaming more broadly, that should lead one to be cautious that practice in one area will transfer successfully to another area. One of the major differences relates to the level and type of NGO activity. Another relates to the level of knowledge and understanding among civil society, politicians and the Civil Service about equality and human rights.

DIFFERENT WAYS OF USING THE EQUALITY MAINSTREAMING MODELS

There are different ways of viewing the relevance of the equality mainstreaming models to the human rights mainstreaming debate. A proposal has recently been made, for example, for broadening the Northern Ireland equality duty itself to incorporate a 'socio-economic' ground into the list of protected categories, on the basis that this would have the effect that socio-economic rights of the type discussed above would then need to be taken into account more broadly within government.[25] This is not the place to discuss this issue in detail, but that particular proposal seems to me to be deeply problematic. The existing equality-mainstreaming model has not yet bedded down in the Northern Ireland context, and remains controversial.[26] How far it will be successful is anything but clear, even as regards its current limited scope. For the existing model to be subject to major revision at this time is likely to be severely disruptive, and thus to further delay the implementation of the existing obligations. It is also likely to provide an opportunity for the existing model to be weakened rather than strengthened, and likely to overburden an already intensive process. In this chapter, I will be concerned, then, to discuss the use of the equality mainstreaming models only as a potential model for a new, separate, self-standing human rights mainstreaming initiative.

[23] S 71.

[24] Race Relations Act 1976 (Statutory Duties) Order 2001.

[25] G McKeever and F Ní Aoláin, 'Enforcing Social and Economic Rights at the Domestic Level—A Proposal' [2004] *European Human Rights Law Review* 158.

[26] A recent official review illustrates this: E McLaughlin and N Faris, *The Section 75 Equality Duty—An Operational Review* (November 2004).

PROCESS REQUIREMENTS OF EQUALITY MAINSTREAMING

The novel and detailed provisions for the enforcement of the Northern Ireland equality duty are what marks out the mainstreaming approach as particularly interesting from a human rights viewpoint. In brief, all public authorities are required to submit an equality scheme to the Equality Commission. Where it thinks appropriate, the Commission may request any public authority to make a revised scheme. An equality scheme shows how the public authority proposes to fulfil the duties imposed by section 75 in relation to the relevant functions, and to specify a timetable for measures proposed in the scheme. Before submitting a scheme to the Equality Commission, a public authority must consult, in accordance with any directions given by the Commission, with representatives of persons likely to be affected by the scheme, and with such other persons as may be specified in the directions. An equality scheme is required to state the authority's arrangements for assessing and consulting on the likely impact of policies adopted or proposed to be adopted by the authority on the promotion of equality of opportunity. On receipt of a scheme from a Northern Ireland department or public body, the Commission either approves it or refers it to the Secretary of State. Where the Commission refers a scheme to the Secretary of State, the Commission is required to notify the Northern Ireland Assembly in writing that it has done so and send the Assembly a copy of the scheme. When a scheme is referred to the Secretary of State, he has three options: to approve the scheme, to request the public authority to make a revised scheme, or to make a scheme for the public authority.

A somewhat different approach is taken under racial equality mainstreaming in Britain. In addition to the general duty discussed above, more specific duties are imposed on some public bodies for the purpose of ensuring the better performance of the general duty. The Order imposes on these specified bodies a duty to publish a race equality scheme, that is a scheme showing how it intends to fulfil the general duty and its duties under this Order. The Order imposes on specified educational bodies duties to prepare a statement of its race equality policy, to have arrangements in place for fulfilling duties to assess and monitor the impact of its policies on different racial groups, and to fulfill those duties in accordance with such arrangements. The Order imposes on bodies a duty to have in place arrangements for fulfilling duties to monitor, by reference to racial groups, various aspects of education and employment at educational establishments, and to fulfill those duties in accordance with such arrangements. The Order also imposes on other specified bodies a duty to have in place arrangements for fulfilling duties to monitor, by reference to racial groups, various aspects of employment by those bodies, and to fulfil those duties in accordance with such arrangements. The Secretary of State has approved the Commission for Racial Equality Code of Practice relating to these statutory duties.

ADDRESSING THE MARGINALISATION OF HUMAN RIGHTS

Underlying the Northern Ireland and British attempts at equality mainstreaming is an important perception: that unless special attention is paid to equality in policy making, it will become too easily submerged in the day-to-day concerns of policy makers who do not view that particular policy preference as central to their concerns. The motivation for mainstreaming equality lies not only, therefore, in the perception that anti-discrimination law, positive action initiatives, and even traditional methods of constitutional protection of equality, are limited, but in the perception that questions of equality and non-discrimination may easily become sidelined. Mainstreaming, by definition, attempts to address this problem of sidelining directly, by requiring all government departments to engage directly with equality issues. The need to avoid the marginalisation of human rights thinking is equally pressing, particularly in the context of ensuring state compliance with those positive obligations of protecting and promoting human rights.

IMPACT ASSESSMENT

A particularly important technique has been developed to make this idea of equality mainstreaming effective in Northern Ireland. There is a requirement that 'impact assessments' be carried out as part of the process of considering proposals for legislation or major policy initiatives. (There is somewhat less emphasis in practice on impact assessment under the racial equality mainstreaming model.) Put simply, the idea of an impact assessment involves an attempt to try to assess what the effect of the legislation or policy is, or would be, on particular protected groups, such as women or minorities. Mainstreaming should, thereby, encourage greater resort to evidence-based policy making and greater transparency in decision-making, since it necessitates defining what the impact of policies is at an earlier stage of policy making, more systematically and to a greater extent than is currently usually contemplated. And, to the extent that mainstreaming initiatives can develop criteria for alerting policy makers to potential problems before they happen, it is more likely that a generally reactive approach to problems of inequality can be replaced by pro-active early-warning approaches. Current government policy in many countries in the area of equality has often been criticised as tending to be too reactive to problems that might well have been identifiable before they became problems.

As importantly, impact assessment and the duty to promote equality combine to produce an approach that encourages a more positive approach to equality, rather than the largely negative approach often adopted hitherto. In the equality context, this leads to an examination of how far the public body can and should exercise its discretion in such a way as to advance equality. This involves examining alternative ways of delivering policies, and examining ways of moderating any adverse effects that may occur. This approach of emphasising the effect of policies on the human right in question and what the public body can do about it, rather than one that narrowly concentrates on the direct responsibility of the public authority for any breach of human rights, seems particularly well suited as a method of addressing the two obligations of promoting and protecting human rights.

However, the Northern Ireland experience demonstrates that the use of impact assessment is not unproblematic, even in the context of equality. It is clear that there needs to be greater organisational learning on the part of government, and an end to being seen to constantly 'reinvent the wheel' by periodically asking the same people the same questions. Furthermore, with respect to collecting data there does seem to be a danger of the 'best becoming the enemy of the good.' The purpose of impact assessment is not to engage in a purely academic exercise. The purpose ought to be to produce information on which public policy makers can assess whether there is likely to be an issue or a problem. There needs to be greater recognition that perfect data just does not exist. Policy makers however make decisions all the time on the basis of data that is second best—the same principle must apply in relation to promoting greater equality. Data is relevant only insofar as it is useful in ensuring greater equality; data should not be gathered simply for more and more analysis. An equivalent danger exists if impact assessment becomes incorporated more generally in human rights mainstreaming.

PARTICIPATION

A second important feature of the mainstreaming experience in Northern Ireland, almost entirely absent in the racial equality mainstreaming approach, is the extent to which groups inside and outside the mainstream political process have attempted to use impact assessment as part of a strategy to construct a more participatory approach to public policy debate. In short, groups have used the mainstreaming process to become involved in influencing governmental decision-making. From this perspective, mainstreaming should not only be a technical mechanism of assessment within the bureaucracy, but an approach that encourages the participation of those with an interest. It is true, of course, that good decision-making should require policy makers to seek out the views of those potentially affected by the decisions. Unlike more traditional mechanisms of consultation, however, mainstreaming in Northern Ireland does this by requiring impact assessments of a degree of specificity that establishes a clear agenda for discussion between policy makers and those most affected. We can see, therefore, the interlinked nature of the two crucial features of mainstreaming: impact assessment and participation.

One of the most far-reaching 'by-products' of mainstreaming becomes the development of a crucial link between government and 'civil society'. This development encourages greater participation in decision making by marginal groups, thus lessening the democratic deficit. The requirements in Northern Ireland of extensive consultations throughout equality mainstreaming processes aim to empower individuals collectively to engage with public authorities to address equality issues of relevance to the public authority.

If there is a significant absence of effective NGO activity, mainstreaming of the type envisaged in the Northern Ireland model will not work. Even if there are such NGOs in existence, the involvement of such groups is not unproblematic, since their participation raises issues regarding competence, including their access to information and resources. In principle, however, a major argument in favour of mainstreaming is that it may contribute to increased participatory democracy.

This aspect of the Northern Ireland equality mainstreaming process has, however, stimulated much debate. Three issues have been identified that need to be addressed if mainstreaming along these lines were to be applied in the human rights context more broadly. There is the problem of the ability of those encouraged to participate becoming overwhelmed by the sheer number of consultations that they are drawn into. Indeed some have recently complained of 'consultation fatigue'. Undoubtedly there is a major problem with the form consultation appears to be taking. Better *targeting* of consultation is required. So too is providing funding to those consulted to enable them to participate effectively.

Other ideas that have been suggested, however, appear to miss the point of the consultation envisaged by the legislation. One idea that has been suggested (but that happily seems to be being ruled out of consideration) falls clearly into this category. There has been a school of thought that argues that because government departments are having problems with consultation, there should be some centralised mechanism within government for handling these consultations. There should perhaps be a sort of one-stop shop where the consultation efforts of several different bodies are centralised in another body that acts on their behalf. In this model, the consultation takes place at one remove from the policy makers. In my view, that is a mistaken approach to adopt. The very objective of participation is precisely to engage with those who are directly responsible for dealing with the problem. Transferring consultation away from the decisionmakers to a centralised body that does the consultation on their behalf is a mistake. Mainstreaming is about building relationships between those who are protected, between civil society, politics, politicians, and government. Clearly, relationships will not be developed if there is a centralised body 'doing the participation for you.' Equally the idea of contracting out equality impact assessments to consultants is a mistake. It is precisely the people who are making the decisions on policy that ought to be doing the equality impact assessments, since only they can address effectively issues of defining the policy, assessing its impact, and imagining appropriate mitigating options.

PUBLIC SERVANTS AND MAINSTREAMING: DOES IT WORK?

There are, then, dangers in mainstreaming that the Northern Ireland approach seeks to address. But has it worked in practice, particularly in ensuring that a wider epistemic community is formed that is favourable to human rights thinking, one that avoids handing over human rights interpretation to ill-equipped or hostile public servants? Despite all the arguments for mainstreaming, one should not overlook the fact that building such a requirement into Civil Service decision-making requires considerable cultural change in public bodies. Apart from practical issues of competing priorities and risk aversion, there are the problems of departmental exclusiveness and collective responsibility. Mainstreaming may well cut across the working practices, and even, potentially, the ethos, of the Civil Service bureaucracy.

Clearly public servants are no more homogenous a group than 'consultees' or 'politicians'. In Northern Ireland, there has been significant variation with respect to how the various elements of the public service have engaged with equality mainstreaming. At the risk of generalisation it seems that those working 'at the sharp end', generally at more middle and lower levels within the public service, are often producing the best practice. In relation to the upper echelons of the public service however, and particularly within central government, the picture is generally not a favourable one. Indeed, there seems to be almost distaste for equality mainstreaming within elements of the higher Civil Service, and that distaste clearly needs to be recognised and addressed. This appears to have contributed to a lack of commitment to making the equality provisions of the Northern Ireland Act 1998 work. This aversion to equality mainstreaming is not consistently exhibited, and certainly not all senior civil servants share it, but there appears to be a sufficient dragging of the heels, for the equality agenda to be failing to deliver to the extent that it should.

There are also emerging problems regarding the role of civil society in the mainstreaming process. Clearly, a key priority for these groups is developing the skill of asking the right questions of the right people. That is not necessarily always the case at present. Civil society needs to focus on what is essential. NGOs need to consider more systematically what they think is important for their constituencies and then try to seek ways of using mainstreaming to deliver on those priorities. They have often yet to develop a coherent campaigning strategy around the use of mainstreaming, and develop the necessary technical capacity. Clearly trade unions have a major role to play in capacity building, not least because they have been there for the last 150 years in terms of much of this work. Collective bargaining is not that dissimilar from some of the aspects of consultation and participation that we have been discussing and obviously is one of the earliest forms of participation.

The implications for mainstreaming human rights of this analysis are significant. Mainstreaming requires active, well-resourced and politically savvy civil society actors. And it requires a significant cultural shift within the public service, if human rights mainstreaming is to be successful. The extent to which these developments can be delivered by the type of mainstreaming practised in Northern Ireland remains to be seen. The implications for generalising the Northern Ireland model beyond Northern Ireland and beyond equality need considerable thought, therefore. In particular, given the incomprehension and apathy regarding human rights in much of the public sector, mainstreaming human rights seems even more necessary but also more difficult than mainstreaming equality in Northern Ireland.

LEGAL UNDERPINNINGS WITHOUT LITIGATION?

The Northern Ireland experience of mainstreaming equality suggests the inadequacy of a 'soft law' approach. There needs, therefore, to be some authoritative legal requirement on government to ensure that mainstreaming is consistently applied, according to common standards. For some, however, 'law' equals 'litigation'. But another novel approach to compliance in the Northern Ireland mainstreaming model is the extent to which a regulatory regime has been established that attempts to avoid a concentration on litigation. The approach adopted in the Northern Ireland legislation is not one that, so far, has encouraged litigation before the ordinary courts.

We have seen that the Equality Commission plays an important role in approving equality schemes. The functions of the Commission are broader than that, however. If the Commission receives a complaint of a failure by a public authority to comply with an equality scheme approved by the Commission or made by the Secretary of State, then it is required to investigate the complaint, or to give the complainant reasons for not investigating. If a report recommends action by the public authority concerned and the Commission considers that the action is not taken within a reasonable time, then the Commission may refer the matter to the Secretary of State. The Secretary of State may give directions to the public authority in respect of any matter referred to him or her. Where the Commission refers a matter to the Secretary of State it is required to notify the Assembly in writing that it has done so. Where the Secretary of State gives directions to a public authority, he shall notify the Assembly in writing that he has done so. The remedy for failure to mainstream appropriately is, then, to take action in the political domain, rather than through litigation. Given the potential difficulties identified above in using the courts to implement the positive human rights duties, this is an attractive approach were human rights mainstreaming to be adopted in the form of the Northern Ireland model.

It will be successful in practice, however, only if each element in the compliance structure operates as the legislation envisages. The compliance strategy is, essentially, akin to a three-legged stool. If any one of the legs (civil society, the Secretary of State, the Equality Commission) is broken, then compliance will be less than optimal. Unfortunately, a much stronger approach by the Equality Commission is needed than has so far been forthcoming. There should be more staff working on compliance with mainstreaming than is the case at the moment. There has to be much more mainstreaming of the equality duty and linkage between the different sectors within the Commission itself. When some of the worst kinds of equality impact assessments appear, and the Commission is alerted to the problem, they must have the capacity and the willingness to address the problem by indicating what is not right and what is unacceptable. As with the community and voluntary sector, the Commission also needs to develop an enforcement strategy. A mainstreaming compliance strategy needs to be developed by the Commission. The Commission also needs to more actively publicise good practice.

It remains to be seen, therefore, whether a regulatory structure that essentially eschews litigation will work. A litigation strategy may need to be developed if civil society is to have the capacity to offer a serious threat if there is not adequate progress. Significant advances have, on occasion, been made because trade unions involved have been able to threaten judicial review convincingly. Clearly it would be preferable to have a situation where judicial review is not used; section 75 should be more of a carrot than a stick. On the other hand, we cannot ignore the fact that it was a judicial review that played a major role in shifting mainstreaming from an essentially non-legal to a legal requirement. If we want a situation where there is trust and where judicial review is not resorted to, there has to be real progress. Civil society seems to be on the verge of using judicial review. I hope this will not prove necessary, and that change will be embraced willingly rather than at the end of a court case.

A somewhat different approach is adopted under the race equality mainstreaming model. If the Commission for Racial Equality (CRE) is satisfied that a person has failed to comply with any duty it may serve on that person a compliance notice, which requires the person concerned to comply with the duty concerned and to inform the CRE, of the steps that the person has taken, or is taking, to comply with the duty. The CRE may also require the person concerned to furnish it with such other written information as may be reasonably required by the notice in order to verify that the duty has been complied with. The CRE may apply to a designated county court for an order requiring an authority subject to the statutory duties to furnish any information required by a compliance notice if the person fails to furnish the information to the CRE in accordance with the notice, or the CRE has reasonable cause to believe that the person does not intend to furnish the information. If the CRE considers that a person has not, within three months of the date on which a compliance notice was served on that person, complied with any requirement of the notice for that person to comply with a duty imposed by an order, it may apply to a designated county court for an order requiring the person to comply with the requirement of the notice. The advantages, if any, of this approach over the Northern Ireland approach have yet to be tested.

'FULFILLING' EQUALITY AND THE PROBLEM OF RESOURCES

A final issue involves the question of resources. We saw above that one objection to the positive rights enterprise is that positive rights potentially have considerable resource implications, if taken seriously. So too, the approach taken to equality in Northern Ireland is one that is significantly redistributive. Redistribution is essentially what a good equality mainstreaming process should result in. What this requires is the reallocation of resources to, or the targeting of resources at, those most in need. This is where the need to link mainstreaming and other social spending programmes becomes crucial. Clearly one of the problems with the Northern Ireland model of mainstreaming is that it does not have a budget attached to it. So once a public body discovers adverse effects through impact assessments, or decides that it should exercise its discretion in a different way to further equality of opportunity, it is still left uncertain as to where to secure the resources to address those issues. There should be much more attention paid to how social spending programmes can be linked to equality mainstreaming to provide more resources to tackle the social and economic disadvantages that are revealed by way of impact assessments. The use of mainstreaming in the equality context in Northern Ireland also demonstrates the need to consider seriously how best to address the question of resources, if human rights mainstreaming is to be adopted.

CONCLUSION

'Mainstreaming' human rights is, in many ways, an attractive additional mechanism for ensuring greater compliance with human rights obligations, particularly those requiring the 'protection' and 'promotion' of human rights. The Northern Ireland model of equality mainstreaming addresses several of the problems that mainstreaming might be said to involve. However, there are several as yet unresolved aspects of the operation of the Northern Ireland approach even in the context of equality which mean that adopting the Northern Ireland model beyond Northern Ireland is potentially problematic. In addition, the implications of the differences between mainstreaming equality and mainstreaming human rights generally need more thought. We have seen that there are differences in the level and type of civil society involvement in the two issues, that there are differences in the attitudes of government to the two agendas, and in the institutional arrangements for promoting compliance (the role of equality and human rights commissions). In particular, the somewhat more focused nature of the equality guarantee may enable mainstreaming to be more effective. More thought, then, needs to be given to how best to incorporate the potential benefits of human rights mainstreaming, which are considerable, while avoiding the problems that too quick a resort to adapting existing methods of equality mainstreaming to human rights might lead to. We need to ensure that human rights are advanced, rather than retarded, by mainstreaming.

3

Partner Rediscovered: Human Rights and Equality in the UK

SARAH SPENCER

INTRODUCTION

THERE IS AN irony that it has taken the proposal to establish a single equality commission in Britain, with speculation on its potential role, to provoke a long-needed debate in the UK on the relationship between equality and broader human rights standards. The Government's intention to proceed with a new equality body, while resisting the establishment of a human rights commission, inevitably led to a compromise proposal—now accepted—that the equality body itself be given a broader human rights mandate. A White Paper proposing the establishment of a commission on equality and human rights was published in 2004.[1]

In contrast to common practice abroad, equality and human rights work in Britain has operated in almost entirely separate spheres. Activists and policy makers working on equality or human rights only recently began to think through the implications of bringing together these apparently separate bodies of work. Yet the debate on institutional arrangements could not be put on hold. The intention is to establish the new commission in 2006—as EU-inspired legislation on age discrimination comes into force. So the institutional cart has driven the agenda: but will it nevertheless reach the right destination?

The international and European human rights standards which were agreed after the Second World War embraced equality provisions among broader human rights agreements. Subsequently, race and gender discrimination became the focus of their own UN Conventions (in 1966 and 1979 respectively), as did the rights of national minorities at the Council of Europe (1995). But this

---

[1] Department of Trade and Industry and Department for Constitutional Affairs, *Fairness for All: A New Commission for Equality and Human Rights* (Cm 6185, May 2004).

international dimension had little impact on the development of the UK's own anti-discrimination legislation: on the race discrimination legislation that was first introduced in the 1960s, the sex discrimination and equal pay legislation of the mid-1970s, nor the Disability Discrimination Act in 1995.

In the absence of domestic legislation incorporating broader human rights standards into UK law, legislation and practice to address discrimination in employment, goods and services has developed largely in isolation from related human rights concepts. Meanwhile, the language of human rights has often been associated in the public mind either with extreme practices abroad, or with controversial cases taken against the UK Government under the European Convention on Human Rights (ECHR) and latterly the Human Rights Act 1998 (HRA). Neither image has connected with an equality agenda—particularly one dominated by discrimination not by the state but by employers.

Human rights activists, responding to government agendas on criminal justice, surveillance or censorship issues, have rarely focused on the mainstream equality agenda, while those working on equality had little reason to see human rights language and activism as offering them a constructive way forward. When a colleague and I at the Institute for Public Policy Research first proposed in 1998[2] that a human rights commission be established and that the equality commissions—the Commission for Racial Equality, Equal Opportunities Commission and (then proposed) Disability Rights Commission—be brought within its umbrella, we met resistance even to the notion that equality is a human rights issue, and institutional fears that equality would, within such an institution, be dwarfed by a vast and controversial human rights agenda. In Northern Ireland, the Human Rights Commission secured by the Good Friday Agreement was indeed duly established in 1999 as an entirely separate body from the single Equality Commission.

There has subsequently been a remarkable shift in this debate in Britain in a short space of time. Each of the three equality commissions now insists that any new statutory equality body must have a human rights mandate, a view supported by the network of national organisations working on equality issues, the Equality and Diversity Forum.[3] The Joint Committee on Human Rights in Parliament, meanwhile, said in 2003 that the case for a statutory body on human rights is 'compelling' and that its preferred option was for provision within the body addressing equality issues,[4] in which it was supported by the principal

---

[2] S Spencer and I Bynoe, *A Human Rights Commission: Options for Britain and Northern Ireland* (London, IPPR, 1998).

[3] Equality and Diversity Forum response to *Equality and Diversity: Making it Happen*, February 2003 http://www.equalitydiversityforum.org.uk/publications/SEBResponse0203.doc

[4] Joint Committee on Human Rights, *The Case for a Human Rights Commission* 2002–03 (6th Report, vol 1, HL 67–I, HC 489–I). See also Joint Committee on Human Rights, *Commission for Equality and Human Rights: Structure, Functions and Powers* 2003–04 (11th Report, HL78, HC 536 and the Government Response, Department for Constitutional Affairs, 21 July 2004).

human rights NGOs.[5] Finally, after a flurry of debate within government, it was announced on 30 October 2003 that the new commission will indeed have a human rights mandate. This approach was subsequently confirmed in the White Paper. That this consensus has emerged after decades of separate development, requires explanation. What, beyond political pragmatism, has brought these two agendas together and led, despite continuing reservations in some quarters,[6] to some genuine excitement at the scope for delivering change if equality and human rights are delivered, side by side?

DEVELOPING AGENDAS

The most significant factor has been the simultaneous development in the equality and the human rights agendas towards a broader canvas in which their priorities now overlap. Whereas the gender and race agendas were once dominated (by no means exclusively) by the need to address discrimination in employment—reflected in the permanent places on the Equal Opportunities Commission (EOC) and Commission for Racial Equality (CRE) held by the TUC and CBI—recent years have witnessed greater attention to equality in service provision. The Stephen Lawrence report, highlighting discrimination within criminal justice, focused the spotlight on institutional racism in other parts of the public sector and led to innovative legislation to address it: the Race Relations (Amendment) Act 2000. Not only extending discrimination provisions to parts of the public sector that had previously been excluded, the Act imposed a statutory duty on all public bodies (some 43,000) to take active steps to promote race equality (and good race relations), leading to a step change in focus on key services such as health, housing and education.

The Race Relations (Amendment) Act provided a long awaited catalyst for systemic change within public institutions—in employment and service delivery—addressing not only discrimination, but broader causes of inequality. In so doing it has embedded race equality—at least in theory—within the mainstream of the public service reform agenda, in which a central goal is the delivery of services that meet the needs of a diverse population. For people with disabilities, a majority of whom are not in work, the prevalence of discrimination in goods and services was always going to be significant and has indeed been a priority for the Disability Rights Commission, established in 2000. Public services are equally a major focus for those addressing discrimination against older people. The NHS Framework for Older People initiated a significant

---

[5] Human Rights NGO Forum response to the consultation by the Joint Committee on Human Rights on the Structure, Functions and Powers of a Human Rights Commission, 2003.

[6] The CBI (Confederation of British Industry) and the TUC (Trades Union Congress) have both expressed concern that the inclusion of human rights could lead to a dilution of focus on equality issues. See 'Equality and Diversity: Making it Happen, the CBI response' (February 2003); TUC press release (6 March 2003) http://www.tuc.org.uk/equality/tuc-6343-f0.cfm

programme of action in 2001 intent on 'rooting out age discrimination,' an unprecedented acknowledgement by government of the prevalence of age discrimination within health and social care.[7]

Meanwhile, the introduction of the HRA led to some rethinking of the goals of public policy in relation to human rights standards. The initial objective of incorporation of the ECHR into UK law was 'to bring rights home', to enable individuals to seek remedies in the domestic courts, rather than have to take the long road to Strasbourg. As it was assumed by the Government when the plans were drawn up that the UK largely conforms to ECHR standards, few cases were anticipated. Once lawyers and the press began to speculate on the kinds of cases that might be taken, however (including some absurd and highly controversial examples), the fear grew within government that the Act could prove a litigants' charter. At that point, the Home Secretary, Jack Straw, began to emphasise an alternative rationale for the Act that at once had the potential to be more popular, and to reduce the need for litigation.

HUMAN RIGHTS AS CULTURE CHANGE

Ministers from the Home Office and (then) Lord Chancellor's Department stressed that, while the HRA would indeed provide further remedies for individuals in the domestic courts, the intention was primarily that the Act should have a preventive function, ensuring that the culture within government and public bodies is one which respects people's rights, so that such remedies are rarely necessary. As such, it was not simply a constitutional reform of interest to lawyers and NGOs but part of the public service modernisation agenda.

Thus the Home Office Minister, Lord Williams of Mostyn, QC, said that: 'Every public authority will know that its behaviour, its structures, its conclusions and its executive actions will be subject to this culture.'[8] The Home Secretary stated that:

> The Act points to an ethical bottom line for public authorities. It's what you call a fairness guarantee for the citizen . . . This new bottom line, the fairness guarantee, should help build greater public confidence in our public authorities. And that's a vital part of our strategy for getting more public participation. For building the society we want to see.

With rare exceptions, the rights the Act protects are not absolute and a culture of rights within public bodies was thus not intended to give priority to individual rights above all other considerations. Rather, ministers said that the Act provides a framework in which the rights of the individual, for instance to privacy,

---

[7] Department of Health, *National Service Framework for Older People* (2001). See 'Age Equality in Health and Social Care' in S Fredman and S Spencer (eds), *Age as an Equality Issue: Legal and Policy Perspectives* (Oxford, Hart Publishing, 2003).

[8] Second Reading Human Rights Bill *Hansard* HL, col 1308 (3 November 1997).

can be balanced against the rights of others or of society as a whole, for instance to protection from crime. Learning how to balance rights in this way, using human rights language, was the culture shift which ministers envisaged would take place.

There was a further dimension to the rationale for the Act that the Home Secretary proposed. The intention was not only that the Act should contribute to the public service reform agenda, but that it should influence the culture of wider society:

> Consider the nature of modern British society. It's a society enriched by different cultures and different faiths. It needs a formal shared understanding of what is fundamentally right and fundamentally wrong if it is to work together in unity and confidence. . . . The Human Rights Act provides that formal shared understanding.[9]

This role for human rights was subsequently taken up in a White Paper on migration, *Secure Borders, Safe Haven* (2002) in which Jack Straw's successor as Home Secretary, David Blunkett, stressed the importance of human rights in uniting a diverse society:

> We want British citizenship positively to embrace the diversity of background, culture and faiths that is one of the hallmarks of Britain in the 21st Century. The HRA can be viewed as a key source of values that British citizens should share. The laws, rules and practices which govern our democracy uphold our commitment to the equal worth and dignity of all our citizens.[10]

There was, nevertheless, little sign that this broader rationale for a human rights agenda had been accepted across government. Neither its role in public service modernisation nor in uniting a diverse community were echoed in speeches by ministers running departments responsible for the services, like health and education, in which this shift in culture might have been expected to happen. Even within the terrain of the Home Office, while the human rights agenda was taken up with qualified enthusiasm by some agencies, notably the senior ranks of the police, it was less evident in others, like the prison service.

CASE FOR A HUMAN RIGHTS COMMISSION

It was in part perhaps because there was little buy-in across government for this broader rationale for the HRA that ministers were not convinced that a statutory human rights body was needed. Parliamentarians, however, did make the case for such a body, during the passage of the Human Rights Bill, envisaging a role that later found resonance in the select committee's report.

---

[9] Jack Straw, 'Building on a Human Rights Culture' (address to Civil Service College, 9 December 1999).

[10] *Secure Borders, Safe Haven, Integration with Diversity in Modern Britain* (Cm 5387, 2002) paras 2.2–2.3.

Thus Baroness Amos, then a backbench Labour peer (and former chief executive of the EOC) told the House of Lords:

> We need a body which will raise public awareness, promote good practice, scrutinise legislation, monitor policy developments and their impact, provide independent advice to Parliament and advise those who feel that their rights have been infringed. I am particularly keen to see the promotion of an inclusive human rights culture which builds on the diversity of British society. That would be a key role for any human rights body to play.[11]

And Baroness Shirley Williams, a former Secretary of State for Education stated:

> The great advantage of a Human Rights Commission or Commissioner is that it would make human rights open to the public, it would encourage the public to own human rights in a way that would not be exclusive either to Parliament or to the legal profession but should be the beginning of a real and profound change in the democratic ethos and sense of freedom in this country.
>
>   I (also) believe the training and education of public bodies is just as important as the establishment of case law . . . I fear that, for failure to train them in what the Bill means, we shall see a great deal of litigation that is unnecessary, expensive, slow, tedious and repetitive.[12]

While Lord Woolf, then Master of the Rolls, wrote:

> The most important benefit of a Commission is that it will assist in creating a culture in which human rights are routinely observed without the need for continuous intervention by the courts. Human rights will only be a reality when this is the situation.[13]

The Government neither accepted nor rejected this view, insisting that it would await the report of the Joint Committee on Human Rights (JCHR), which would hold an inquiry on whether a commission was needed. Meanwhile each Whitehall department would take responsibility for ensuring that the public bodies within its sphere of influence were alert to their responsibilities under the Act, and a task force was set up to advise on the content of the guidance and on the implementation strategy.[14]

In practice, Whitehall proved to have neither the capacity, resources nor the political backing to drive through the change in culture that Jack Straw had envisaged. Later, when giving evidence to the JCHR inquiry in April 2002, the then Lord Chancellor, Lord Irvine, was asked whether he thought that public authorities outside Whitehall had injected human rights thinking into their

---

[11] House of Lords, 24 November 1997, prior to Baroness Amos becoming a government minister.

[12] Committee stage Human Rights Bill, HL, 24 November 1997, cols 845 and 844.

[13] Foreword to S Spencer and I Bynoe, *A Human Rights Commission: Options for Britain and Northern Ireland*, above n 2.

[14] The author was a member of the task force which included representatives from NGOs such as Liberty, Justice, and the 1990 Trust, and the Law Society and Bar Council, as well as key agencies including the police and Crown Prosecution Service. It was initially chaired by Home Office minister Lord Williams of Mostyn, QC, subsequently by the minister then responsible for human rights in the House of Commons, Mike O'Brien MP.

service delivery. He replied that he had not sensed any reluctance to embrace human rights but added, 'Really, there is a limit to what the centre can do to encourage such a culture.'[15]

In the time that has passed since the HRA came into force, it is indeed debatable whether a human rights culture has yet begun to shift practice in public bodies, or take hold in the public at large. A survey by District Audit (now within the Audit Commission)[16] found that, contrary to government advice, the majority of local authorities and NHS Trusts had not reviewed their policies and procedures for compliance with the Human Rights Act and 42 per cent of health bodies had not even taken action to raise staff awareness. Few had mainstreamed human rights considerations into decision making, were monitoring compliance on an ongoing basis, nor acted to ensure that contractors providing services for them were taking reasonable steps to comply. Authorities complained of a lack of guidance and 'staff felt that they were operating in a vacuum.' Good practice local authorities, in contrast, had embedded human rights within their 'Best Value' process and existing training programmes and procedures; coupling it, for instance, with training on implementation of the new positive duty to promote race equality.[17]

Research for the British Institute of Human Rights by Jenny Watson, deputy chair of the EOC and a human rights consultant, investigated the impact of the Act on children, disabled people, older people and refugees and asylum seekers.[18] While she found examples of good practice, the Act generally had a low impact on the service received by these groups. There were varying levels of awareness of the Act by service providers and, where awareness was high, it was generally being used to challenge treatment through individual cases rather than to achieve systemic changes in policy and practice. In relation to older people, she records:

> Participants from this sector presented overwhelming evidence that older people are routinely treated with a lack of dignity and respect that would simply not be accepted in relation to other social groups.[19]

Whereas the equality legislation is accepted in the care field as a standard that has to be met, this was not the case with the Human Rights Act. It had not been used as a lever to generate systemic change.

The JCHR, when it reported its conclusions in March 2003, reflected this broader conception of a human rights agenda, arguing that a culture of human rights has two dimensions—institutional and ethical:

---

[15] Joint Committee on Human Rights, *The Case for a Human Rights Commission: Interim Report* 2001–02 (22nd Report, HL 160, HC 1142, Minutes of Evidence at 8, April 2002).

[16] District Audit, *The Human Rights Act, A Bulletin for Public Authorities* (May 2002).

[17] Under the Race Relations (Amendment) Act 2000.

[18] J Watson, *Something for Everyone: the Impact of the Human Rights Act and the need for a Human Rights Commission* (London, British Institute of Human Rights, 2002) supported by Comic Relief.

[19] *Ibid.*

The key to the effective protection of rights lies in creating a culture in public life in which these fundamental principles are seen as central to the design and delivery of policy, legislation and public services. In their decision making and their service delivery central government, local authorities, schools, hospitals, police forces and other organs and agencies of the state should ensure full respect for the rights of all those involved.[20]

Each individual, the committee concluded, should understand that they enjoy certain rights as a matter of right, as an affirmation of their equal dignity and worth, but this understanding should go with a sense of personal responsibility to protect the rights of others, so that we create 'a climate in which such respect becomes an integral part of our dealings with public authorities of the state and with each other.'

In practice, the committee found little awareness of human rights either within public authorities or among the public at large and concluded that a human rights commission was needed to drive the agenda forward. It saw considerable congruence between the work required to promote equality and that required to promote wider human rights, while recognising that the detailed measures needed to address discrimination would not always be appropriate in promoting human rights standards. An integrated human rights and equality commission thus emerged as its preferred option.[21]

VALUABLE COMPLEMENT TO EQUALITY AGENDA

The most significant factor in bringing together the human rights and equality agendas has thus been the stronger focus within both agendas on systemic change within public services. This has included the addition of a new, scarcely yet articulated, interest in human rights as a contributor to the social cohesion agenda.

In practice, those working on equality issues have indeed begun to find human rights law and principles to be valuable in pursuing their objectives, complementing the powers and arguments that they have traditionally used. Thus, the Disability Rights Commission relies on Article 2 ECHR, the right to life, when challenging the withdrawal of medical services; the EOC has cited Article 8, the right to family life, in support of its demand for employment practices which support work–life balance; and the CRE uses the same provision in support of the right of Gypsies and Travellers to have legal sites on which to live.

---

[20] Joint Committee on Human Rights, *The Case for a Human Rights Commission* 6th Report, above n 4, at 5. See also J Croft *Human Rights and Public Authorities*, a report prepared for the Joint Committee and included in vol. II of its report, HL Paper 67-II, HC 489-II.

[21] Joint Committee on Human Rights, *The Case for a Human Rights Commission* 6th Report, above n 4, at 8–9.

The commissions' right to use the HRA is limited to discrimination cases. They have no free-standing power to take a human rights case unless the case also addresses discrimination within the terms of the race relations, sex discrimination or disability discrimination legislation. This is problematic as a case may arise, for instance relating to accommodation for a disabled person, which is a potential breach of Article 8, but in which no discrimination within the terms of the Disability Discrimination Act has occurred. This restriction will be particularly limiting in relation to the new discrimination legislation on age (2006), sexual orientation and religion and belief (December 2003), which only addresses discrimination in employment and occupational training—not in services. An ability to use the HRA to challenge degrading treatment in a residential home for the elderly or denial of religious freedom for Muslims in prison, for instance, would thus be a valuable human rights tool for a new commission to protect the disadvantaged groups for whom it is being established. In relation to these new strands, equality issues such as religious discrimination in education or criminal justice will similarly, by default, have to be litigated in the human rights arena.[22] There is the further advantage that the HRA provides some protection from discrimination on grounds beyond the six strands, and can address several grounds of discrimination together.

There is a significant range of issues affecting disadvantaged groups which fall within a broad human rights canvas but are not strictly discrimination issues, certainly within the terms of existing discrimination law. Domestic violence, for instance, is known to affect one in four women in the UK in their lifetime, yet is beyond the remit of the statutory body that exist to address sex discrimination, the EOC. Bullying in schools may be motivated by racism, religious intolerance or homophobia (in which case it would nevertheless, as education is a service, be outwith the recent regulations on employment discrimination). It may anyway be more effectively addressed in the round as a human rights issue—protection from degrading treatment and the value placed on respecting the dignity of each individual, regardless of ethnicity, gender, disability, sexual orientation, weight or any other characteristic which bullies consider warrant prejudicial treatment.

There is a further reason in principle to complement an equality focus with a human rights framework, and one that translates into a real need on the ground. Discrimination law only provides grounds for action if one person, or group, is being treated less favourably than another, or if the individual is suffering detriment *because of* their race, gender or other characteristic. Where everyone is treated equally badly, there is no discrimination. It is indeed not unknown, when the equality commissions are investigating practices within an institution, for those running the institution to give them the 'bastard' defence: 'we treat everyone like this'. In those circumstances, it is protection from ill treatment per se that is needed, which is what human rights standards provide.

---

[22] S Fredman, 'The Future of Equality in Britain' (Working Paper Series 5, Equal Opportunities Commission, 2002).

Sandra Fredman addresses this point when she explores different concepts of equality—from equal treatment through to equality of opportunity—and argues that each is inadequate unless underpinned by equal respect for the dignity of each individual. Without the dignity principle, equality can be achieved by levelling down to a lower standard of protection so that the treatment is equally bad. Moreover, if we perceive the pursuit of equality not only as being about how people are treated, but as an agenda to achieve positive outcomes, the ultimate goal must be equality of choice, autonomy and dignity.[23] In the words of the Universal Declaration,

> recognition of the inherent dignity and of the equal and inalienable rights of all members of the human family is the foundation of freedom, justice and peace in the world.[24]

DELIVERY IN PRACTICE

What might this mean in practice within a single commission and, more important, in those institutions where there is the greatest need to promote human rights and equality standards? The extent of the new commission's mandate has not yet been agreed, but a broad outline of functions is proposed in the White Paper. Within the public sector, we can anticipate that respect for human rights would be promoted by the commission alongside its statutory duty to promote racial equality and, in time, the duty to promote broader equality standards. (The Government is extending the duty to promote equality to disability and gender, but no such commitment in relation to the new 'strands'—age, religion and belief and sexual orientation.) Effective implementation of human rights standards by public bodies could then be monitored by the existing audit and inspection bodies such as the Audit Commission and Ofsted, as the race equality duty is now. This monitoring role is particularly important in the absence of any explicit statutory duty on public bodies to mainstream human rights standards into their work.

It will be important that the commission's mandate also allows it to include human rights standards within its powers to conduct inquiries and then to make recommendations on how to enhance protection, whether to government or the body concerned. That mandate should equally cover the private sector. Although the HRA currently only has limited scope within that sector (because of the case law restricting the definition of 'public functions'), the fact remains that many institutions responsible for vulnerable people, from residential homes to penal establishments, are run by the private sector and would benefit from guidance on human rights standards, even if not enforceable in law.

---

[23] S Fredman, 'The Age of Equality' in S Fredman and S Spencer (eds), *Age as an Equality Issue: Legal and Policy Perspectives* (Oxford, Hart Publishing, 2003); and in S Spencer and S Fredman, *Age Equality Comes of Age: Delivering Change for Older People* (London, IPPR, 2003).

[24] Preamble to the United Nations Universal Declaration of Human Rights, 1948.

Similarly, for the public at large, the drive to raise awareness and acceptance of equality and broader human rights principles could be holistic—emphasising the common principles of fairness, dignity and proportionality; or focusing on the specifics of different equality or human rights issues where appropriate.

The Government has been wary of establishing a statutory human rights body that could challenge its human rights record with more authority than the frequent existing challenges by NGOs. It has therefore excluded the possibility of the new commission being able to take freely standing human rights cases, or indeed any kind of enforcement role. Human rights NGOs, understanding that *real politik*, have not insisted on such a role. NGOs will themselves continue to be able to take cases and the HRA itself provides the legal teeth behind the commission's good practice, partnership approach. But there will remain concern that individuals, without the support of a statutory body, may be unable to take meritorious cases. The Government is nevertheless unlikely to change its mind to allow representation on human rights cases that have no equality dimension. The commission will, as the existing commissions can now, be able to address the human rights issues that arise in a discrimination case and a key question is whether the commission will be able to pursue the case if the discrimination element in the litigation proves unsustainable.

STRATEGIC FOCUS

The proposal to bring all of the equality issues together within one commission, even before the inclusion of human rights, has raised concerns among each strand that 'their' issue could be marginalised in the new body. The Government has been at pains to stress that the commission will not be staffed with generalists but need expertise on each issue, including human rights. The benefits of addressing equality issues in the round will indeed not outweigh the permanent need to address the specifics of each equality dimension—there are aspects of disability, for instance, that are qualitatively different from addressing the discrimination faced by ethnic minorities or that experienced by gays and lesbians—and the skill within the new commission and for employers and service providers will be in securing the right balance between a holistic equality and human rights agenda and addressing the specificities of each separate issue.

The fear that bringing together the equality issues will result in one or more of the strands being marginalised by the others has been the central obstacle to be overcome in moving towards a single equality commission. That fear is exacerbated in relation to human rights by a concern that some human rights issues are not only far removed from the traditional equality agendas but inherently controversial and, in challenging the state in high profile cases, confrontational. Many of those in the equality world who see the benefits of working on human rights and equality issues side by side nevertheless wanted to find a way to curtail the human rights mandate to ensure that, within a new commission, human rights complements but does not eclipse their agenda.

In part this is a question of mandate, in part of structure and governance. The mandate could be curtailed, as we have seen, by a restriction on taking free-standing human rights cases; by requiring any investigation to be triggered by an equality issue; or limiting the human rights mandate solely to promotion. That path, however, would perpetuate the current difficulty in relation to cases in which the evidence of discrimination has been successfully challenged, leaving only the human rights point to be pursued. It could also result in legal uncertainty and challenge, as establishing whether there was an equality 'trigger' might not always be clear cut.

An alternative approach, if the intention were to ensure that human rights does not dominate the body, could be to provide that those appointed to run the body are predominantly drawn from an equality background, and secondly that human rights is mainstreamed into the work of the organisation (its legal, research and policy departments for instance) rather than established as a separate directorate. However, those concerned to see a statutory body that can effectively challenge the state on controversial human rights issues may argue for a stronger and more distinct human rights presence within the body.

A third consideration is the governance arrangements. Should the new commission fall under the Department of Trade and Industry, which currently has lead responsibility for the single commission project, and may be well placed to ensure a strong focus on employment, under another department which already has an equality focus (like the Home Office, currently responsible for race) or the Department for Constitutional Affairs, which has the lead on human rights but currently little experience on equality issues? Should the commission have a stronger relationship of accountability to Parliament than the current commissions, perhaps to the JCHR, to a select committee on equality (as exists in the Scottish Parliament), or a revamped Joint Human Rights and Equality Committee? Finally, should the statute require a stronger relationship with external stakeholders and, if so, to whom should that be? The answer to those questions would, with the mandate of the body and its internal structure, determine the balance in its work between human rights and equality issues.

CONFLICTING RIGHTS

Some fear that inclusion of human rights would bring within the body a tension between certain human rights principles and equality issues: between free speech, for instance, and the right of ethnic minorities to be protected from incitement to racial hatred. This is not grounds to exclude human rights, for three reasons. First, human rights are not (with rare exceptions like freedom from torture), absolute. The human rights agreements like the ECHR anticipated the need to balance the rights of individuals and communities, and allow rights to be restricted if necessary and proportional—hence the UK's legislation to make incitement to racial hatred unlawful is perfectly compatible with the protection for free speech in the HRA.

Disagreements over where the balance between rights should lie will certainly arise; but this is equally so between the equality strands themselves, for instance between the right of gays and lesbians to be free from discrimination and that of religious minorities to be able to refuse to employ someone whose sexuality they consider incompatible with their beliefs. Far from being unhelpful in these circumstances, setting those differences within a human rights framework would be essential. Human rights both set a minimum standard of protection which cannot in any circumstances be trumped by the rights of others, while above that level allowing restrictions on rights where the restriction is necessary and proportional to protect the rights of others.[25]

CONCLUSION

The resolution of these issues should rest on the tangible outcomes which can be achieved for individual members of the public: can we deliver better outcomes if human rights and equality standards are promoted and protected side by side, or if the current separation is perpetuated? Looking at the public sector, where the broader reform agenda has put services under enormous pressure, neither human rights nor equality standards will be mainstreamed into the planning process unless there is both significant leadership and public measurement of progress in practice. NGOs have an invaluable role to play in pressing for change and supporting individuals. But the chance of securing progress must be far greater if organisations are receiving a consistent joined up message from one, statutory, agency—with the additional authority and resources it would command—and not separate messages from a range of agencies urging different action plans to differing time scales. For individuals, it must be preferable if the commission can advise and represent on all dimensions of their case.

For the public at large, fairness and respect for the dignity of each individual will be a more powerful message than a disjointed promotion of what may appear sectional interests. The goal is a society in which each individual is treated fairly and with respect by the state, their employer, parent, spouse and others in positions of power—regardless of who they are. A single Commission on Equality and Human Rights could—with the right powers, resources, and governance arrangements—be a powerful driver to take us there.

---

[25] Discussed in S Fredman, *The Future of Equality in Britain*, above n 22.

4

Social and Economic Rights as Agents for Change

MAGGIE BEIRNE

INTRODUCTION

HUMAN RIGHTS DISCOURSE is a relatively recent phenomenon in Britain. This seems in large part to be due to the fact that, until the entry into force of the Human Rights Act (HRA) in 2000,[1] the issue of human rights was seen as an international rather than a domestic issue. While incorporation of the European Convention on Human Rights (ECHR) into domestic law has changed, and will continue to change this situation dramatically, it has also posed new challenges. There is a considerable risk that, at least in the minds of the general public, rights will be seen as limited to those rights enshrined in the HRA, rather than the whole range of other regional and international human rights treaties to which the UK is a party.[2]

Incorporation of the ECHR into domestic law was however, in some senses, merely a legal technicality, to ensure that individuals could seek redress for an abuse of their rights in the domestic courts. Their fundamental rights were in no way changed or even improved—simply their potential to seek an effective remedy. While the securing of a domestic remedy should in no way be underestimated, it is vital to recognise that the breadth of rights that ought to be enjoyed by UK citizens, by virtue of the UK's international commitments, goes

---

[1] The Human Rights Act 1998 gives 'further effect' to the European Convention on Human Rights in the domestic law of the United Kingdom.

[2] Eg, the rights laid down in the International Covenant on Civil and Political Rights, the International Covenant on Economic, Social and Cultural Rights, the International Convention on the Elimination of All Forms of Discrimination Against Women, the International Convention of the Elimination of All Forms of Racial Discrimination, the Convention on the Rights of the Child, the Convention Against Torture, and regional instruments such as the Council of Europe's Revised Social Charter and many others.

beyond those guaranteed in the HRA. The particular challenge posed in Britain in the wake of the passage of the HRA, given its focus on civil and political rights, is that relatively little is still known of the whole world of economic, social and cultural rights.

This chapter will argue that all rights are interdependent and indivisible, but that it is economic, social and cultural rights that touch the vast majority of people's lives, and therefore that, if taken fully on board in British political culture, the promotion of socio-economic rights could bring about a revolutionary attitude to human rights generally. The chapter will also argue that while all rights offer the potential to act as agents for change, social and economic rights have a particular role in this regard. In making this case, the chapter will draw extensively on the experience of Northern Ireland, where the symbiotic relationship between civil, political, economic, social and cultural rights has long been a recognised feature of political life.[3]

RIGHTS AS AGENTS FOR CHANGE

Rights can never be 'given'. Rights inhere in us by virtue of our very humanity, so slaves in ancient Rome, Jews under the Nazis, and women under the Taliban, all possessed rights, even if those rights were abused egregiously. Part of the modern debate about rights has been an exploration of how to ensure that these rights, deriving from our very humanity, are more respected than they have been in previous generations. The consensus has been that improvements must be made in two complementary domains. First, those holding power[4] must accept that there are limits to their power, and that one of the most important limitations imposed on them is the requirement to uphold the human rights of all those over whom they exercise power. Secondly, human beings must be agents of their own change in this process, for it is only in asserting rights that change is effected both on the governors and the governed.

Successful efforts to secure human rights effect changes in the power relationships within society, and vice versa. In Europe, we can be grateful to the struggles of the ancient Greeks and Romans in beginning to give meaning to concepts of democracy, the rights of citizenship, and the risk posed by absolute power. In Britain, the early assertion of rights in the form of the Magna Carta (albeit the rights of the aristocracy in relation to the king) secured fundamental

---

[3] The key demands of the 1960s civil rights struggles related to jobs, housing and votes, see B Purdie, *Politics in the Streets: The Origins of the Civil Rights Movement in Northern Ireland* (Belfast, Blackstaff Press, 1990).

[4] For the purpose of this discussion, states are considered as the main holders of power, and it is states' use and abuse of power that has been the main focus of political struggles. There is however a lively current debate about the extent to which the obligation to uphold and respect human rights extends in the twenty-first century beyond states to multinational companies, international financial institutions, and others. See A Clapham, *Human Rights in the Private Sphere* (Oxford, Clarendon Press, 1993).

protections such as habeas corpus that are still enjoyed today. A few hundred years later, the English Bill of Rights of 1689, followed thereafter by the American and French revolutionary struggles, dramatically changed society's power relationships, and imposed certain duties on those in authority to respect basic civil and political liberties. Of course, this growing consciousness of human rights was both slow and far from universal—slaves, women in general, and many others throughout the generations were denied their human dignity. Nevertheless, important gains have been made and assertions of, for example, one's right to freedom of association (with others of the same religion, same labour union, same political belief), which were previously the site of divisive and difficult power struggles, are now deeply entrenched in British political culture.

Clearly, however, certain economic, social and cultural rights are not nearly as well established, either in law or even in rights discourse. There are many fundamental reasons for this. Of most immediate historical relevance were the political antagonisms that arose in the wake of the Second World War—the Cold War. Just at the time when the nations of the world were trying to agree on a modern concept of human rights—one that might help avoid a repeat of the horrors of war—major new political divisions were underway. In 1948, the then Member States of the United Nations could agree on the indivisibility and interdependence of rights, as encapsulated in the Universal Declaration of Human Rights. But, by the mid-1960s the world had changed, and the elaboration of two distinct covenants—one emphasising the importance of civil and political rights and actively promoted by the West, and the other emphasising the importance of economic, social and cultural rights, and actively promoted by the then Soviet Union—conveyed a very different message. The vision enunciated by the Declaration was seriously undermined by these divisions, not least because the discourse of rights itself was used as a weapon in the political posturing. The West was able to comfortably criticise the communist world for abusing the civil and political rights of its people; and abuses of human rights in the capitalist world (unemployment, lack of universal healthcare etc) were cited by communists as symptomatic of the failings of the capitalist economic system. This legacy of Cold War rhetoric has greatly hobbled the debate of social and economic rights in Britain since then.

THE DISTINCTIVENESS OF SOCIO-ECONOMIC RIGHTS
AS AGENTS FOR CHANGE

However, it is the contention of this chapter that it is the promotion and protection of socio-economic rights (alongside, not in contra-distinction to civil and political rights) that can prove a particularly effective force for change in our society. There are many different, if complementary, reasons for this contention.

First, the very fact that economic, social and cultural rights are the 'poor relation' in British human rights discourse can be turned to advantage by those working for change. Civil and political liberties have ancient roots in political struggle and are therefore accepted as largely self-evident. The current 'war on terrorism', which seeks to challenge long-established rights, is the exception that proves the rule. Proponents of limitations on the right of association, the right to due process, freedom from torture, etc realise that these rights are so well entrenched in society's value system that they must be argued in terms of a 'necessary evil' or of only 'temporary' duration. The upholding of socio-economic rights has nothing like the same level of societal protection and support. But perhaps—as with earlier civil and political struggles—the very assertion of certain rights will effect a change in people's thinking about the power arrangements in society. Educational efforts, campaigning, advocacy and organising to change this reality can, in and of itself, empower those who will most benefit from a wider respect of social and economic rights.

Secondly, economic, social and cultural rights are likely to be particularly important in effecting social change simply in terms of the sheer numbers of people affected. Everyone needs nourishment, an adequate standard of living, a roof over one's head, and basic education and health services. While civil and political rights are often thought to be more fundamental (and perhaps even pre-requisites to securing effective economic and social rights), it is arguable that they touch fewer lives directly. Most people in Britain live their lives without risk of torture, detention, or state interference in their desire to move freely and associate with others. Indeed, even in highly despotic societies, often relatively few people are made to suffer so as to ensure the compliance of the vast majority. So, while improvements in the protection and promotion of civil and political rights are vital to a thriving democracy, such improvements are unlikely to affect large numbers of people as directly as would dramatic changes in addressing poverty, or providing effective public health services.

Thirdly, the assertion of, and debates around, human rights in the past, has often been limited to the 'elites' in society. A focus on socio-economic rights would not merely engage more people in the debate of rights; it is likely also to engage a qualitatively different support base. Traditional human rights discourse is often characterised as being overly legalistic, and of particular interest to lawyers, given its emphasis on certain kinds of rights, and current constitutional debates in Britain—about devolution to separate parliaments for the different UK regions, the appropriate role of a second chamber, and institutions such as royalty or the established church—confirm this characterisation. These issues are all of interest to the media, the political and legal worlds, but propose no fundamental changes relevant to the redistribution of economic power. Human rights activists should learn from the bad press given to the HRA, which is all too often portrayed as either a vehicle for promoting the right to privacy of wealthy film stars or a 'charter for terrorists'. These criticisms are due in part at least to the failure of human rights campaigners to make the link between international human rights standards and the needs and aspirations of those most in need of those standards. Why, for example, does the media report extensively on problems in the health service but rarely, if ever, refer to the right to healthcare? Human rights campaigns against homelessness, or for good healthcare and for good educational provision, are likely to attract not only more people, but a much wider and more diverse constituency of interest.

This is not the place to comment in detail on feminist critiques of traditional human rights approaches. Nevertheless, as just one example of the potential for the socio-economic rights debate to galvanise 'new' constituencies as agents for their own and society-wide change, the gender perspective is an interesting one. Women, as a group, have long been excluded from the various civil and political rights advances secured in earlier centuries, and suffer still the legacy of persistent socio-economic exclusion. The strict public/private divide in traditional human rights discourse has been accused of hindering the empowerment of women, but the increasing international emphasis on the interdependence and indivisibility of rights could radically challenge this.

Fourthly, the protection of economic, social and cultural rights requires positive, proactive measures on the part of government, and sometimes the deployment of major resources. As such, debates about how best to protect economic, social and cultural rights often require and/or elicit broader society-wide debates. Obviously, the general public have strong views about the protection of civil and political rights, but it is nevertheless true that debates about criminal justice and policing (and the burden they create for the taxpayer) are likely to engage many fewer people than would a debate about education or health provision. The latter debate is also likely to be much richer and more complex. As suggested earlier, good practice in the civil and political realm is reasonably well established internationally. There are shared understandings about due process, appropriate detention periods, and other such standards, that can be applied relatively easily in the domestic context. Few people challenge the expense that the principle of due process entails for the public purse. This situation does not prevail when discussing how to effectively ensure, for example, the right to education. What does this right mean in differing circumstances, and how does one secure the right to education regardless of gender, geography, age, class, religious or political convictions, and within finite public resources? The securing of this right is far from being defined at the international level, still less interpreted or applied universally.

Fifthly, economic, social and cultural rights not only directly affect large numbers of people, from very diverse backgrounds; they also, for the most part, require expression in common. Whereas civil and political rights often focus on the inherent dignity of the individual and an individual's right to be different, economic, social and cultural rights complement this approach by celebrating people's common humanity and their inherently social nature. Values of human solidarity imbue these rights and indeed flow from the exercise of those rights. As such, the exercise of economic, social and cultural rights often act as agents for change for whole groups within society. Obviously, one should not be oblivious of the possible tensions this may create—since addressing group disadvantage can sit uneasily with traditional civil liberties approaches that elevate the rights of individuals. Yet marrying the concepts is vital since, if we do not, the language of human rights will come to be seen as a tool by which the privileged seek to undermine initiatives designed to address historic group disadvantage. In the very search, however, for ways of marrying these rights, there will be unique opportunities created to bring about social change.

But perhaps most importantly, it is worth noting that experience in many jurisdictions suggests that the assertion of socio-economic rights empowers the rights' bearers themselves to become agents of their own change. This phenomenon is explored in some detail in the next section, with regard to the experience of Northern Ireland. There is no suggestion that Northern Ireland is unique—quite the reverse—but the example provides a practical model of how, with appropriate modifications for different jurisdictions, the language of rights might begin to be effectively used in domestic discussions and campaigns as a means of social change.

THE NORTHERN IRELAND CASE

Apart from the author's own interest in the area, there is a clear justification for exploring the lessons that Northern Ireland can offer other jurisdictions in its operationalisation of socio-economic rights to secure change. Given the long history of political conflict, discrimination, and disadvantage experienced on a whole range of socio-economic indicators, people in Northern Ireland have had to be both innovative and creative in trying to promote change, and provide an alternative to the language of state and non-state violence.

The conflict cannot be simplified to issues of poverty and social exclusion, but few would doubt that these problems fed and fuelled the conflict, and that it is necessary to address these issues to bring about a more just and peaceful society. Accordingly, in Northern Ireland one can find a range of initiatives that both seek to secure socio-economic rights in practice, and which seek to use the process of securing of these rights to empower people to act as the agents (not recipients) of change.

These initiatives can be exemplified in three different arenas—international, Northern Ireland, and at community level. For the purposes of study, they are explored separately below, but the interrelationship and interdependence of the three domains will be explored in some concluding remarks.

The International Arena

Individuals and groups in Northern Ireland have often turned to the international arena, and to international human rights treaty mechanisms, in the hope of finding solutions to their domestic problems. This search for external remedies, or guidance and support, is due in large part to the fact that Northern Ireland experienced nearly thirty years of 'democratic deficit'. Between 1972 and 1998,[5] all crucial political decisions were taken by ministers based either in London, or in their constituencies, which were to be found in the length and breadth of Britain. These ministers rarely had any Northern Ireland roots, and never had a Northern Ireland electorate. The usual mechanism by which politicians are held to account—elections—was therefore unavailable to the people in whose names they were making decisions. The few indigenous political structures that were maintained—for example district councils—had nothing like the potential power of parallel institutions in Britain. Effective power was in the hands of civil servants and public policy makers, who made a virtue of being unresponsive to public opinion and the normal democratic process of competing political claims. In reality, the decisionmakers were not as removed from the political fray as they liked to think, but it was not in their interest to seek out ways in which to be held democratically accountable for their actions. In response to this vacuum, people sought to exercise political muscle differently, and turned to the international arena.

In human rights terms, this meant that campaigners in Northern Ireland— much more so than their British (or indeed Irish) counterparts—saw the need to exert external leverage, and accordingly resorted to international human rights treaty bodies as often a first, rather than a last, port of call. Early on, they saw the added value of working with the network of UN treaty bodies, which routinely require the UK Government to report and account for its treatment of its citizens. Many individuals and groups invested time and energy in making submissions, attending hearings, and publicising the recommendations of international human rights treaty mechanisms. Results were not always immediate, but there were some important early gains that reassured people that the effort was worthwhile.

Two examples of early success may suffice. Campaigners credit interventions by the UN Committee Against Torture for a dramatic drop in allegations of psychological ill treatment in the early 1990s. Local campaigning was all too easily dismissed as politically partisan; concerns expressed by the UN had to be taken seriously, and were. Similarly, interventions by the UN Committee on the Elimination of Racial Discrimination are thought to have been pivotal in having race relations legislation extended to Northern Ireland. Introduced in 1976 in Britain, politicians resisted local pressure to extend these race protections to Northern Ireland; it required the concerted efforts of local non-governmental organisations (NGOs), and their effective lobbying of the UN, to effect the necessary change.

---

[5] There was a brief period of devolution in 1974 (after the Sunningdale Agreement), but the period from 1972 (the proroguing of Stormont) until 1998 (the passage of the Good Friday/Belfast Agreement and subsequent elections of a local parliament) was essentially one of direct rule from Westminster (see www.cain.ulst.ac.uk).

In terms of advancing socio-economic rights, it was early successes such as these that encouraged active engagement by Northern Ireland groups with the UN Committee on Economic, Social and Cultural Rights (CESC), when the Committee examined the United Kingdom (most recently in 2002). Trade unions, local NGOs, and wider civil society were now made aware of the existence of a covenant guaranteeing social, economic and cultural rights, of the Government's obligations in this regard, and of the opportunity provided by the UN monitoring process to bring about improvements. Accordingly, the UN received a number of submissions from and about Northern Ireland, which facilitated their assessment of the Government's assertions, and led them to make a series of recommendations of particular relevance to the jurisdiction.[6]

For example, the Committee recommended that any Northern Ireland Bill of Rights should include effective protection for socio-economic rights; that the poverty experienced by vulnerable groups and in areas like Northern Ireland be tackled with urgency; and that additional facilities be provided for integrated education. Other recommendations touched on the problems of domestic violence, fuel poverty, housing provision, and the needs of ethnic minorities. Assessing the impact of these recommendations will of course require time. Local campaigners, however, are actively using these findings in their work, and indeed in their requests for funding support. Of course, the very fact that a wide range of activists—on issues of housing, health, education, poverty, domestic violence, trade union rights—were made more aware of the obligations of the Government to uphold basic socio-economic rights was in itself an important advance. Those activists, and the people they work for and with, are more likely in future to couch their work in the context of 'rights' rather than 'hopes' or 'aspirations', and this trend should lead to the development of a wider culture of respect for human rights.

For those who fear that the language of rights breeds irresponsibility, it is worth noting that it is the lived experience of Northern Ireland that campaigns to promote rights invariably expose people to a greater awareness of the rights of others, and of the value in working together for the good of all.

The Northern Ireland Arena

Experience suggests that the assertion of socio-economic rights lend themselves particularly well to the development of cross-cutting alliances. Whereas civil and political rights often focus on the individual's right to be different, and the right of minorities to be protected against majoritarianism, socio-economic rights often emphasise the importance of solidarity and social cohesion. Again, references to ways in which this is being put into effect in Northern Ireland may be useful.

---

[6] Concluding Observations of the UN Committee on Economic, Social and Cultural Rights: the United Kingdom of Great Britain and Northern Ireland, E/C/12/1/Add/79, 5 June 2002.

One of the building blocks in the Good Friday/Belfast peace agreement was the commitment to a society which, not only countered discrimination, but actively promoted equality for all.[7] A broad alliance of groups, working to promote equality on grounds of political and religious opinion, race, gender, sexual orientation, age, and disability, had lobbied hard to ensure that such a commitment would be part of the political negotiations, and would be translated into legislation. The subsequent equality duty (often called the section 75 duty)[8] offers an extremely important tool for change, for a variety of reasons.

First, if fully implemented, the duty should result in greater equality of opportunity for all within society. The duty requires that public authorities consider all those likely to be affected by a particular policy—not just the white, heterosexual males that often constitute society's senior policy makers—and actively promote greater equality for all. Secondly, and of particular importance when considering people as agents of their own change, the equality duty requires public authorities to engage with the people most directly affected by their decisions. Instead of people having things done 'to' or even 'for' them, they must be enabled to participate in a timely and meaningful way in the decision making process itself. Decisions that might have an adverse impact on particular sectors of society must be examined with those most directly affected, with a view to seeking alternatives or mitigation. Accordingly, section 75 offers not just an opportunity to change policies to bring about greater equality; it creates a new kind of policymaking that relies upon a more participative democratic approach.

The loose coalition that lobbied in the mid-1990s to create this equality duty has been subsequently formalised, and the Equality Coalition now meets on a monthly basis to share information and strategise.[9] Unsurprisingly, given its breadth of concerns, there are occasions when members agree to disagree. The equality concerns of women are not necessarily the same as for those with disabilities, or for those campaigning against Catholic/nationalist discrimination. At the same time, some women do have disabilities, and some are Catholics and nationalists, and indeed some will have all these identities. The fact that human beings have multiple identities is particularly important to recognise when people suffer discrimination on several grounds simultaneously. The existence of a pool of activists working together to promote the equality agenda highlights the multiple disadvantages that many in society face.

---

[7] 'We are committed to partnership, equality and mutual respect as the basis of relationships within Northern Ireland, between North and South, and between these islands' (The Agreement, preambular para 3, April 1998).

[8] The Northern Ireland Act 1998 (which gives the Agreement legislative effect) requires in s 75(1) that each public authority, in carrying out its functions relating to Northern Ireland, have due regard to the need to promote equality of opportunity between persons of different religious belief, political opinion, racial group, age, marital status and sexual orientation; men and women generally; persons with a disability and persons without; and persons with dependants and persons without.

[9] The Equality Coalition is co-convened by UNISON and the Committee on the Administration of Justice (CAJ). For information on the work of the coalition see CAJ's website—www.caj.org.uk

A coalition is also particularly effective in countering the 'divide and rule' strategy that is so often used by those supportive of the status quo. More positively, it can effectively build upon the strengths of its individual constituencies, to make the combined agenda difficult to withstand. Certainly the experience of Northern Ireland's Equality Coalition is that 'all boats rise with the rising tide,' with groups working to promote equality regardless of sexual orientation, or disability, or community background, all able to share tactics, strategies, and lend political clout to the struggle for greater equality, at different times and in different ways.

So, what has this coalition achieved in terms of having social and economic rights act as agents for change? Well, apart from the advance mentioned earlier—the securing in legislation of a commitment to equality and of the right for people to be involved in the decision-making processes directly affecting them—a number of other important achievements can be noted. For example, before the creation of an equality duty, and the need to create a coalition of forces lobbying for its operationalisation, the issue of sexual orientation was a largely hidden issue in Northern Ireland. Yet, in response to a need to develop a strong voice for lesbian, gay, bisexual and transgendered individuals in the lobbying for greater equality, an umbrella group, the Coalition on Sexual Orientation (COSO), came into being. This means that a previously 'invisible' and almost entirely disregarded community is developing its own voice and creating the mechanisms by which its voice (or indeed its many voices) will be increasingly influential.

Other constituencies are visible, but nonetheless, relatively powerless in terms of legal remedies. Older people, for example, have as yet limited protection against discrimination in international and domestic law. The equality duty provides such constituencies with some leverage for the first time. Given that the elderly now have a right to be involved in decisions affecting them, officials working in health, education, employment etc must begin to address the long-standing concerns that have been enunciated by older people, but previously ignored with impunity.

As indicated earlier, the issue of multiple identities is also more effectively addressed in this new equality framework. Trade unions and other representative groups have been able to be effective in overturning a number of decisions that would have worked to the disadvantage of their low paid and often highly vulnerable members.[10]

Nor is the Equality Coalition a lone example of how at the Northern Ireland level people have come together and found that social and economic rights have proved to be agents for change. For example, there has long been cross-party support for a Bill of Rights for Northern Ireland,[11] but the idea was given

---

[10] See report of Equality Coalition conference in Spring 2003—www.caj.org.uk

[11] See, *A Bill of Rights for Northern Ireland: Through the years—the views of the political parties* (Belfast, Committee on the Administration of Justice, July 2003)(www.caj.org.uk).

particular impetus by the Good Friday/Belfast Agreement. The Northern Ireland Human Rights Commission (NIHRC), which itself was instituted as part of the peace agreement, was tasked with consulting and advising on the scope for 'rights supplementary to those in the ECHR, to reflect the particular circumstances of Northern Ireland, drawing as appropriate on international instruments and experience.'[12] To support the Commission in this work, a Human Rights Consortium came into being to lobby for a strong and inclusive Bill of Rights for Northern Ireland.[13]

The Consortium initially had as its sole organising theme the value of promoting discussion of a Bill of Rights, and took no position in principle about the value or otherwise of a Bill of Rights. However, this changed over time and, after working together for many months, and having deepened its reflections on the topic, the 100+ groups that make up the Consortium have determined that such a Bill of Rights (if strong and inclusive) could make an important contribution to Northern Ireland's future. The diversity of the groups subscribing to this common platform for action is very striking: groups working in republican and loyalist areas, groups who disagree on the issue of abortion, and groups reflecting very different class perspectives, are all members of the Consortium. There is no attempt to agree on the content of a Bill of Rights—indeed, it would be extremely unlikely that there could be any such agreement between Consortium members. The members do, however, agree that the discussion about, and the adoption of, a Bill of Rights for Northern Ireland is an important objective for society as a whole.

The Consortium—in its very existence and in its work—has been effective in highlighting how rights can affect change. Its breadth of membership indicates that rights belong to no one group in society. In a deeply divided society like Northern Ireland, the existence of the Consortium confirms that rights transcend political and community divisions and focuses the debate on people's common humanity. Members are obliged, in campaigning for respect for the rights of their particular constituency, to accept the logic that requires that equal respect must be accorded to all other human beings. In so doing, they are encouraged to find ways in which everyone's rights are respected to the fullest extent. In its work with political parties across the spectrum, and in its dealings with government, churches, trade unions and all other social actors, the Consortium encapsulates the kind of society that a Bill of Rights would help secure—a society respectful of difference, and one in which humanity is seen to be enriched not impoverished by such differences.

It is noteworthy that—at least in Northern Ireland—it is the agenda of socio-economic rights that has proved particularly effective in creating a cohesive and shared agenda. Whereas civil and political rights (issues such as policing,

---

[12] The Agreement, April 1998, 'Rights, Safeguards and Equality of Opportunity' para 4.

[13] For more information on the composition and work of the Human Rights Consortium, see its website www.billofrightsni.org

emergency laws, and prisoners) have often been the source of much division between the two major traditions, many unionists and nationalists can find common cause around issues of poverty, housing, health, and other socio-economic rights. Indeed, an early opinion poll carried out by the NIHRC, high-lighted very high levels of cross-community support for the inclusion of socio-economic rights.[14] There have been many attempts by different political groups and parties over the years to develop support along class rather than communal lines, all to little effect. No one would suggest that this is likely to change in the near future, but it is interesting to note that socio-economic cleav-ages have their salience, and may be subject to mobilisation in particular cir-cumstances. In fact, the extent to which the debate around socio-economic rights in the Bill of Rights has allowed non-traditional cleavages to come to the fore has led to expressions in some quarters of serious dissatisfaction with the Human Rights Commission's somewhat timid, potentially contradictory, and lacklustre reference to socio-economic rights in its draft proposals.[15]

A third quite different but innovative and creative approach to the promotion of socio-economic rights is arguably to be found in the principles underlying the Government's programme to 'target social need' (ie, skew resources to those most in need). Unfortunately, the operationalisation of this measure is far from satisfactory, and few of the intended beneficiaries of the new Targeting Social Need (TSN) programme would recognise it as addressing the need for change. Nonetheless, it is worth commenting upon, albeit briefly, if only to explore why its apparent potential is so far from fruition.

In 1992, a leaked government memo revealed that, despite many years of anti-discrimination legislation intended to promote greater equality between Catholics and Protestants, the legacy of discrimination and disadvantage was proving stubbornly resistant to change. Despite its age, it is worth quoting the 1992 memo directly: 'on all the major social and economic indicators, Catholics are worse off than Protestants' (internal memo from the then Department of Economic Development). Government concluded that its practice of solely focusing on discrimination at the point of recruitment needed to be supple-mented by a much broader and more proactive programme, aimed at levelling the playing field in terms of education, health, housing and all public services. In future, it was determined that government should target resources at those most in need. The policy was to be 'religion and politics-neutral', in that Protestants and unionists in need would be treated exactly on a par with Catholics and nationalists, but it was explicitly recognised that, given the

---

[14] Research and Evaluation Services, Northern Ireland Omnibus Survey, July 1999. This indi-cated that over 80 per cent of respondents in both main communities supported the inclusion of rights in respect of health, housing and employment in the Bill of Rights.

[15] See series of articles in *Just News* (May, July/August, and September 2002), Committee on the Administration of Justice, www.caj.org.uk and, for responses generally to the Human Rights Commission's proposals, see *Summary of Submissions on a Bill of Rights* (NI Human Rights Commission, August 2003) www.nihrc.org

differentials between the two communities, a targeting of social need would result in more resources going to the Catholic nationalist community. It was equally realised that this result was both appropriate and necessary to secure fundamental change in ending poverty and social exclusion.

Unfortunately, apart from making the decision of principle, government did little to give practical effect to the TSN programme. Research published in 1996 for the Standing Advisory Commission's review of employment equality concluded that TSN had not been a public expenditure priority as intended but rather that it was 'a principle awaiting definition, operationalisation, and implementation.'[16] Government's response to these criticisms was to launch a 'New Targeting Social Need' programme, which was supposedly intended to be more targeted and more easily operationalised.[17] Unfortunately, few intended beneficiaries of either TSN, or New TSN, can point immediately to visible signs that the programmes have been effective[18] and a review of the policy is currently underway.

The reasons for the failure of New TSN to deliver on the ground are complex. However, it is worth noting the extent to which this failure might be due, in part at least, to the argument being made in this chapter. The TSN programme was rarely if ever seen or presented by government as a question of human rights. Despite the substantive rights content—TSN after all was intended to tackle social exclusion and poverty—it had no explicit rights language or construct. Moreover, the TSN programme is a centrally directed, top-down, measure: it has not sought to involve the intended beneficiaries in determining how to operate most effectively. TSN, and New TSN, both seem to have been intended to effect change (at least in the important question of the distribution of resources), while ensuring that the agents for change would remain the central policy makers who had consistently failed to secure any substantial change in the preceding decades.

The Equality Coalition, discussed earlier, has increasingly sought to make clear the link between its own efforts to promote equality, and the requirement on government to effectively target social need. The harnessing of these two measures—one aimed at greater equality and the other aimed at tackling socio-economic disadvantage—clearly offers enormous potential. In recent campaigning, the coalition has highlighted the extent and differential nature of socio-economic disadvantage across Northern Ireland, and across different social groupings. A particular strength the coalition brings to the debate about the distribution of resources is the ability to be non-partisan in a deeply contested political space. Arguing the language of equality, non-discrimination and human rights, changes the dynamic of debate from that of the 'zero-sum game'

[16] P Quirk and E McLaughlin, 'Targeting Social Need' in their *Policy Aspects of Employment Equality in Northern Ireland* (Standing Advisory Commission on Human Rights, 1996) 183.

[17] *Partnership for Equality* (Cm 3890, 1998).

[18] P McGill, *Re-new TSN: Now Let's Target Social Need* (Northern Ireland Council for Voluntary Action, 2002).

in which politics in Northern Ireland are often conducted. It is much too early to say how successful this campaigning is likely to be; suffice it to say that the need for real change is very great and that the current arrangements leave a lot to be desired.

Socio-economic rights are gravely abused in Northern Ireland: serious differentials in unemployment between the two communities persist, infant mortality among Travellers is ten times higher than for the settled population, and the educational system produces both the best and the worst qualified young people throughout the UK, thereby failing to tackle social differentials and the inter-generational legacy of underachievement. Research into the selective educational system (11+) that Northern Ireland still retains, has shown that schools where there were more children eligible for free school meals were less likely to have children securing good grades, or to retain pupils after reaching school-leaving age. It would be quite wrong if the focus of this chapter, which is on innovative measures and attempts to tackle these problems, encouraged anyone to lose sight of the extent of work still to be done.

The Local Arena

This last remark leads naturally to a discussion of the 'sharp end' of the rights debate. Who in Northern Ireland is experiencing the denial of basic socio-economic rights, and are they endeavouring, or succeeding, to have socio-economic rights effect change? There is no simple answer, but a difficult and exciting project is currently underway to try and address these issues in a more systematic way.

Several years ago, organisations in Northern Ireland and the Republic of Ireland,[19] launched a wider debate on questions of poverty, participation and rights. The purpose of the initiative was to address the topic of 'rights as agents of change' in a very direct and concrete way. A number of people from trade unions, anti-poverty and human rights groups, came together to discuss how rights could effectively be put at the service of those who most need to challenge their situation and to benefit from the promise of governments' various international commitments. Organisations and groups who had long used the language of rights, and who had found their engagement with the treaty mechanisms to be of value, wanted to put their know-how and reflections at the service of those who most needed to benefit from these mechanisms. Other organisations and groups, who had long worked at the sharp end of social exclusion, marginalisation and poverty, were looking for new tactics and techniques

---

[19] The organisations involved were the all-island Irish Congress of Trade Unions, human rights groups north and south, ie, the Committee on the Administration of Justice and the Irish Council for Civil Liberties, and anti-poverty groups north and south, ie the Combat Poverty Agency and the Northern Ireland Voluntary Trust (now Community Foundation).

to address these long-standing and persistent problems. It was agreed to roll out a series of consultations with local community groups to explore this topic.

Accordingly, groups working in very deprived communities in inner city Dublin and Belfast, in rural areas, and with particularly vulnerable social groups (the homeless, the elderly, Travellers etc), sat and discussed with lawyers, UN experts, trade union activists and rights campaigners, what would be the best way of putting the language, tactics, and mechanisms evolved for rights protection at the service of local communities. Everyone had to reflect profoundly on the value of deliberations around the protection of rights that take place in Geneva, New York, and other corridors of power: if these deliberations do not secure changes on the ground they are useless and indeed counterproductive. More constructively—since all involved are inveterate campaigners who wanted to bring about change—how could one ensure that those deliberations in far-off places do have an impact at the local level?

As indicated already, the discussion has been difficult. The answers are far from self-evident. The purpose of the debate is to put the international standards and mechanisms at the service of change at the local level—not to turn local activists into international lobbyists. So, while an early finding was that local community workers want to know more about the standards that exist, how they came into being, and how they could be strengthened, they are equally clear that this process of discovery must assist and not divert them from their primary goal, which is to effect change in their own impoverished communities. At the same time, the potential for learning at the international as well as the local level is very obvious: one of the goals of the project is to put some substantive interpretation on the meaning of the international commitment to the progressive realisation of socio-economic rights. If this concept is to facilitate, and not undermine, the securing of greater socio-economic rights protection at the local level, there needs to be some common understanding of what is meant, how improvements can be measured, and how those responsible can be held effectively to account for the international commitments they have freely taken upon themselves.

Everyone involved in this project is convinced that the work is at a very early stage, and it would therefore be invidious to attempt to be too definitive about the conclusions that can or should be drawn from the work to date. There are, however, a few very tentative remarks that can be distilled from the work so far.

First, the thirst for information, and the energy and commitment to work through difficult concepts, have surprised and excited most of those involved. It should be remembered that, for the most part, the people engaged in the project are long-term campaigners, working with some of the most intractable problems and most deprived areas on the island of Ireland. They are therefore somewhat cynical; they are people who are not attracted by quick-fix solutions. Yet, many of them have found the process of debate useful, and believe that the dimension of rights, which has not been tried before by many of them, may well bring something new to the table.

Secondly, many have already decided that the problems in effecting change to date can be very usefully addressed by the language and construct of rights. On the one hand, there is a shared belief that the authorities that are elected and appointed to secure the well-being of people are not being held effectively to account when they fail. In Northern Ireland, as indicated earlier, there has been a total absence of local democracy, but even in more effective democracies like the Republic of Ireland or Britain, the system of voting for politicians every few years is not delivering change for the most deprived in our communities. On the other hand, people also believe that those who should be holding the authorities to account are not doing so, either because they are not sufficiently aware that they should be doing this and how best to do so, or because their interventions have proved fruitless in the past, and they become alienated. Accountability is at the heart of the rights debate, and therefore the language, tactics and construct of rights, offers the potential of bringing about an end to the lack of accountability that many believe explains why poverty and marginalisation is 'allowed' to persist in relatively rich nations like Britain and Ireland. Other rights principles, such as transparency, impartiality, and human dignity, have also been recognised as of self-evident importance in any attempt to effect change, and local campaigners want to create a sense of ownership of these principles within their communities.

Last but not least, those working to end poverty and marginalisation have long argued that a top-down process cannot effectively address these problems. Spending £1million on developing a Traveller site without proper consultation with Travellers will most likely result (and has resulted) in wasting £1m of taxpayers' money. Local campaigners have long argued that better decision making will only occur if the people most directly affected by the decisions are seen as part of the solution (not part of the problem). The principle of participation has long been a central tenet of all community development approaches, but this debate is encouraging people to think of participation as a basic right, which of necessity creates a concomitant duty on the authorities. Community activists are eager to discover how they can reformulate their 'request' to be allowed to participate in decision making, into a 'right' which the relevant authorities are obliged to respond to.

The project is in its early stages. It is attempting to model the very process that it believes needs to be promoted with policy makers, ie, participation and bottom-up leadership and mobilisation. It is too early to indicate how successful it will be, but there seems little doubt already that it will offer some important lessons to the debate about how socio-economic rights can become ever more effective agents of change.

INTERDEPENDENCE

As indicated earlier, it was necessary in this last section where the Northern Ireland experiences were looked at in some detail, to separate the three levels of intervention (international, Northern Ireland wide, and local) for the purposes of clarity. When drawing conclusions about the way forward, however, it would be quite wrong to overlook the extent to which these three arenas are in fact mutually inter-dependent and interlocking.

Reference was made, for example, to the important catalyst for change provided by international human rights treaty bodies. This will not happen, however, or is much less likely to happen, if these bodies do not receive the necessary input and assistance from knowledgeable non-governmental groups (NGOs). The latter will not be knowledgeable if they do not have the ability to tap into real on-the-ground experiences of the abuse of rights. Then, once the treaty body has reported (in Geneva or New York), their potentially very influential recommendations will have little or no impact if they are not 'brought home' and made the object of determined campaigning. The international system has extremely limited capacity to follow up its recommendations, and governments can comfortably rely on not being challenged on their human rights record for another four or five years (until the next reporting cycle), unless local media, politicians, church groups, trade unions, NGOs, and concerned citizens choose to keep up the domestic pressure for change.

THE RELEVANCE OF THE NORTHERN IRELAND EXPERIENCE TO BRITAIN

There is no doubt that, for all the many differences that Northern Ireland displays, much of what has been said earlier would or could apply to other jurisdictions in these islands. The work being done locally and on a cross-border basis by way of information exchange and common strategising is clearly transferable. The mainstreaming of equality provisions into Northern Ireland's policy making may hold some lessons for how the protections offered by the HRA could be more effectively mainstreamed in central government processes than is currently the case. The development of participative approaches to decision-making, so as to complement normal democratic channels of influence, may also be of relevance. It would be wrong, however, to overlook the fact that the focus on Northern Ireland in this study has at least one serious disadvantage, and that is its limited emphasis on the role that elected politicians can and ought to play in securing socio-economic rights. That, for reasons given elsewhere, is something that the people of Northern Ireland can hope to look forward to, but have limited experience of.

It is not intended to compensate for this deficiency here, other than to commend the exciting development underway at the UK parliamentary level in this regard. The determination by Parliament to hold government to account for its international commitments to uphold human rights, is relatively new, but offers great potential in the cyclical process of trying to operationalise socio-economic rights as an agent for change in society. The parliamentary Joint Committee on

Human Rights,[20] consisting of members of both Houses of Parliament, is beginning to make a real impact in the 'domestication' of rights protection. Inquiries have been launched into the Government's response to recommendations arising from the UN Committee on the Rights of the Child, and the Committee on Economic, Social and Cultural Rights.[21]

Previously, NGOs, and indeed many government departments (including those with specific responsibility for implementing the decisions), were not even routinely informed of the UN's findings and recommendations. Now, government will be required to account for its actions—and inactions—to a powerful parliamentary committee.

Perhaps even more importantly, the parliamentary committee is incorporating many international human rights standards by a process of stealth. It has become common practice for the Joint Committee, when monitoring proposed new legislation for its compliance with the HRA, to ascertain from the responsible government departments whether the draft legislation also complies with other relevant international and regional human rights standards to which the UK is a party. In so doing, the parliamentary committee is performing a vital dual function: educating the machinery of government as to the extent of its international human rights obligations, and seeking to ensure compliance with those obligations.

CONCLUSIONS

This chapter has argued that if social and economic rights are to act as agents for change, they need to be operationalised at several different levels. Indeed, a cycle (rather than a hierarchy) of interlocking measures is required. The cycle includes, but is not limited to, the following elements:

— Rights need to be recognised and asserted as a body of principles that are independent of (though clearly not alien to) local circumstances and belief systems. Rights need to be 'universalised' in time and geography if they are to be accessed by all. Rights cannot be made the subject of political expediency, or cut in accordance with the cloth available.
— International rights principles need to be translated into practical effect—in legislation, policy and practice—in specific jurisdictions and at specific times, in such a way as to allow for different cultural, historical, economic, political, legal and other more localised realities. Rights cannot and do not exist in a vacuum.

---

[20] See www.parliament.uk/parliamentary_committees/joint_committee_on_human_rights
[21] *Ibid. Inquiry into the United Nations Convention on the Rights of the Child*, 10th report (24 June 2003), Joint Parliamentary Committee Session 2002–2003. The Joint Committee report on the International Covenant on Economic, Social and Cultural Rights was published in November 2004.

— The legislation, policy and practice that is developed at the national or sub-national level needs to empower rights bearers to exercise their rights to the full. This will require equipping rights bearers with the information, resources, and access necessary to influence the decision making that affects them. Rights are not 'given' to rights bearers; they must be interpreted, asserted, and given practical effect by rights bearers themselves.

The thrust of the chapter in this book is to engage with a variety of issues, perhaps most importantly, the challenge of how rights can be made 'real' for those most in need of them, namely the socially and economically excluded. This chapter contends that the answer to that question must be in involving the most marginalised in society in operationalising the different elements of the above cycle.

The poor, socially excluded, and marginalised need to see that rights are universal and apply to everyone by virtue of their humanity, and therefore that they, and the community they form a part of, cannot be denied basic rights because of transient political dogma or expediency. Rights cannot be an occasional preoccupation of government (at best), but instead the promotion of rights must be a central tenet and purpose of governance. Governments can have very different political, economic, legal, social and other policies, but they cannot pursue these policies at the expense of people's basic rights. Moreover, the intended beneficiaries of a programme targeting exclusion and poverty need to be party to translating the principles of rights into practical effect, in determining what the criteria for success and failure will be, and in contributing to the monitoring of the extent to which those criteria are met in reality. For this cycle of empowerment to even begin to operate, everyone (but particularly the most vulnerable in society) need to be facilitated in access to information and need in particular to know that they have rights. Rights bearers can only assert their rights, and begin to effect change, when they are aware that they have rights (not merely demands), and that rights cannot be 'given' to them, but must be asserted.

As noted at the outset, the introduction of the HRA in Britain is beginning to extend the popular understanding of rights. A veritable sea change in the use of the language and concepts of rights is taking place, and there is a growing awareness that human rights are relevant domestically as well as internationally. Unfortunately however, the nature of the HRA has largely confined this revolution in thinking to the field of civil and political rights. Few inroads have been made in educating public opinion as to the extent and nature of the social, economic and cultural rights guaranteed to people by virtue of the UK's European and international commitments. Moreover, some high profile successes under the Human Rights Act have arguably contributed to negative perceptions of human rights in general.

Yet, it is economic, social and cultural rights that touch the vast majority of people's lives. There can be little doubt that embedding the pursuit of economic and social rights as a staple of British political culture could, as in Northern

Ireland, begin to address a multiplicity of needs, and create a much broader commitment to human rights protection.

Moreover, such a debate would contribute to the intellectual debate around modern issues of governance. Representative democracy served society relatively well in the nineteenth and twentieth centuries, but is it enough for the twenty-first? Has the unintended political vacuum of Northern Ireland allowed for experiments that should no longer be seen as 'second best' but as mechanisms that can usefully complement the more traditional forms of political engagement? If this were to occur, social and economic rights would truly serve as radical agents for societal change.

5

Building a Human Rights Culture

➤•◄

FRANCES BUTLER

THE MEANING OF 'HUMAN RIGHTS CULTURE'

P ARLIAMENT'S JOINT COMMITTEE on Human Rights (JCHR), in
its report on the case for a human rights commission, provided a comprehensive explanation of the origins and fundamentals of a human rights
culture. It reconciles the different elements that are involved and forms the basis
for considering in this chapter how such a culture could be built; the committee's approach therefore merits extensive quotation:

> The claim of human rights to universality springs from a recognition of the common
> humanity and equal dignity of all human beings, as proclaimed in the UN Universal
> Declaration of Human Rights. These rights are anchored in the UN Covenants, the
> various specialised international human rights conventions and the European
> Convention on Human Rights (ECHR). They are not the property of any one political
> party, political philosophy, or religious creed. But human rights cannot form the sole
> basis or define the whole extent of a political culture based on democracy and the rule
> of law. They do, however, form an integral part of moral and political life and lay
> down fundamental standards that may be violated, if at all, only under stringent and
> clearly specified conditions. By a culture of human rights we mean, therefore, not one
> that is concerned with rights to the neglect of duties and responsibilities, but rather
> one that fosters basic respect for human rights and creates a climate in which such
> respect becomes an integral part of our way of life and a reference point for our deal-
> ings with public authorities and each other.

> A culture of human rights has two dimensions—institutional and ethical. So far as the
> former is concerned, it requires that human rights should shape the goals, structures,
> and practices of our public bodies. In their decision making and their service delivery,
> schools, hospitals, workplaces and other organs and agencies of the state should
> ensure full respect for the rights of those involved. Under the various international
> human rights instruments, it is the state that has positive duties to secure the effective

protection of human rights. The legislature, the executive and judiciary share responsibility for the protection and promotion of human rights. What is essential is that the principles enshrined in human rights are translated into practice. Achieving that requires public authorities to understand their obligations both to avoid violating the rights of those in their care, or whom they serve, and to have regard to their wider and more positive duty to 'secure to everyone . . . the rights and freedoms' which the Human Rights Act (HRA) and the other instruments define.

But making a culture of human rights a reality also requires that individuals are able to understand what their rights are, and are able to seek advice, assistance, redress and protection if they believe that their rights have been violated or are threatened with violation. It also requires that they understand their responsibilities for upholding those rights in their dealings with others.

So far as the moral or personal dimension is concerned, a culture of human rights could be characterised as having three components. First, a sense of entitlement. Citizens enjoy certain rights as an affirmation of their equal dignity and worth, and not as a contingent gift of the state. Secondly, a sense of personal responsibility. The rights of one person can easily impinge on the rights of another and each must therefore exercise his rights with care. Thirdly, a sense of social obligation. The rights of one person can require positive obligations on the part of another and, in addition, a fair balance will frequently have to be struck between individual rights and the needs of a democratic society and the wider public interest.

That is what is meant by a culture of human rights—or, as we would prefer to term it, 'a culture of respect for human rights'. In the absence of a written constitution, the HRA, and the various international human rights instruments to which the UK has acceded, may be seen to serve in place of a comprehensive constitutional concept of the positive rights and duties of those who live in this country.[1]

This vision of a human rights culture is not alien to our society but complements existing cultures and philosophies. In public services it relates both to the modernisation and improvement of those services as well as to the public service ethos of those who are delivering them. In the private sector it resonates with corporate social responsibility. In wider society it encourages the ascendancy of benevolent attitudes towards others founded on moral principles.

This chapter will examine the different elements in more detail but will first describe how the idea of a human rights culture appeared in political discourse.

---

[1] Joint Committee on Human Rights, *The Case for a Human Rights Commission* 2002–03 (6th Report, HL 67-I, HC 489-I, vol I, 11–12). See also Joint Committee on Human Rights, *Commission for Equality and Human Rights: Structure, Functions and Powers* 2003–04 (11th Report, HL 78, HC 536 HL78/HC 536 and the Government Response, Department for Constitutional Affairs, 21 July 2004).

WHAT DID THE GOVERNMENT INTEND?

Government statements in 1998 on the Human Rights Bill introduced the concept of 'a human rights culture' as something extra that the new law would bring. During the Bill's passage through Parliament, its purpose was described as follows:

> ... to give access to Convention rights in our courts, rather than people having to incur the cost and delay of going to Strasbourg. Remedies will be nearer home, and I believe that people will seek them ... The result will be the beginning of the strong development of a human rights culture in this country.[2]

The Government, however, did not want to suggest that what it meant by a human rights culture was more domestic litigation. Later pronouncements suggested that the legislation would offer the citizen something else:

> The Human Rights Act will help us rediscover and renew the basic common values that hold us all together. And those are also the values which inform the duties of the good citizen. I believe that, in time, the Human Rights Act will help bring about a culture of rights and responsibilities across the UK.[3]

This statement was both ambiguous and ambitious. The Act, as a technical vehicle for incorporating articles of the ECHR, neither imposes legal requirements on citizens nor sets out a mechanism for renewing values. But the Home Secretary was pursuing a desirable goal when he said of the Act that it is,

> ... an ethical language we can all recognise and sign up to, a ... language which doesn't belong to any particular group or creed but to all of us. One that is based on principles of common humanity.[4]

Statements of this sort, with their open-ended potential, are more an illustration of governmental aspiration for transforming society than any kind of practical guide to legislative effect. The Government, however, did not sufficiently pursue these ideas and they had little impact on the citizens to whom they referred.

The Government also intended that the Act would bring about reform in public services. The Home Secretary talked about the 'ethical bottom line for public authorities ... a fairness guarantee for the citizen' which should 'help build greater confidence in our public authorities.'[5] The Lord Chancellor explained it in the following way:

> What I mean and I am sure what others mean when they talk of a culture of respect for human rights is to create a society in which our public institutions are habitually,

---

[2] Mike O'Brien MP, Parliamentary Under-Secretary of State for the Home Department HC Deb col 1322 (21 October 1998).

[3] Secretary of State for the Home Department, Rt Hon Jack Straw MP (29 March 2000).

[4] *Building a Human Rights Culture,* address by Rt Hon Jack Straw MP to a Civil Service College seminar (9 December 1999).

[5] *Ibid.*

automatically responsive to human rights considerations in relation to every procedure they follow, in relation to every practice they follow, in relation to every decision
they take, in relation to every piece of legislation they sponsor.[6]

This approach, however, did not take root either across Whitehall departments
or within public authorities. Instead legal departments took the lead in
conducting risk analyses of possible legal challenges under the forthcoming legislation.

The Government's priority in implementing the HRA had in fact been ensuring minimum compliance by public authorities and containment of the legal system. Following the comprehensive training programme for all levels of the
judiciary, the Act entered judicial consciousness in a reasoned and moderate
way. After the Act came into force in 2000, the Government could regard itself
as having successfully achieved incorporation of the ECHR into UK law without a revolution in the courts. The Government then left it to Parliament's Joint
Committee on Human Rights to start an inquiry into whether a human rights
commission was really needed to support the new legislation. As a consequence,
the ambitions for a human rights culture within public authorities and in civil
society were not realised.

THE ABSENCE OF A HUMAN RIGHTS CULTURE

The HRA has now been in force for four years, yet there is little visible evidence
of the existence of a human rights culture. So far as public authorities are concerned, research commissioned by the Joint Committee found that:

> . . . the need to comply with the Act has become an integral part of the work of public
> authorities [however] the Act has not given birth to a culture of respect for human
> rights or made human rights a core activity of public authorities.[7]

The consequences for the vulnerable groups whom the HRA was supposed to
protect, have been predictable. A report by the British Institute of Human
Rights found that:

> . . . there is little serious attempt by any organisation . . . to use the Human Rights Act
> to create a human rights culture that could in turn lead to systemic change in the pro-
> vision of services by public authorities.
>
> Consequently, many vulnerable people remain open to abuses of their rights,
> despite the theoretical protection the Act affords.[8]

In reporting on its inquiry into the case for a human rights commission, the Joint
Committee found that a human rights culture had failed to materialise and that:

---

[6] Rt Hon The Lord Irvine of Lairg (19 March 2001).
[7] Report by Jeremy Croft, Joint Committee on Human Rights, 6th Report, vol II Ev 252.
[8] J Watson, *Something for Everyone: the Impact of the Human Rights Act and the Need for a
Human Rights Commission* (London, British Institute of Human Rights, 2002) 7.

Too often human rights are looked upon as something from which the state needs to defend itself, rather than to promote as its core ethical values. There is a failure to recognise the part that they could play in promoting social justice and social inclusion and in the drive to improve public services. We have found widespread evidence of a lack of respect for the rights of those who use public services, especially the rights of those who are most vulnerable and in need of protection.[9]

There is little evidence of the development of a human rights culture in wider civil society or that many people are speaking the 'ethical language that [they] can all recognise and sign up to,' as the Home Secretary had hoped. Instead, media references to the HRA concentrate on its assistance to criminals in avoiding justice, celebrities dodging the press and promotion of a 'compensation culture'. It has been suggested to *Daily Mail* readers that 'We need a human rights culture like we need a hole in the head'.[10] In this interpretation, a human rights culture suggests a culture of selfish entitlement and is, ironically, the opposite of the human rights culture as already defined.

MISUNDERSTANDINGS ABOUT HUMAN RIGHTS

These examples reveal the lack of consensus in wider society about what human rights mean and what their value is. Because international human rights standards were developed in response to the horrors of the Second World War, they still tend to be seen in extreme terms (torture is prevalent in foreign and despotic regimes) and therefore as irrelevant domestically. An Asian man who fled to Britain thirty years ago phoned in to tell a radio audience: 'I came here because Britain is a free country. We don't need a bill of rights.'[11]

The corollary of this view is that human rights are looked on as a British export and they have not been 'marketed' at home. There was little public consultation before the HRA was passed and the slogan 'bringing rights home' appeared to be aimed at reducing the opportunity for 'European' judges to interfere in domestic issues. As a consequence, outside a small group of enthusiasts, there is little understanding of the potential that the HRA could contribute to achieving a culture of respect for human rights.

To the extent that human rights do reside in the national consciousness, they are perceived to be more about the civil liberties of individuals than social issues relating to vulnerable groups. Historically, human rights have been understood as guarantees of life, liberty, privacy, free speech and the right to protest and when threatened by excessive state action, they require the protection of the courts. As fundamental rights in a liberal democracy, we defend them with tenacity.

---

[9] Joint Committee on Human Rights, 6th Report, vol I, at 7.
[10] Melanie Phillips, *The Daily Mail,* 2003.
[11] Radio 5, Late Night Live, 2 October 2002.

The predominance of civil and political rights in the ECHR meant that incorporation did not dispel this impression. The HRA operates as a vehicle providing legal remedies for breaches of Convention rights. The absence of any culture-building provisions on the face of the statute, such as a positive duty to promote compliance or the establishment of a commission, meant that the Government's stated intention (that the Act should encourage a cultural change decreasing the tendency to litigation) could hardly have been realised. One consequence of the emphasis on legal remedies is that human rights tend to be seen in narrow legalistic terms and largely of interest to lawyers.

HUMAN RIGHTS: OTHER INTERPRETATIONS

Because human rights have tended to be considered as relevant only to the protection of the individual against abuses of the state, there is a misconception that they only involve extreme scenarios, such as freedom from torture. But human rights principles also have a part to play in ordinary circumstances affecting groups of people as well as individuals subjected to unacceptable conditions and treatment. Consider Article 3 and the prohibition on torture. No institution responsible for the care of the young, the elderly or mentally ill would consider that they could engage in torture. But Article 3 also prohibits degrading treatment; and what other description can one give to the practices that are too often revealed to be prevalent in some of these institutions?

It needs to be demonstrated more widely that human rights concern day-to-day issues which affect people's lives; and that they can be used to improve the standard of public services and provide better protection for those who use them. There needs to be greater recognition that human rights are '. . . something for everyone . . . for the good of the people'.[12] In this analysis, human rights principles are as much about majority concerns as minority interests. The opportunities that these principles offer for social policy reform and greater achievement of social justice need to be explored. There are signs that these are now being recognised. The chairwoman of the Social Care Institute for Excellence, when asked 'what is the key to better social care?' answered, 'it should be underpinned by a human rights ethos.'[13]

Although a human rights ethos may be difficult to identify and measure in practice, it should not be regarded as merely aspirational or condemned as vague 'do-goodery'. The tendency to think that a human rights culture is from Venus whereas legal enforcement is from Mars needs to be avoided. Proponents of the preventive rather than litigation approach to human rights protection need to overcome this stereotype at the same time as avoiding a descent into well

---

[12] C Monteith, Refugee Support Centre, quoted in *Something for Everyone*, above n 8.
[13] *Guardian Society*, 10 December 2003.

meaning platitudes. Jack Straw, when Home Secretary, recognised the potential problem when he told civil servants:

> The culture we need is one which is not always soft when an individual's rights are in play. The true culture of rights and responsibilities may actually sometimes require us to be quite robust about an individual's rights to maintain the rights of others. It's a question of the interdependence of rights.[14]

In the frequent situations in ordinary life where one person's rights conflict with another's, a balancing exercise is required to resolve the particular dispute. The process of identifying and then balancing the rights and responsibilities involved should be conducted within a human rights framework so that participants are able to recognise and respect the different rights which are engaged. The mere assertion of rights does not mean the claimants can expect to win the argument, but that they can expect the discussion to proceed with a recognition that human rights are at issue. Human rights, therefore, are capable of more than one interpretation and have the potential to be an agent for positive change in society. The foundation for a human rights culture will be laid when human rights are more widely understood in these terms. Those who care about human rights, however, will have to work hard to demonstrate the value that they have in society, dispel negative impressions and win popular support for a positive vision of human rights. As the evidence has shown, a human rights culture is unlikely to evolve on its own. Developing such a culture is a project that needs encouragement and commitment from the centre and elsewhere.

STEPS TOWARDS ACHIEVING A HUMAN RIGHTS CULTURE

A fully realised human rights culture would mean that:

— The vulnerable would be better protected from violations of their human rights;
— Government would operate within a human rights framework promoting human rights standards;
— Public authorities would institutionalise human rights thinking and treat people with fairness and respect thus safeguarding their dignity;
— In wider civil society, human rights standards would be popularly accepted as the principles by which we all live and treat each other and by which conflicts can be resolved; and
— People would recognise and value both their own rights and the rights of others and would be genuinely tolerant of difference.

Who is or should be engaged in the process of building a human rights culture and what tools do they need? First, the Government should provide leadership

---

[14] *Ibid.*

and impetus to make a reality of this vision. Secondly, public authorities need to institutionalise human rights thinking when making law and policy and in their day-to-day decisions so that they avoid infringing people's human rights. Thirdly, vulnerable people and the organisations representing them need to be made aware of the relevance of human rights and how to access them effectively. Fourthly, citizens should be encouraged to recognise that human rights have a 'moral and personal' dimension. Other actors like Parliament, inspectorates, commentators, academics and the media also have important roles to play.

The Government's Continuing Role

The Human Rights Division in the Department for Constitutional Affairs has, with limited resources, pursued efforts to encourage human rights best practice within public authorities. There is a continuing programme of 'road shows' for public authorities, a help desk and the department's website sets out the Government's continuing vision for a human rights culture. But as Lord Irvine, then Lord Chancellor, conceded in his evidence to the Joint Committee, 'there is a limit to what the centre can do to encourage such a culture.'[15] In its report published in March 2003, the Joint Committee found that:

> The development of a culture of respect for human rights is in danger of stalling, and there is an urgent need for the momentum to be revived and the project driven forward. Since the Government is committed to developing a culture of respect for human rights it has a duty of leadership.[16]

In October 2003, the Government responded to this challenge by announcing the establishment of a Commission for Equality and Human Rights which will have the following role:

> It will promote an inclusive agenda, underlining the importance of equality for all in society as well as working to combat discrimination affecting specific groups. It will promote equal opportunities for all and tackle barriers to participation.
>
> It will play a key role in building a new, inclusive sense of British citizenship and identity in which shared values of respect, fair treatment and equal dignity are recognised as underpinning a cohesive, prosperous society. It will promote a culture of respect for human rights, especially in the delivery of public services.[17]

The Government's White Paper, published in May 2004, set out in more detail the possible structures, functions, and powers of this new body.[18] There is no

---

[15] Joint Committee on Human Rights, *The Case for a Human Rights Commission: Interim Report*, 2001–02, 22nd Report, HL 160, HC 1142 Ev 8.

[16] Joint Committee on Human Rights, 6th report, vol I at 7.

[17] Rt Hon Patricia Hewitt MP, Secretary of State for Trade and Industry and Minister for Women and Equality, written statement, 30 October 2003.

[18] Department for Trade and Industry and Department for Constitutional Affairs, *Fairness for All: A New Commission for Equality and Human Rights* (Cm 6185, May 2004). See also Joint Committee on Human Rights, above n 1.

doubt that the establishment of a commission will be the single most significant development towards achieving a culture of human rights. But there are two caveats. First, the earliest that the new commission will be constituted is 2007; and the culture-building work needs to be progressed now. Secondly, its function should not be to assume anyone else's responsibilities to promote and protect human rights but to check that they are being met sufficiently.

The Government therefore needs to continue to lead by example. This means policy across government, particularly within departments responsible for health, social care, education and local government, should be developed within a human rights framework. Public pronouncements should demonstrate that this has occurred. There is evidence that this is not happening yet. For example, the JCHR, in its report, published in May 2003, on the Government's compliance with the UN Convention on the Rights of the Child recommended,

> . . . particularly in relation to policy-making, that Government demonstrate more conspicuously a recognition of its obligation to implement the rights under the Convention.[19]

In September 2003, the Government published its Green Paper on services to children and that month it also responded to the Joint Committee's UNCRC report. Despite the JCHR's exhortation, neither of these documents was explicitly set within a children's rights framework. In this respect, the Government has failed to comply with the culture of human rights that it expects from everyone else. When responding to calls to change law and policy, for example on the corporal punishment of children, the age of criminal responsibility and conditions in young offender institutions, the Government should seek to win support for its policies on human rights grounds.

These human rights grounds are not limited to those incorporated by the HRA but include those contained in the international human rights covenants which the Government is required by treaty law to implement. Both the Children's Rights Convention and the Covenant on Economic, Social and Cultural rights (which is referred to below), for example, contain measures for the progressive realisation of human rights across society. They are useful tools for developing a culture of respect for human rights and the Government, in addition to meeting its legal obligations under them, should recognise their potential to inform public debate about human rights.

Public Authorities

Building a culture of respect for human rights within public authorities is a priority because of continuing failures to protect human rights which are not

---

[19] See further, the reports of the Joint Committee on Human Rights on the case for a children's commissioner: 9th Report (2002–03), HL 96, HC 666; and on the UNCRC: 10th Report (2002–03), HL 117, HC 81 and 18th Report (2002–03) HL 187, HC 1279.

remedied by litigation. Difficulties with access to justice mean that the courts cannot provide comprehensive protection of human rights. It would also be the wrong approach. Public authorities should not regard human rights as something to be complied with defensively. Instead they should use human rights principles to inform decision-making and to improve the delivery of services.

At a seminar held by the Audit Commission in June 2003, a public sector ombudsman reflecting on the significance of human rights for public authorities explained it as follows: 'If you adopt human rights thinking then you'll get service delivery right.' This observation illustrates what the Joint Committee meant by the 'institutional dimension' of a human rights culture. In October 2003, the Audit Commission published a report and guidance booklet for public authorities, *Human Rights: improving public service delivery* explaining that: 'The Human Rights Act can help to improve public services, as it seeks to ensure the delivery of quality services that meet the needs of individual service users.'[20] Most of the report is devoted to practical examples of how human rights can be used by public authorities as a framework for delivering public services. It therefore represents a valuable contribution to the development of a human rights culture. Administrative competence and confidence on these issues need to be developed within departments developing policies and providing services as well as with the legal advisers. Public authorities need to be encouraged to absorb human rights thinking within an environment of competing demands on time and resources.

There are other hurdles too. As one delegate at the conference held to launch the report remarked, the Audit Commission were 'preaching to the converted and that it is the political leaders who need convincing as well.' The challenge is to communicate the vision and advantages of a human rights culture in less sympathetic areas. There is a view that public authorities need do little more than the letter of the law requires of them and that building a human rights culture is not a priority. The statutory inspection process is likely to be the most significant mechanism for judging whether public services can be effectively delivered to the expected standard without a cultural change. This will shape the decisions and priorities of public bodies.

Another difficulty is that not all public services are now provided by the public sector. Culture-building work is underpinned by statutory requirements imposed on 'public authorities' and the stick of legal liability lurks behind the carrot of good practice. The definition of a 'public authority' within the meaning of section 6 of the HRA has, however, been restricted by the courts and is now narrower than the Government intended when the legislation was passed. The effect is that users of public services provided by the private sector may not enjoy proper human rights protection and that whether they are entitled to it or not depends on the status of the provider of the service. This is both unjust and

---

[20] Audit Commission, *Human Rights: Improving public service delivery* (Audit Commission, London, 2003).

discriminatory and needs to be addressed. This development also comes at a time of increasing private sector provision of public services and therefore affects more people.

A mechanism that has been underplayed in educating public authorities is the concept of 'positive obligations'. Article 1 of the ECHR requires states 'to secure' Convention rights 'to everyone' and the principle has been further developed by the European Court of Human Rights (ECtHR), though it is interpreted narrowly by domestic courts. Because it defines the way public authorities should approach their legal responsibilities under the Human Rights Act, however, it is fundamental to making progress on a culture of human rights. The guidance booklet distributed to public authorities before the Act came into force explained it as follows:

> All public authorities have a positive obligation to ensure that respect for human rights is at the core of their day-to-day work. This means that you should act in a way that positively reinforces the principles of the Human Rights Act . . . you have a crucial human rights role to play, not only in ensuring that you always act in accordance with the Convention rights, but also in supporting a positive attitude to human rights issues throughout the community. This is a vital responsibility for all of us.[21]

As has already been noted, however, at that time there was more emphasis within public authorities on avoiding unlawful action rather than promoting positive compliance and the concept did not take root. When properly explained to public authorities, it should propel them from negative risk assessment to positive securing of human rights and will be a useful tool in developing a culture of human rights.

The 'positive obligation' to secure human rights is comparable to the duty under the Race Relations (Amendment) Act 2000 to promote racial equality and good community relations in addition to tackling discrimination. The draft Disability Bill published in December 2003 creates a new duty on public authorities to promote equality of opportunity for disabled people and something similar for gender equality has been promised but not yet delivered. There is a rationale for extending the positive duty to equality as a whole. There is also a concern that legislation underpinning promotional work for human rights should be at least equal to that provided for equality. The introduction of positive duties will encourage public authorities to adopt proactive measures to achieve greater equality in the delivery of services, but also to adopt an integrated approach to delivering equality and human rights strategies. This process will be enhanced with the establishment of the Commission for Equality and Human Rights.

---

[21] Home Office Human Rights Task Force, *A New Era of Rights and Responsibilities: Core Guidance for Public Authorities* (2000) 16–17.

Vulnerable Groups

The development of an all-embracing culture of respect for human rights, equality and diversity within public authorities would undoubtedly improve the delivery of services and so benefit users. This will not happen overnight and pressure for reform needs also to come from users themselves. There is considerable work to be done to communicate a vision of human rights that makes them more meaningful and useful to the disadvantaged and vulnerable people whom the HRA was supposed to protect. As the head of policy at a leading advice agency remarked: 'We've all got the poster on the wall, but there's no one telling us what it means for the people that we represent.' There is also a tendency for the voluntary sector to avoid the language of 'rights':

> . . . we would be careful about using [the Human Rights Act] overtly in campaigning directed at the general public, rather than professionals, as there's a perception that it would be an own goal.[22]

Aside from litigation, human rights should be a helpful tool for users and their representatives in negotiating with public authorities for better conditions and treatment in individual cases as well as in wider policy campaigns. The British Institute of Human Rights is running a three-year outreach project in London (funded by the Community Fund). Its purpose is to raise awareness of human rights in the voluntary sector and among community groups in four specific sectors (refugees, mental health, disability and the elderly).

The effect of initiatives like these, as other contributors in this collection show, is not yet sufficiently widely spread. There are still many groups representing interests which have not participated in current debates, particularly those which may fall outside the remit of the existing equality commissions and the three 'new strands' of age, sexual orientation and religion and belief. These include travellers, homeless persons, refugees and asylum seekers, victims of crime, domestic violence sufferers and healthcare patients.

Socio-Economic Rights

Many groups concerned with social exclusion have not participated in debates on human rights because of the perception that they are confined to civil liberties issues. Increasing awareness of the relevance of socio-economic rights could change this. The UN Covenant on Economic, Social and Cultural Rights 1966 targets social injustice in areas outside the civil and political fields such as health, work and education; but both the Covenant and the UN Committee's recommendations have been largely ignored by successive governments. There is insufficient recognition within the voluntary sector that these human rights

---

[22] B Badham, 'Children's Society', quoted in *Something for Everyone* above n 8, at 29.

standards can be used as a tool in campaigning for greater relief of poverty, provision of satisfactory housing and better healthcare. The lack of a rights-based approach to socio-economic questions is a serious missed opportunity for developing a human rights culture in the mainstream of society. As Maggie Beirne writes in her chapter:

> [E]conomic, social and cultural rights are likely to be particularly important in effect-ing social change simply in terms of the sheer numbers of people likely to be affected. Everyone needs nourishment, an adequate standard of living, a roof over one's head, and basic education and health services.[23]

Greater prominence of socio-economic rights will also encourage a much needed alliance between human rights and work that the Government is priori-tising on social inclusion. The lessons learned in Northern Ireland about the value of socio-economic rights have resonance for the divided and excluded communities in Britain. It is to be hoped that the JCHR's recent report on com-pliance by government with its obligations under the UN Covenant will open up a debate about the importance of these rights.

Civil Society

This chapter has concentrated so far on the legal responsibilities of government and public authorities to promote a human rights culture in order to have the necessary impact on those who need human rights protection. Achieving a human rights culture across society is a much harder task since the misunder-standings about human rights described above need to be overcome and because, in the main, the culture-building process has a moral rather than legal basis.

Children need to know that they have human rights and that these are applic-able to their own concerns about bullying, privacy, discrimination and lack of participation in decisions that affect them. The introduction of citizenship edu-cation has been an opportunity to achieve this aim and the revised guidelines for schools suggest that primary school children should be taught '. . . that there are different kinds of responsibilities, rights and duties at home, at school and in the community and that these can sometimes conflict with each other'.[24] At sec-ondary school this becomes more specific as pupils are taught '. . . about the legal and human rights and responsibilities underpinning society and how they relate to citizens'.[25]

The debate about these issues should be widened beyond school children and the forthcoming Commission for Equality and Human Rights will provide this opportunity. Public debate is a necessary foundation for the Commission's

---

[23] See this volume ch 4.
[24] Qualifications and Curriculum Authority, *Citizenship Programme of Study Guidelines*, 2003.
[25] *Ibid.*

legitimacy, but human rights advocates will have to work hard to win over public opinion. It is inevitable that as human rights are talked about more in the media, the voices of detractors will get louder. In the face of a sceptical press, it is certain that human rights and the value of a human rights culture will need to be vigorously, frequently and conspicuously defended. Public figures who can command media attention should communicate a positive vision of human rights. They need also to provide leadership so that discussions about controversial issues like asylum, antisocial behaviour and the corporal punishment of children can be conducted in measured and civilised terms within a human rights framework.

As progress is made in placing human rights concerns at the centre of social policy and everyday concerns affecting larger numbers of people, so the reputation of human rights should improve and their values become internalised. Gradual permeation into national consciousness is likely to be more productive than a publicity campaign. People will not be convinced of the value of human rights because they are told to be but rather because they see rights in action. This will happen when human rights principles are used to redress wrongs done to the majority as much as minorities, for example, to improve the conditions of the elderly in residential care. When human rights are referred to in popular television and radio dramas like *EastEnders* and *The Archers* in terms of human dignity, rather than unpopular causes, then a human rights culture will be taking root.

The Commission for Equality and Human Rights

This chapter's purpose is not simply to describe the work being done, and which needs to be done to build a human rights culture, but to demonstrate that it should continue when the commission is operational. Expectations of what a commission can achieve in promoting a human rights culture should be realistic. With a wide remit, but finite resources, it will have to be innovative and catalytic, prompting and co-ordinating activity rather than doing the work itself.

In any event, this is a more appropriate role. The commission should not attempt to replace existing efforts and responsibilities to develop a human rights culture. Instead it should encourage and complement them by occupying an independent space checking that human rights are being promoted properly and defended effectively. Like the director of a play, the commission should show the actors how to perform without doing the performance for them. In order to avoid any temptation in government or public authorities to cede responsibility for human rights to the commission, it should maintain a watchdog role.

To succeed in communicating the message that human rights are 'something for everyone,' the commission will need to be seen to be, in theory at least, 'for everyone' too. This is what Article 1 of the ECHR requires as well. To be credible and effective, it will need adequate powers to demonstrate its independence from government and its ability to protect human rights as well as to promote their value.

Measuring the Existence of a Human Rights Culture

We are clearly a long way from reaching the elusive goal of a human rights culture, but the aim is to progress gradually towards it. Measuring achievements along the way helps the process. Indicators of a human rights culture within public authorities can be measured in specific ways, for example, reduction of deaths in custody other than through natural causes, eradication of institutional racism in the police and positive reports from public service inspectorates. Currently, these would be reported as successes in their own field, but as they also contribute towards the realisation of a human rights culture they should be recognised as such. The New Zealand Human Rights Commission is involved in work which aims to measure human rights outcomes. As the New Zealand Commission explains it:

> Like many organisations, the Commission is one of a complex array of actors that contribute to progress towards the realisation of human rights in New Zealand. The Commission has an interest in not only managing for outcomes by identifying the impact of its own interventions, but also understanding whether the activities of others contribute to improving human rights outcomes in New Zealand.[26]

This project could suggest useful methodology that can be used by its British counterpart to identify tangible outcomes, whether or not they can be said to be attributable to its own work in promoting and protecting human rights.

A measure of how successfully a culture of human rights has been accepted by the general public, as Michael Wills MP, then Minister for Human Rights, described it, would be:

> . . . how rights are talked about in the media . . . how is the language of rights being used, is it being used positively, is it being used pejoratively or is it being used at all.[27]

The JCHR saw the achievement of a human rights culture in the following terms:

> The culture of respect for human rights would exist when there was a widely-shared sense of entitlement to these rights, of personal responsibility and of respect for the rights of others, and when this influenced all our institutional policies and practices. This would help create a more humane society, a more responsive government and better public services, and could help to deepen and widen democracy by increasing the sense among individual men and women that they have a stake in the way in which they are governed.[28]

---

[26] A Boyd, *Measuring Human Rights Outcomes* (Commission Paper, New Zealand Human Rights Commission, November 2002).

[27] Evidence to the Joint Committee on Human Rights, 21 March 2002.

[28] Joint Committee on Human Rights, 6th Report, vol I, at 12.

CONCLUSION

A human rights culture is another way of describing what brings out the best in all of us in our relations with our fellow human beings. This has always been a foundation of our culture and its effect as a force for good is quietly recognised. George Eliot described it as follows:

> . . . the growing good of the world is partly dependent on unhistoric acts; and that things are not so ill with you and me as they might have been, is half owing to the number who lived faithfully a hidden life, and rest in unvisited tombs.[29]

---

[29] George Eliot, *Middlemarch* (any edition, 1872).

Part II: Using Human Rights

6

Education: Hard or Soft Lessons in Human Rights?

NEVILLE HARRIS

INTRODUCTION

T HIS CHAPTER CONSIDERS the impact of the Human Rights Act (HRA) 1998 in the field of education from two main perspectives. First, it assesses the advancement of human rights resulting from the courts' response to individual claims to and in respect of educational provision. Secondly, it considers the extent to which the UK Government's commitment towards increased respect for the human rights of its citizens has been manifested in recent wide-ranging education reforms.[1] It also examines evidence concerning the way that education bodies as 'public authorities' for the purposes of the HRA[2] have responded to the new legal environment in which they exercise their functions.

---

[1] The relevant Acts comprise the School Standards and Framework Act (SSFA) 1998; the Teaching and Higher Education Act 1998; the Learning and Skills Act 2000; the Special Educational Needs and Disability Act (SENDA) 2001; the Education Act 2002; and the Higher Education Act 2004.

[2] Universities would be regarded as public authorities (PAs) for the purposes of a majority of their functions: A Bradley, 'Scope for Review: The Convention Right to Education and the Human Rights Act 1998' [1999] *European Human Rights Law Review* 395, at 409. Schools (or more particularly their governing bodies) in the maintained (state) sector and local education authorities are also PAs, as are head teachers when carrying out certain functions, such as exclusion from school: see *A v Headteacher and Governors of The Lord Grey School* [2004] EWCA CIV 382, [2004] All ER (D) 544 (Mar), per Sedley LJ at paras 36–38. As far independent (private) schools are concerned, it seems that they would only be classed as PAs in the very limited circumstances when they exercise public functions, such as when administering the (now abolished) assisted places scheme: *R v Cobham Hall School ex p S* [1998] ELR 389; *R v Muntham House School ex p R* [2000] ELR 287; *R v Fernhill Manor School ex p A* [1994] ELR 67. As hybrid (public–private) bodies, city technology colleges (CTCs) are amenable to judicial review (*R v Governor of Haberdashers' Aske's Hatcham College Trust ex parte T* [1995] ELR 350) and are likely to be considered PAs for the purposes of the Act.

One of the problems in evaluating the actual contribution made by incorporation of the European Convention on Human Rights (ECHR) is the absence of definitive benchmarks. Like so much of the Convention, the provisions concerned with education are expressed in open-textured language that fails to set clear standards beyond bare minima, as in the requirement in the first part of Article 2 of Protocol 1 (A2P1): 'No-one shall be denied the right to education.' Not only the 'margin of appreciation,' but also the constraining effects of resource limitations on states' ability to provide public/welfare services to a particular standard or in the way desired by individual parents, have made for uncertainty as to the precise obligations of public authorities in this area. In terms of the Strasbourg jurisprudence, it is not even completely certain that A2P1, while considered to be concerned primarily with elementary education and not necessarily advanced studies, applies to higher education;[3] it probably does, and in the UK the Court of Appeal recently concluded—in a case brought by a student undertaking a Higher National Certificate course in counselling—that it applied to tertiary education.[4] Nonetheless, it remains the case that access to a university may in any event be restricted to those persons 'who have attained the academic level required to most benefit from the courses offered'.[5]

Pre-implementation academic and professional predictions about the potential effects of the HRA in this field were necessarily speculative and cautious, viewing it as likely to have an extensive but uncertain impact.[6] One consistent expectation was that human rights arguments would become pervasive in education litigation, which itself has proliferated over the past decade, especially in the areas of admission to school, exclusion from school and special educational needs. A critical factor behind this trend has been a general cultural shift towards provider accountability and parental choice and involvement, precipitated to a large extent by a range of national policy initiatives and the introduction, via statute, of formal procedures for expressions of preference, democratic participation (such as voting on grammar school status) and appeal and other redress mechanisms. Together with governmental commitment to raise standards in education, these developments have generated increased expectations among parents with regard to the advancement of education rights. The HRA has arguably raised these expectations still further. Moreover, as education is not only an end in itself but is also central to many concerns about fundamental

---

[3] See *Sulak v Turkey* (1996) 84 DR 101. See also *X v UK*, Application no 5962/72 (1975) 2 DR 50. See further K Starmer, *European Human Rights Law* (London, LAG Books, 1999) 568; K Kerrigan and P Plowden, 'Human Rights and Higher Education' (2002) 3 *Education Law* 16.

[4] *R (Douglas) v (1) North Tyneside Metropolitan Borough Council and (2) Secretary of State for Education and Skills* [2004] ELR 117, CA, per Scott Baker LJ at paras 43 and 44, Thorpe and Jonathan Parker LJJ concurring. The European Court of Human Rights will in due course have an opportunity to consider this question in *Eren v Turkey* (Application no 60856/00), the complaint having been declared admissible.

[5] *X v UK* Application no 8844/80 (1980) 23 DR 228 at 229.

[6] Eg, Bradley, above n 2; H Mountfield, 'The Implications of the Human Rights Act 1998 for the Law of Education' (2000) 1 *Education Law* 146.

rights, including those related to respect for personal integrity and beliefs, the coming of the 1998 Act was bound to ensure that disputes over education provided a significant share of human rights challenges in the UK.

EDUCATION AND THE EUROPEAN CONVENTION ON HUMAN RIGHTS

Article 2 of Protocol 1

Article 2 of Protocol 1 (A2P1) leaves as a matter of conjecture the precise minimum level of provision or its aims or content that would be consistent with the notion of 'education' for the purposes of the Convention. Some guidance is contained in the judgment of the European Court of Human Rights (ECtHR) in *Belgian Linguistics*,[7] however. The Court viewed as within the ambit of this right access to institutions providing education, education in the national language (or languages) and official recognition of studies successfully completed; while the state's duty (under A2P1) to respect parents' religious and philosophical convictions as regards the education of their children applied 'not only to the content of the curriculum and the manner of its teaching, but to other factors such as the organising and financing of public education, and matters relating to internal administration such as discipline.'[8] The state is clearly viewed as having competence over such matters,[9] and the Court would be unwilling to rule on them unless there had been a clearly unjustified interference with parental convictions. In *Valsamis v Greece*,[10] for example, the Court refused to rule on the expediency of schools instilling historical memory of the country's military struggle against fascist Italy via history lessons rather than through the compulsory participation of pupils in national day parades (see below).

Almost every citizen is the recipient of formal education at some point in their lives, indeed the Government currently promotes 'lifelong learning'. Significant numbers will become concerned and interested parties in the education of their own children. For the most part, education is provided in institutions funded and regulated by the state. At school, the formal and affective or hidden curricula not only provide the individual with a framework of knowledge and the skills to enhance and evaluate it, but play a key role in the socialisation of future citizens, helping to shape personal and collective values and the capacity for social participation. The drafting of the part of the ECHR that deals specifically with education—A2P1—thus acknowledged the need, at a time when totalitarianism in Europe was in retreat but still present, to ensure that the individual

---

[7] *Belgian Linguistics (No 2)* (1979–80) 1 EHRR 252.

[8] Citing *Campbell and Cosans v UK* (1982) 4 EHRR 293; *Kjeldsen, Busk Madsen and Pedersen v Denmark* (1979–89) 1 EHRR 711; and *Valsamis v Greece* (1997) 24 EHRR 294.

[9] See *Kjeldsen* and *Campbell and Cosans* above n 8.

[10] Case no 74/1995/580/666 (1996) 24 EHRR 294; [1998] ELR 430.

could be insulated from the full scope of the state's potential ideological power, which might be manifested in indoctrination. After its prohibition of a denial of the right to education (above) the Article continues:

> In the exercise of any functions which it assumes in relation to education and to teaching, the State must respect the right of parents to ensure such education and teaching in conformity with their own religious and philosophical convictions.

In relation to the UK, this is subject to a reservation to the effect that the principle of adherence to parents' religious or philosophical convictions in relation to the right to education is accepted only so far as is compatible with the provision of efficient instruction and training and the avoidance of unreasonable public expenditure.[11] It reflects an identical condition attached to the general principle under statute that 'pupils are to be educated in accordance with the wishes of their parents,' originally contained in the Education Act 1944 and later consolidated in the Education Act 1996.[12] Education law contains several similar caveats to the upholding of parental wishes, for example in the field of special educational needs, where parents' choice in respect of a maintained school placement for their child is subject to its compatibility with, inter alia, the 'efficient use of resources,'[13] and in the context of school admissions generally, where the law permits a denial of parental choice where compliance would 'prejudice . . . the efficient use of resources.'[14]

In any event, the ECtHR in *Belgian Linguistics* noted that the scope of the A2P1 right is not fixed and is subject to prevalent economic or social conditions at the particular time or place. In holding that the French-speaking parents in an area designated as Flemish-speaking were not being denied their right to education by the state's failure to grant their wish to have their children educated in accordance with their linguistic and cultural preferences, and by its withholding of financial support from schools that did not comply with the linguistic requirements, the Court noted that 'the Contracting Parties do not recognise such a right to education as would require them to establish at their own expense, or to subsidise, education of any particular type or at any particular level.'[15] A different and arguably more enlightened approach was taken in *Cyprus v Turkey*,[16] however, when Greek Cypriots living in northern Cyprus were denied the opportunity for their children to be taught through the medium of Greek beyond primary school. The Court held that there had been a violation of the Article 'in so far as no appropriate secondary-school facilities are available.'[17] Moving their children

---

[11] As regards the possible invalidity of the UK's reservation, however, see K Williams and B Rainey, 'Language, Education and the European Convention on Human Rights in the Twenty-first Century' (2002) 22 *Legal Studies* 625, at 641.

[12] S 9 (formerly s 76 of the 1994 Act).

[13] Education Act 1996, sch 27, para 3(3)(b).

[14] School Standards and Framework Act 1998, s 86(3)(a).

[15] *Belgian Linguistics (No 2)* (1979–80) 1 EHRR 252.

[16] Application no 25781/94 (2002) 35 EHRR 731.

[17] *Ibid*, para 280.

to the south for teaching in the Greek medium was not feasible 'having regard to the impact of that option on family life.'[18] This more recent case might presage a shift towards greater recognition of pluralism by the Court on this issue, but this will still play against a traditional sympathy for the resource constraints on the state. For example, in *X v UK*[19] it was held that the Government was entitled not to fund fully a new non-denominational (integrated) school in Northern Ireland, as the state was under no positive obligation to fund a particular form of educational provision in furtherance of a particular citizen's religious or philosophical beliefs. Similarly, in *Simpson v UK*,[20] when a dispute arose between the parents of a boy with dyslexia and the LEA over an independent school placement that the parents wanted but the LEA resisted on cost grounds, the European Commission of Human Rights acknowledged that authorities needed to enjoy 'a wide measure of discretion . . . as to how to make the best use possible of the resources available to them in the interests of disabled children generally.'[21] Respect must be paid to parental views, but the state is not under a strict obligation to provide particular forms of education desired by parents.[22]

In cases where decisions are less driven by resource considerations the Convention education right has proved to be more potent. For example, the right of parents to pay for their children to have a private education has been upheld[23] and the state has no obligation to subsidise it.[24] But even so, the state may be entitled to subjugate the wishes of individual parents to wider social goals, albeit that democracy requires that 'a balance must be achieved which ensures the fair and proper treatment of minorities and avoids any abuse of a dominant position.'[25] In *Kjeldsen*,[26] the state in Denmark was held to be entitled to make sex education compulsory in schools in the public interest, and thereby override the views of parents who argued that it conflicted with their Christian beliefs and values, as long as the 'information or knowledge is conveyed in an objective, critical and pluralistic manner' and not via 'indoctrination that might be considered as not respecting parents' religious and philosophical convictions.'[27] A key factor here was that the parents could avoid sex education

---

[18] *Ibid*, para 278.

[19] Application no 7782/77 (1978) 14 DR 179.

[20] (1989) 64 DR 188.

[21] *Ibid*, at 7.

[22] See, eg, *X, Y and Z v Germany* Application no 9411/81 (1982) 29 DR 224 (parents demanding a particular form of scientific/mathematical education) and *W and DM v UK* (1984) 37 DR 96 (parents demanding places at single-sex selective schools rather than comprehensive school with different ethos).

[23] *Jordebo v Sweden* Application no 11533/85 (1987) 51 DR 125. The right to establish a private school is also recognised: *Verein Gemeinsam Lernen v Austria*, Application no 23419/94 (1995) 82 DR 41 (1995) 20 EHRR CD 78.

[24] *W and KL v Sweden* Application no 10228/82 (1985) DR 143; *X v UK* Application no 7782/77 (1978) 14 DR 179.

[25] *Young, James and Webster v United Kingdom*, 13 August 1981, Series A no 44, at 25 § 63.

[26] Above n 8.

[27] *Ibid*, at 731. See also *Campbell and Cosans v UK* (1982) 4 EHRR 293, and *Valsamis v Greece*, above n 8.

by sending their children to private schools or by educating them at home.[28] In *Campbell and Cosans v UK*,[29] however, the Court confirmed that parental convictions that corporal punishment was wrong required respect, on the basis that the views related to:

> a weighty and substantial aspect of human life and behaviour, namely the integrity of the person, the propriety or otherwise of the infliction of corporal punishment and the exclusion of the distress which the risk of such punishment entails.[30]

They were therefore worthy of respect in a democratic society, compatible with human dignity and not in conflict with the child's fundamental right to education. In *Valsamis v Greece*[31] the complainants were Jehovah's Witnesses who, as such, abhorred any conduct or practice connected, directly or indirectly, with war or violence. Under the national law, children could be excused participation in religious education or observance but not national events. The children were required to participate in school parades on the national day marking the military struggle between Greece and fascist Italy and there was a sanction of short-term suspension for non-participation. The Court held that there was no violation of A2P1, because there was:

> nothing, either in the purposes of the parade, or in the arrangements for it, which could offend the applicants' pacifist convictions to an extent prohibited by the second sentence of [A2P1].[32]

The Court noted, as in *Kjeldsen*, that the parents were not deprived of their right to educate their children themselves about matters that were important to their religious and philosophical convictions. The minority judgments, however, supported the claim of breach of A2P1 and also Article 9 (on freedom to manifest one's religion). They considered that the symbolism of the parade touched upon matters rooted in the religious or philosophical convictions of the parents and that the parents' perceptions should be respected unless unfounded or unreasonable.

Parental convictions were therefore upheld over the matter of corporal punishment in *Campbell and Cosans* but not over compulsory sex education in *Kjeldsen* or compulsory participation in a national parade in *Valsamis*; and in *Belgian Linguistics* linguistic preferences were not considered to amount to a religious or philosophical conviction within the understood meaning of the term for the purposes of the Convention.[33] A rationalisation for the different out-

---

[28] An obligation on home-educating parents in the UK to assist the authorities in evaluating their children's education was held not to be inconsistent with the parent's right under Art 2 of Protocol 1: see *Family H v UK* Application no 10233/83 (1984) DR 105.

[29] Above n 8.

[30] Paras 33–36.

[31] Case no 74/1995/580/666 (1996) 24 EHRR 294; [1998] ELR 430.

[32] *Ibid*, para 31.

[33] For a full analysis of the decision, including the Court's rejection (save in one respect) of a claim that there was discrimination against the French-speaking families contrary to Art 14 read with A2P1, see K Williams and B Rainey, above n 11. See also H Cullen, 'Education Rights or Minority Rights?' (1993) 7 *International Journal of Law and the Family* 143.

comes might be that, in the course of seeking an appropriate balance between the rights of the individual and the state's authority over matters of education at the time, decisions over corporal punishment were considered more fundamental to the integrity of the individual and represented a more severe interference by the state than compulsory sex education, non-mother tongue teaching or participation in a parade. Williams and Rainey argue that even if choice of language for education were now to be regarded as a conviction recognised by A2P1, it might still fail to be upheld if the state had sound resource grounds for denying it.[34] Kilkenny makes a similar point in relation to parental views on special educational needs, which a series of Commission decisions[35] failed to recognise as amounting to philosophical convictions and which arose in a field where resource demands tend to be high and of necessity to compete against other areas of required education expenditure.[36]

Of course, the Convention is a 'living instrument' and views on what might amount to a religious or philosophical conviction might be expected to change over time. Yet the ECtHR, whose decisions (and those of the Commission) must be taken into account by UK judges in construing Convention rights,[37] has established in respect of A2P1, 'a threshold whereby only those views which are serious, important and coherent will require respect under the provision' and has imposed 'a significant burden of proof on the parent seeking to rely on [that provision],' thereby limiting the protection which it could offer.[38] Overall, the prospects were therefore not all that strong for successful HRA challenges based simply on A2P1.

One final point concerns the issue of children's rights. A2P1 is seen as conferring a right on the *child* to education but, in the second sentence, to upholding the right of the *parents* to have their religious and philosophical convictions considered.[39] The way that education law in England and Wales has traditionally excluded children from the enjoyment of independent education rights has been much commented upon; for example, the UN's Special Rapporteur on the right to education referred to 'the inherited legal status of the child as the object of a legally recognised relationship between the school and the child's parents rather than the subject of the right to education and of . . . rights in education.'[40]

---

[34] *Ibid*, at 641.

[35] *PD and LD v United Kingdom* (1989) 62 DR 292; *Graeme v United Kingdom* (1990) 64 DR 158; *Klerks v Netherlands* (1995) 82 DR 41. See also *W and KL v Sweden* (1983) Application No 14688/83; *Simpson v United Kingdom* (1989) 64 DR 188; *Cohen v United Kingdom* (1996) 21 EHRR CD 104.

[36] U Kilkenny, *The Child and the European Convention on Human Rights* (Aldershot, Ashgate, 1999) 79–80.

[37] HRA 1998, s 2.

[38] Kilkenny, above n 36, at 77.

[39] See *Eriksson v Sweden*, Series A no 156 (1989) 12 EHRR 183 §93.

[40] UN Commission on Human Rights, *Report submitted by Katarina Tomaševski, Special Rapporteur on the right to education, Addendum. Mission to the United Kingdom 18–22 October 1999*, E/CN4/2000/6/Add 2 (www.unhcr.ch/Huridcoda) (Centre for Human Rights, Geneva, 2000), para 90. On the exclusion of children's rights in education, see, eg, C Hamilton, 'Rights of the Child: A Right to Education and a Right in Education', in C Bridge (ed), *Family Law Towards the*

Unlike in Scotland,[41] the relevant statute law is not expressed in terms of a right to education as such, but instead in terms of a duty on the authorities to ensure that the required educational provision is made by the provision of suitable schools or through alternative arrangements.[42] Rights of choice and redress over matters of education have tended to rest exclusively with parents. While much of the concern focuses on the matters of principle that the absence of children's independent education rights raise, there are also practical concerns about disagreements between parents and children over decisions concerning matters such as attendance at sex education lessons (the parents have a right to withdraw the child)[43] or a school placement (the parents are entitled to express a preference).[44]

Other ECHR Provisions

As *Valsamis* indicated, the basic education right in A2P1 interacts with a number of other Convention rights. Indeed, in *Kjeldsen* the Court stated that the two sentences of the Article 'must be read not only in the light of each other but also, in particular, Articles 8, 9 and 10 of the Convention.'[45] Article 8 (the right to respect for privacy and family life) is particularly relevant, since many education decisions of necessity impinge upon matters central to personal or family integrity, such as sex education, discipline/punishment or the language that forms the medium of teaching. But arguments based on a breach of Article 8 were rejected in *Belgian Linguistics* (on the basis that if the parents sent their children to another region to receive teaching in the French language it would be their choice rather than an interference by the state) and *Kjeldsen*. In *Simpson v UK*[46] a complaint that an LEA decision to send a child with dyslexia and a 'delicate' personality to a comprehensive school would infringe Article 8 by causing a deterioration in the boy's mental condition and ability to be educated was not rejected out of hand, but the Commission considered that the particular complaint was too hypothetical in nature. In *Costello-Roberts v UK*,[47] the Court commented that 'the sending of a child to school necessarily involves some degree of interference with his or her private life' and that in the context of corporal punishment (and thus by implication other forms of punishment) a

---

Millennium: Essay for PM Bromley (London, Butterworths, 1997) 201–33; P Meredith, 'Children's Rights in Education', in J Fionda (ed), *Legal Concepts of Childhood* (Oxford, Hart Publishing, 2001); N Harris, 'Education Law: Excluding the Child' (2000) 12 *Education and the Law* 31–46; and J Fortin, *Children's Rights and the Developing Law* (London, LexisNexis Butterworths, 2003).

[41] See the Standards in Scotland's Schools Etc Act 2000, ss 1 and 2.
[42] Education Act 1996, ss 13, 14 and 19.
[43] *Ibid*, s 405.
[44] SSFA 1998, s 86.
[45] Above n 8 at para 52.
[46] Above n 35 at para 4.
[47] Case no 89/1991/341/414 [1994] ELR 1.

violation of Article 8 would need to entail sufficiently adverse effects for a person's physical or moral integrity.[48] The Court also confirmed that corporal punishment was not in itself necessarily in conflict with Article 3 of the Convention (prohibition against torture or inhuman or degrading treatment), which could also be relevant to other forms of treatment, such as school detention.

Article 9 was noted above and clearly has relevance to matters such as the school curriculum, especially, but not exclusively, religious education and worship, and the wearing of particular forms of dress. It provides for freedom of thought conscience and religion and, inter alia, for the individual's freedom 'either alone or in community with others and in public or private, to manifest his religion or belief, in worship, teaching, practice and observance'; subject to such limitations as are 'prescribed by law and are necessary in a democratic society in the interests of public safety, for the protection of public order, health or morals, or for the rights and freedoms of others'. In the context of education it is clearly a right enjoyed by the child, as was acknowledged in *Angeleni v Sweden*.[49] Here the national law provided for exemption from religious education only for children belonging to a religious community. The parents were atheists and on that basis the authorities refused full exemption. The Commission held that the head teacher had accommodated the applicants' wishes to some extent but in any event was clearly influenced by the way that the school curriculum did not seek to *promote* any particular religion in focusing on Christianity at junior level and thus avoided indoctrination.[50] There will be questions in relation to Article 9 as to the kinds of beliefs that would be protected; in *Valsamis* (above), for example, the Court seems to have accepted the argument, supported by the Commission's opinion in *Arrowsmith v UK*,[51] that pacifist beliefs fell within its ambit.[52] The Court did not uphold the claim that there had been a violation of Article 9, but the majority decision interlinked the parents' right concerning the upholding of religious or philosophical convictions under A2P1 with the child's right under Article 9:

> The Court . . . has already held . . . that the obligation to take part in the school parade was not such as to offend her parents' religious convictions. The impugned measure therefore did not amount to an interference with her freedom of religion either.[53]

It has been argued that the Article 9 right should protect the child from being compelled to participate in collective worship, but that the position is less clear with regard to participation in religious education at the behest of the parents, in view of the parents' right under A2P1.[54]

---

[48] *Ibid*, para 36. See *X and Y v Netherlands* Series A no 91, paras 22–27.

[49] Application no 10491/83 (1988) 10 EHRR CD123.

[50] *Ibid*, para 4.

[51] Application no 7050/75, Decisions and Reports no 19, 5 (69).

[52] For a list of those beliefs recognised in the cases, see K Starmer, above n 3, at para 27.5.

[53] *Valsamis v Greece*, above n 8, at para (37).

[54] E Craig, 'Accommodation of Diversity in Education—A Human Rights Agenda?' (2003) 15 *CFLQ* 279 at 293. Fortin (above n 40, at 356) notes that: 'The Strasbourg institutions have not considered what rights, if any, children might have if they disagreed with their parents regarding decisions over religion.'

Many claims concerning the protection of the rights of religious and other minorities in relation to education would be pursued under Article 14 read with A2P1. Article 14 provides that Convention rights and freedoms 'shall be secured without discrimination on any ground such as sex, race, colour, language, religion, political or other opinion, national or social origin, association with a national minority, property, birth or other status.' It has been argued that, for example, the statutory requirement in England and Wales that collective worship in schools should be 'wholly or mainly of a broadly Christian character'[55] might not violate Article 9 because of the parental right of withdrawal and the right for the child to pursue religious observance away from school, but that it could be discriminatory for the purposes of Article 14.[56] Article 14 prohibits discrimination or differential treatment which has no reasonable and objective justification. Such justification will depend upon the aim and effect of the measure in question (thus positive discrimination may be legitimate if aimed at redressing a pre-existing situation of inequality) and on whether the means employed are proportionate to the aim.[57] The onus is on the state authorities to show that justification.[58] In *Angeleni v Sweden*, for example, the Court accepted the justification for exempting from Christian-orientated religious knowledge lessons only those children from other religious communities (but not atheists), namely that they would be expected to learn about religion from their community. The overriding aim was to ensure that all children received 'sufficient factual religious knowledge.'[59] Similarly, no unlawful discrimination occurred in relation to all but one of the complaints in *Belgian Linguistics* because the state's objective of securing linguistic unity was a legitimate aim and the action was proportionate to it.[60] In *X v UK* the accepted justification for the discrimination against integrated schools in terms of funding was that the state enjoyed far greater control over the schools that attracted full funding.[61]

Article 10 provides for the right to freedom of expression, including 'freedom to hold opinions and to receive and impart information and ideas without interference by public authority . . .' The Article could affect the way that pupils express themselves, both verbally and non-verbally (such as through dress or body adornment). It is a necessary condition for interference with the Article 10 right that the restriction is 'prescribed by law,'[62] but there is likely to be considered sufficient legal authority for this purpose in the head teacher's statutory power to define acceptable and unacceptable forms of behaviour and to main-

---

[55] SSFA 1998, sch 20 para 3(2). See also *R v Secretary of State for Education ex p R and D* [1994] ELR 495.

[56] C Hamilton, 'Freedom of Religion and Religious Worship in Schools', in J De Groof and J Fiers (eds), *The Legal Status of Minorities in Education* (Leuven, Acco, 1996) 165–79.

[57] Above n 15.

[58] K Starmer, above n 3, at 687–90.

[59] Above n 49, at para 4.

[60] See further H Cullen, above n 33.

[61] Above n 24. See also *Verein Gemeinsam Lernen*, above n 23.

[62] Art 10(2).

tain discipline and 'otherwise regulate the conduct of pupils' (whether through school rules or otherwise).[63] The restriction must in any event be such as is necessary in a democratic society in the interests of, inter alia, public safety, the 'prevention of disorder' and 'the protection of health or morals', which seems to justify interference with many of the more outlandish, disruptive or obscene expressions of individuality on the part of pupils. It must also be 'proportionate to the legitimate aim pursued', which, in *Vogt v Germany*,[64] meant that there was a violation of Article 10 when a teacher who engaged in various political activities was dismissed for failing to meet the statutory requirement that civil servants maintain loyalty to the Constitution. Protection for the expression of a teacher's personal views might be sought in Article 10, but it seems unlikely that a court would hold as incompatible with the Convention the statutory requirement that the LEA, governing body and head teacher must forbid 'the promotion of partisan political views in the teaching of any subject in the school.'[65] Indeed, as the right to education, in the light of *Kjeldsen*, requires that education be provided in an objective manner, interference with freedom of expression would be justified by protecting that right.[66] In *X v UK*[67] a teacher was found by the Commission to have been legitimately forbidden to display religious and anti-abortion stickers on his clothes and briefcase. There was no violation of Article 10, and the complaint was inadmissible, because regard had not been had to the right of parents to have their religious and philosophical convictions respected under A2P1. It was thus a case of conflicting rights where the balance lay in favour of the parents. In *Cyprus v Turkey*,[68] however, the Court found a violation of Article 10 in the 'excessive censorship' in northern Cyprus of school textbooks for use by Greek Cypriots.[69] A rigidly prescribed school curriculum could possibly be challenged on a similar basis, but in the case of the national curriculum in England or Wales any restriction to freedom of expression is likely to be sanctioned by one or more of the legal justifications noted above, including support for the right to education.

It is necessary to discuss one further provision, Article 6. Article 6(1) protects the right to a fair trial in the determination of a person's civil rights and obligations or of any criminal charge against him or her. As it has also arisen in a recent education case in the UK (*Barnfather* below), it is necessary also to mention Article 6(2), providing for the right to the presumption of innocence until proven guilty in the case of anyone charged with a criminal offence. A pivotal question has been whether the right to education within A2P1 is a 'civil right' for the purposes of Article 6(1), thereby making education appeal committees

---

[63] SSFA 1998, s 61(4).
[64] Case no 7/1994/454/535 (1995) 21 EHRR 205 [1996] ELR 232.
[65] Education Act 1996, s 406(1).
[66] See Art 17.
[67] (1979) 16 DR 101.
[68] Application no 25781/94 (2002) 35 EHRR 731.
[69] *Ibid*, para 254.

subject to its fair trial requirement. Widely applied domestically has been the Commission's decision in *Simpson v UK*[70] holding that the right not to be denied an ('elementary') education under A2P1 was not in the nature of a 'civil right' but was 'squarely within the domain of public law' with 'no private law analogy and repercussions on private rights or obligations'; thus Article 6(1) was not fully engaged in respect of the statutory appeal process. A similar rejection occurred in *Lalu Hanuman v UK*[71] in respect of a complaint by a university student concerning the procedure for academic appeals at the University of East Anglia. These decisions appeared to weaken the prospects of successful Article 6(1) challenges before the UK courts,[72] but there was nonetheless some optimism that the judiciary might approach the matter differently.[73] In relation to higher education, it did seem odd that there were no private law rights at issue in *Hanuman* given the clear recognition by the UK courts that students stand in a contractual relationship with their university.[74]

HUMAN RIGHTS AND EDUCATION UNDER THE HUMAN RIGHTS ACT 1998

The approach taken by the Commission and the Court to the education cases brought before them did not suggest that public education authorities in the UK had a great deal to fear from the 1998 Act. Nonetheless, the potential range of human rights challenges was very broad. There were no clear lessons from the relatively few domestic cases where Convention rights were considered prior to the HRA 1998.[75] Between the Act's enactment and full implementation there was, however, a rapid increase in the number of human rights arguments presented in education cases, although (as far as can be ascertained) unsuccessful in every case. In *R v Secretary of State for Education and Employment ex p Begbie*,[76] for example, parents failed to convince the Court that the Government was obliged by virtue of A2P1 to honour pre-election promises to continue assisted places for children moving from primary to secondary departments in the same independent

---

[70] Above n 35.

[71] Application no 56965/00 (admissibility decision) [2000] ELR 685.

[72] See M Hunt, 'The European Convention on Human Rights' in J R McManus (ed), *Education and the Courts* (London, Sweet & Maxwell, 1998) 183–205, at 205.

[73] N Harris and K Eden with A Blair, *Challenges to School Exclusion* (London, RoutledgeFalmer, 2000); J Wadham and H Mountfield, *Blackstone's Guide to the Human Rights Act 1998* (London, Blackstone, 1999); A Bradley, 'The Implications of the Human Rights Act 1998 for Schools' (1999) ELSA Bulletin no 23, 2–13.

[74] *Clark v University of Lincolnshire and Humberside* [2000] 3 All ER 752; [2000] ELR 345, CA; *Moran v University College Salford (No2)* [1994] ELR 187.

[75] See, eg, *R v Secretary of State for Education and Science ex p Talmud Torah Machzikei Hadass School Trust* [1985] *The Times*, 12 April, LexisNexis, where Woolf J said that the Secretary of State had a duty, when determining a complaint relating to an independent school, to have regard to the general principle of taking account of parental wishes, as was 'underlined by Article 2 of Protocol 1 of the European Convention on Human Rights . . .'.

[76] [2000] ELR 445.

school, largely because education was available in the state sector.[77] In *R v London Borough of Richmond ex p JC*[78] the Court of Appeal held on the basis of *Simpson* (above) that Article 6 was not engaged in admission cases and that an Article 8 claim, arising from the LEA's failure to take account of health issues relating to the child and his mother, was without substance.[79] Ward LJ considered that the statutory class size limit which affected the authority's ability to meet everyone's choice was 'necessary in a democratic society' for the purposes of Article 8(2).[80] Choice was also asserted in some special educational needs cases. In *H v Kent County Council and the Special Educational Needs Tribunal*[81] Grigson J held that the LEA's refusal of the parents' request for a formal assessment of the child, upheld by the tribunal,[82] did not give rise to a breach of A2P1. In *L v Hereford and Worcester County Council and Hughes*,[83] the parents asserted that the LEA's placement for their child who had cerebral palsy was contrary to their religious and philosophical convictions; but Carnwath J refused to entertain the argument because it had not been raised before the tribunal. (In such circumstances now, the court would have to consider it.[84]) A similarly hard line was taken in *R v Secretary of State for Education and Employment ex p RCO*[85] over A2P1 and Article 8 arguments concerning the disenfranchisement of parents in relation to parental ballots to determine whether a school should retain grammar school status (ie, a selective admissions system). The Court held that its jurisdiction over Convention claims could not operate retrospectively.[86] Another attempt to invoke A2P1 failed in *R v Carmarthenshire CC ex p White*,[87] when an LEA refused to fund a child's transport to a school to which she was moved by her parents after being bullied in her previous school and the parents claimed that her right to education was being denied. The parents asserted that her enjoyment of that right was dependent upon her being free from psychiatric problems and stress. Tomlinson J agreed that the Article was concerned with 'effective education'[88]; but in his view the LEA had addressed the issue in considering the original school's suitability.

Although parents had met with little success in arguing their Convention rights, it was becoming clear that some rights had considerable potential to reinforce legal arguments in various areas of education litigation. Consideration will now be given to post-2 October 2000 decisions in the key subject areas.

[77] *Ibid*, para [72].
[78] A decision in July 2000; [2001] ELR 21.
[79] *Ibid*, para [35], per Kennedy LJ.
[80] *Ibid*, para [87].
[81] [2000] ELR 660.
[82] The Special Educational Needs Tribunal, recently re-named the Special Educational Needs and Disability Tribunal.
[83] [2000] ELR 375.
[84] HRA 1998, ss 3, 6 and 7.
[85] [2000] ELR 307.
[86] *Ibid*, 313F–G. See also *R (K) v Governors of the W School and West Sussex County Council* [2001] ELR 311.
[87] [2001] ELR 172, decided 20 July, 2000.
[88] *Ibid*, para (55).

Admission to School

Choice of school is central to parental wishes about their children's education. In 2002–03 nearly 91,430 parents lodged appeals[89] when they failed to secure a place at the desired school.[90] Parents have a right to express a preference for a state-maintained school for their child[91] and their choice must be upheld[92] unless a statutory ground applies, the most important of which is that the admission of the child to the school would 'prejudice the provision of efficient education or the efficient use of resources.'[93] Such prejudice is deemed to arise where there is a statutory class size limit—applicable to infant classes only at present—and the child's admission would result in the limit being exceeded.[94] Case law[95] holds that when a school is oversubscribed, rational criteria laid down in the admissions policy may be applied to determine priority for admission. Factors such as having a sibling at the school, living within a school's catchment area, and belonging to a particular religion, have been held legitimate factors.[96]

For children with a record of repeated exclusion from school, however, the duty to comply with parental preference and the parent's right of appeal are explicitly excluded.[97] In *Alperton School*[98] it was argued that this amounted to an unreasonable and disproportionate interference with the excluded child's right to education under A2P1 and the fair hearing right under Article 6 and that because disproportionately more black Caribbean children than others were excluded from schools, there was a breach of Article 14 read with A2P1. Newman J, relying on *Belgian Linguistics*, acknowledged the authority of the state to regulate matters of discipline in schools and in any event found that the right to education was not being denied, because LEAs had a statutory duty to secure the provision of suitable alternative education.[99] He also held that Article

[89] Involving a hearing before an appeal panel: SSFA 1998, ss 94 (as amended in relation to England by the Education Act 2002 s 50) and 95. Appeal panels were previously constituted in England under sch 24 to the 1998 Act but the relevant provisions now are in the Education (Admissions Appeals Arrangements) (England) Regulations 2002 (SI 2002 No 2899).

[90] DfES, *First Release. Admission Appeals for Maintained Primary and Secondary Schools in England 2002/03 Provisional* (London, DfES, 2004).

[91] SSFA 1998, s 86(1).

[92] *Ibid*, s 86(2).

[93] *Ibid*, s 86(3)(a).

[94] *Ibid*, s 86(4). As regards the limit, see *ibid* s.1.

[95] Eg, *Choudhury v Governors of Bishop Challoner Roman Catholic School* [1992] 3 All ER 277, HL; *R v Greenwich LBC ex p Governors of John Ball Primary School* [1990] 88 LGR 589, CA.

[96] *Ibid*. Admissions authorities must also have regard to the *School Admissions Code of Practice* published by the Department for Education and Skills (London, DfES, 2003): SSFA 1998, s 84(3).

[97] SSFA 1998, ss 87 and 95. This applies only when the latest exclusion of the child occurred within the previous two years.

[98] *R (B) v Head Teacher of Alperton Community School and Others; R v Head Teacher of Wembley High School and Others ex p T; R v Governing Body of Cardinal Newman High School and Others ex p C* [2001] ELR 359 (Admin).

[99] Education Act 1996, s 19.

6 was not engaged, because the right to education was not a civil right. (See also discussion of exclusion below.)

It is clear that not only must parents' religious and philosophical convictions be taken into account within the admissions decision-making process, but in view of the positive action required of the state to ensure compliance with A2P1,[100] they must be addressed within admissions policies. Thus, when a parent's preference for a single sex school was identified under an admissions procedure by inferences drawn from the name of the schools listed by the parent on the form, rather than from expressed reasons given by the parents (no space having been provided for them to be stated), the LEA was held to have failed in its duty to give due weight to religious convictions for the purposes of the Article.[101]

Individual admissions cases are throwing up a range of human rights issues, as *School Admission Appeals Panel for the London Borough of Hounslow v The Mayor and Burgesses of the London Borough of Hounslow*[102] illustrates. An admissions policy gave primary school applicants living in priority admission areas proximate to the school a higher priority than those with a sibling already on roll. Four unrelated children who were denied places at a school already had an elder brother or sister registered there. The panel upheld each of the parents' appeals on the ground that the LEA's decision was unreasonable, that being a statutory ground for admitting a child despite exceeding the class size limit by doing so.[103] But in response to arguments based on Articles 8 and 14 and A2P1, the panel said that it was 'not the proper forum to judge the unlawfulness of the criteria under the [HRA]'. As regards the Convention claims, Maurice Kay J in the Administrative Court had found that the panel had in fact been influenced by the HRA and the ECHR but that the case law did not suggest that the admissions criteria offended any of the above Articles.[104] It may be observed that the fact that the panel addressed human rights issues was creditable but untypical of these appeal proceedings. Here the parents' solicitor had argued them forcibly and the LEA had had counsel to oppose them.

The panel's appeal to the Court of Appeal on a number of grounds was dismissed. The principal human rights assertion there was that the discrimination against applicants not living in the priority admissions areas was not proportionate to the LEA's objective in determining priority. Such an issue might legitimately come into play when an appeal panel considers the lawfulness of a panel's decision, although unless the admissions policy is 'intrinsically or obviously unlawful' it will 'scarcely ever be necessary to go further than to

---

[100] *Valsamis v Greece*, above n 8.

[101] *R (K) v London Borough of Newham* [2002] EWHC 405 (Admin) [2002] ELR 390, per Collins J.

[102] [2002] EWCA Civ 900, [2002] ELR 602, CA.

[103] SSFA 1998, sch 24, para 12.

[104] *R (Mayor and Burgesses of the London Borough of Hounslow) v The School Admission Appeals Panel for the London Borough of Hounslow* [2002] EWHC 313 (Admin), [2002] ELR 402, para [81].

consider whether their application to the particular child was perverse.'[105] As regards the substantive discrimination argument, May LJ said:

> If a school is over-subscribed, there will necessarily be discrimination, because not every child whose parents apply for admission can be admitted . . . Discrimination needs to have reasonable objective justification. Some children will have stronger cases than others for admission. A child with an elder brother or sister in a school may well have a strong case wherever they live; but so may a child who lives close to the school. Neither child's case is by definition stronger than the other child's case. Neither child's relevant Convention rights are by definition infringed, nor is it by definition objectively unfair, if either of them fails to gain admission . . . [L]ocal education authorities have to make practical admission decisions which are objectively fair and by a process which is fair.[106]

Thus in order to succeed, the parent would need to present a case 'which is so compelling that the decision not to admit the child is shown to be perverse', while the LEA could succeed if its decision was 'objectively fair'.[107] Overall the Court of Appeal considered that the human rights arguments could legitimately be considered by an appeal panel as a public authority for HRA purposes, but rather downplayed their significance, in this context at least. Certainly the Court disapproved of wide-ranging challenges before admission appeal panels as to the legality of LEA admission policies, which might of course include those focusing on Convention compliance. May LJ saw exploration of the question whether the LEA's policy was lawful and reasonable (which he seemed to accept could legitimately arise not merely in class size limit cases)[108] as 'tending to divert them from their main task.'[109] At the same time, he disagreed[110] with the suggestion by Stanley Burnton J in an earlier post-HRA admissions case, *South Gloucestershire*,[111] that the panels should consider adjourning to enable questions of legality, including infringements of a human right, to be resolved via judicial review. The assumption seems to be that, as Stanley Burnton J put it, an allegation such as discrimination on the grounds of residence can be dealt with 'briefly' by appeal panels.[112]

---

[105]   Above n 102, per May LJ, at para [61].

[106]   *Ibid*, para [62].

[107]   *Ibid*, para [63].

[108]   The view of the majority judges in *R v Sheffield City Council ex p H and Another* [2001] ELR 511 was approved.

[109]   Para [61]. This dictum was applied by Richards J in *R (Khundakji and Salahi) v Admissions Appeal Panel of Cardiff County Council* [2003] EWHC 436 (Admin), [2003] ELR 495, at paras [52–54], when rejecting an argument that an appeal panel had failed to take account of the likelihood that, because of their domestic and other circumstances, the children in question would arrive late at school if not admitted to the school preferred by the parents and that their human rights (presumably—the full basis for the argument is not clear from the judgment—the right to education) would thereby be prejudiced.

[110]   At para [60].

[111]   *R (South Gloucestershire Local Education Authority) v The South Gloucestershire Schools Appeal Panel* [2001] EWHC 732 (Admin), [2002] ELR 309.

[112]   *Ibid*, para [51].

Stanley Burnton J's confirmation that priority on the basis of residence under admissions policies was potentially discriminatory under Article 14 read with A2P1 was clearly accepted by the Court of Appeal in the *Hounslow* case. Thus one might expect to see the relevant Convention rights raised in future in similar cases to *Sikander Ali*,[113] decided in 1994, where Bradford's admissions scheme—which resulted in the Manningham district, which had a high proportion of families of Asian origin, not being placed in a priority admissions area in respect of any particular upper (secondary) school—was held to be lawful.

It has been argued that the separation of siblings might represent an unjustifiable interference with private and family life for Article 8 purposes. In *R (O) v St James RC Primary School Appeal Panel*,[114] however, Newman J accepted, without deciding, that while Article 8 rights could be at issue in admissions decisions (particularly in the case of admission to a religious school), the Article conferred 'no absolute right to have a child admitted to a school already attended by a sibling'.[115] More recently, however, in *R (K) v London Borough of Newham*, Collins J commented:

> The desirability of enabling children to attend the same school as siblings is already recognised and most . . . perhaps all, admissions policies have that as a very important criterion. That is now rendered the more necessary because of the provisions of Article 8 of the Convention.[116]

While all of the human rights challenges to school admissions policies and procedures have failed for various reasons, the decisions to date at least confirm the relevance of the Convention rights to questions relating to school admissions and (if taken into account by those in the field) provide some guidance on compliance.

School Discipline and Organisation

Exclusion, the most severe sanction that may be imposed by a school, is an area ripe for human rights challenges because it has such a serious impact on the child both socially and educationally.[117] The right to education and the right to respect for private and family life are likely to be prejudiced by an exclusion decision. The greater incidence of permanent school exclusion among boys than girls, and among black children of Caribbean origin compared with white children,[118] means that Article 14 may also be engaged. Note, however, that

---

[113] *R v Bradford MBC ex p Sikander Ali* [1994] ELR 299.

[114] [2001] ELR 469.

[115] *Ibid*, para 36.

[116] [2002] ELR 390, para [39].

[117] Social Exclusion Unit, *Truancy and School Exclusion* Cm 3957 (London, The Stationery Office, 1998); see also Harris and Eden, above n 73.

[118] *Ibid*, ch 3 and see also DfES, *Permanent Exclusions from Schools and Exclusion Appeals, England, 2002/2003 (Provisional)* (London, DfES, 2004). Boys were excluded in 82 per cent of the 9,290 cases overall. Black Caribbean children were over three times more likely than white children to be excluded: *ibid* table 2.

exclusion from school is covered by the Race Relations Act 1976 as well as the Sex Discrimination Act 1975 and Disability Discrimination Act 1995.[119]

School exclusion cases have seen perhaps the greatest engagement with the Convention rights in the context of education post the implementation of the HRA. Many of the key issues were dealt with by Newman J in the Administrative Court in the *Alperton School* judgment.[120] There was a question whether the exclusion appeal panels were covered by Article 6(1); this in turn hinged on whether there were civil rights or criminal charges at issue. It was claimed that the civil rights included a right not to have one's reputation damaged, and that exclusion from school arising from serious misconduct was analogous to a criminal matter.[121] A further question was whether the LEA's arrangements for one of the excluded children to be educated at home for ten hours per week amounted to a denial of his right to education and of his Article 8 right to develop a personality (through being part of a school group rather than isolated). Newman J held that there was no private law right to education; that the right to education was not a civil right (applying *Simpson* above); the exclusion proceedings were not to be construed as criminal; and there was no actionable infringement of the right to enjoyment of reputation (an issue which the Court of Appeal recently refused permission to be argued via amended grounds of appeal in another case[122]). Thus Article 6(1) was not applicable. Newman J also held that the right to education was not infringed by the part-time provision, which he considered to be reasonable in the circumstances. Newman J also refused to recognise the existence of a right (under Article 8) in the field of education to develop a personality and said that the child was 'not being denied the opportunity to develop his personality in conjunction with others simply because he is not in mainstream school.'[123]

---

[119] 1975 Act, s 22; 1976 Act, s 17, 1995 Act, s 28A.

[120] *R (B) v Head Teacher of Alperton Community School and Others; R v Head Teacher of Wembley High School and Others ex parte T; R v The Governing Body of Cardinal Newman High School and Others ex p C* [2001] ELR 359.

[121] The criminal matter most likely to be involved in an education case is in fact a prosecution of a parent arising from the non-attendance of the child at school, normally under the Education Act 1996, s 444(1), which creates a strict liability offence. In *Barnfather v London Borough of Islington Education Authority and the Secretary of State for Education and Skills* [2003] EWHC 418 (Admin), [2003] ELR 263 the Divisional Court rejected an argument that this strict liability was contrary to Art 6(2) of the ECHR on the grounds of its disproportionality.

[122] *R (S) v Governing Body of YP School* [2003] EWCA Civ 1306. The appellant had wanted to argue that the head teacher's power to impose a fixed-term exclusion under s 64 of the SSFA 1998 was incompatible with the pupil's civil right of reputation for the purposes of Art 6 because there was no right of access to an independent and impartial tribunal for the determination of that right.

[123] Above n 120, para [67]. In another recent case Art 8 was advanced in support of a contention that the LEA was obliged to make suitable alternative provision (under its duty in s 19 of the 1996 Act) for a child whose emotional well-being was threatened by bullying at school: *G (R on the application of) v Westminster County Council* [2003] EWHC 2149, [2003] ELR 734. His Honour George Bartlett QC saw no need to construe the LEA's duty under s 19 in order to give effect to the requirements of Art 8 because the s 19 duty would in any event only bite where the child's behavioural difficulties made it impossible for him to attend school. The Court of Appeal did not consider Art 8 added anything to G's case given that the court was concerned with statutory provisions that 'go beyond any positive obligations that might be imposed by Article 8': *R (G) by his father and*

When one of these cases progressed to the Court of Appeal (where it was heard with two others)[124] the Article 6 fair trial right was the only Convention right argued, the question being whether either the LEA's role in exclusion appeals cases and the Secretary of State's guidance to independent appeal panels compromised the panels' independence. The Court held that while no civil right was involved in independent appeal panel decisions, domestic human rights law, and arguably the ECtHR, might regard the matter differently now; that was, at least, a 'tenable assumption' that could be made.[125] This aspect of the decision is important because it could presage a change of approach in relation to the idea of the right to education not being a civil right. However, in a more recent judgment Stanley Burnton J held (and counsel conceded) that the right to education was not a civil right.[126] A critical factor in the medium term is likely to be the element of discretion involved in the exercise of the power of exclusion.[127] Meanwhile, exclusion procedures and appeal processes continue to be subject to challenges on more traditional public law grounds.[128]

A number of human rights arguments surfaced as *L* became one of the first exclusion cases to progress through to the House of Lords.[129] *L*, aged 16, was permanently excluded from school following an assault on another pupil. An independent appeal panel directed that he should be reinstated; but the head teacher, in order to prevent industrial action by teachers who did not accept the decision, made arrangements for L to be kept isolated from other pupils and taught separately (although one other pupil later joined him). The question of whether this was reinstatement was the key issue as the case progressed, but Henriques J at first instance[130] also had to consider whether L's isolation infringed his freedoms under Articles 10 and 11 of the Convention. He held that the restrictions were proportionate and necessary to safeguard the right to education and the freedoms of others at the school. He also dismissed an argument based on breach of Article 3. In the Court of Appeal,[131] the human rights

litigation friend RG) v Westminster County Council [2004] EWCA Civ 45, [2004 ELR 135, per Lord Philips of Worth Matrevers MR (judgment of the court) at para 39.

[124] *S, T and P v London Borough of Brent and Others* [2002] EWCA Civ 693, [2002] ELR 556, CA.

[125] *Ibid*, para [30] per Schiemann LJ.

[126] *A v Headteacher and Governors of The Lord Grey School* [2003] EWHC 1533 (QB).

[127] See the House of Lords decision in the homelessness case of *Begum v London Borough of Tower Hamlets* [2003] UKHL 5, [2003] UKHRR 419.

[128] See, eg, *R (N) v The Head Teacher of X School and Others* [2001] EWHC Admin 747, [2002] ELR 187; *R (A) v Governing Body of K School and the Independent Appeal Panel of the London Borough of Enfield* [2002] EWHC 395 (Admin), [2002] ELR 631; *R (MB) v Independent Appeal Panel of SMBC* [2002] EWHC 1509 (Admin), [2002] ELR 676; *R (T by her mother and litigation friend A) v Head Teacher of Elliott School and Others* [2002] EWCA Civ 1349, [2003] ELR 160; *R (S) v The Governing Body of YP School* [2002] EWHC 2975 Admin, [2003] ELR 579.

[129] *Re L (A Minor by his father and next friend)* [2003] UKHL 9, [2003] ELR 309. The other, decided the same day, was *P v National Association of Schoolmasters/Union of Women Teachers* [2003] UKHL 8, [2003] ELR 357.

[130] *R (L) v The Governors of J School* [2001] EWHC Admin 318, [2001] ELR 411.

[131] *R (W) v The Governors of B School; The Queen on the application of L v The Governors of J School* [2001] EWCA Civ 119, [2002] ELR 105.

arguments appear not to have been renewed. In the House of Lords, only Lord Bingham referred to the ECHR. Responding to the argument that L had been denied his right to education under A2P1, Lord Bingham stated briefly that 'there are situations in which educational regimes may have to be adapted to meet particular circumstances . . . and the House was referred to no case in which it has been held that the convention (sic) right to education is violated in a case such as this.'[132] Stanley Burnton J reiterated this point more recently in *A v Headteacher and Governors of The Lord Grey School*,[133] saying that A2P1 did not create a right to be educated in any particular institution or in a particular manner; thus educating a child excluded from school via home tuition or other alternative arrangement was not in conflict with the Article, provided provision was effective. Thus, even though the exclusion of the child and his removal from the school roll were unlawful in the circumstances, there was no liability for damages for breach of the Article.

The Court of Appeal in *A* has recently taken a slightly different view, however.[134] In an important and rather complex judgment of the Court, Sedley LJ explained that there would be a denial of the Convention right if there were an unlawful exclusion (within the terms of domestic law) which 'resulted in the pupil's being unable to available himself of the means of education which presently exist . . . by being shut out for a significant or indefinite period from access to such education as the law provides for.'[135] He said that a period of 'unlawful exclusion during which the pupil is offered no education at all either by the school or the LEA was a different thing in Convention terms from an unlawful exclusion during which adequate or appropriate substitute education is offered.'[136] The boy, A, was at first told by the school to stay away for an indefinite period, which was unlawful, and was then excluded for a fixed period but no information was provided to his parents on the statutory right to attend a meeting at which the governing body would consider the matter, and no such consideration took place, contrary to the requirements of the SSFA 1998. Sedley LJ held that as work was set or offered for A to do at home throughout this period and, in effect, it was not clear that the governing body would more probably than not have overturned the exclusion, there was no breach of the A2P1 Convention right.[137] However, once the permitted period of fixed term exclusion (45 school days) had expired, and the boy's exclusion had still not been made permanent, the continuing exclusion was unlawful *and also* a breach of the Convention right, notwithstanding the school's willingness to provide the boy with substitute work at home during this latter period. He considered that

---

[132] *R (W) v The Governors of B School*; *The Queen on the application of L v The Governors of J School* [2001] EWCA Civ 119, [2002] ELR, para [26].

[133] [2003] EWHC 1533 (QB), [2003] ELR 517.

[134] *A v Headteacher and Governors of The Lord Grey School* [2004] EWCA Civ 382, [2004] All ER (D) 544 (Mar), [2004] ELR 169.

[135] *Ibid*, para 45.

[136] *Ibid*, para 55.

[137] *Ibid*, paras 56 and 57.

at the post-45 days stage the governing body would have concluded that the exclusion (as it stood) could not continue. Moreover, it would 'offend good sense and justice' to hold that there was no denial of the right to education.[138] Thus, from day 46 until A was finally placed at another school some seven months later, his exclusion was unlawful and amounted to a denial of his education right and he was entitled to damages under section 8 of the HRA. Sedley LJ also reminds us that 'if no breach of domestic law is found, it is only if that law materially offends against the Convention that the Human Rights Act moves one on to the question of a remedy.'[139] To date, the compatibility of the school exclusion statutory framework itself with the Convention has not been placed in doubt by the courts.

Another area of discipline where Convention rights have been invoked is corporal punishment. The ban on its use in schools[140] was held by the Court of Appeal in *Williamson*[141] to be consistent with the Convention despite the claims by a group with fundamental Christian views that to proscribe it in all schools could amount to a failure to ensure that education was given having respect to parents' religious or philosophical beliefs. Teachers and parents of pupils at the independent Christian Fellowship school also argued that the ban was incompatible with their rights under Articles 8, 9, and 10. The Court held that Parliament had removed any legal sanction for corporal punishment in all schools. Unlike Elias J in the lower court,[142] their lordships concluded that the teachers and parents who, on the basis of their religion, inflicted or authorised the imposition of physical chastisement of children in their care were practising or manifesting a religious belief or conviction for the purposes of Article 9 and (in the case of parents) A2P1. However, in the majority's view corporal punishment was not an *expression* of religious belief for the purposes of Article 9. Moreover, the ban did not interfere materially with a manifestation of a belief that corporal punishment should be inflicted for breaches of school discipline; this was because the corporal punishment by the parent was permitted by the national law and would satisfy that belief. The Court also cast doubt on a claim that the applicants were a religious organisation for the purposes of section 13 of the HRA, which requires a court to have particular regard to the importance of the exercise by such an organisation (itself or its members collectively) of a Convention right to freedom of thought, conscience or religion, if the court's determination of any question under the Act might affect it.[143] With regard to Article 8, the principal arguments were, first, that the state should interfere with

---

[138] *Ibid*, paras 60 and 61.

[139] Above n 134, para 45.

[140] Education Act 1996, ss 548 (as substituted by the SSFA 1998, s 131) and 549.

[141] *R (Williamson) v Secretary of State for Education and Employment* [2003] ELR 176, CA; [2002] EWCA Civ 1820.

[142] [2002] ELR 214, per Elias J. See H Mountfield, 'Spare the Rod and Spoil the Child: A Philosophical Conviction? Corporal Punishment in Schools and the Human Rights Act 1998' (2002) 3 *Education Law* 9–15

[143] See, in particular, Buxton LJ, above n 141 at paras [47], [48].

the autonomy of the family only in extreme cases and, secondly, that activities within the school were private in themselves or were an extension of the privacy of the home and therefore should not be interfered with. The Court considered that participation in state-required education took the child outside the private and family sphere. Accordingly, '[t]he protection of family values as perceived by the parent can only be achieved in the educational context through Article 2 of Protocol 1.'[144] There was considered to be no interference with the Article 10 right because it could not be said that the infliction of corporal punishment at school or the sending of children to a school where it might be practised had 'expressive content', nor were those who believed in corporal punishment prohibited from expressing their beliefs by other means.[145] *Williamson* is an important judgment and has made a significant contribution to human rights jurisprudence under a variety of heads.[146]

The extent to which views about the management and organisation of education fall within the scope of A2P1 has been tested in a case in Scotland: *Dove v The Scottish Ministers*.[147] A primary school was going to change its status from 'self-governing' to an education authority school. Under self-governing status it was directly financed by central government and was not under education authority control. The prescribed composition of the school's governing body was also different from that of an education authority school in that there was greater parental representation. Some parents argued that the statutory orders revoking the school's self-governing status violated their rights under A2P1 because they would result in changes to the method of managing the school and an alteration in the school's character. They believed these changes would be detrimental to their children's education. The court found, however, that the change of status would not affect the curriculum or teaching at the school. It would only affect its management or administration and those matters did 'not fall with the scope or ambit of the right to education guaranteed by the first sentence of art 2' and did 'not constitute a disadvantage to any of the modalities of the exercise of that right nor are they linked to the exercise of that right.'[148] The court also dismissed the idea that the parents' belief that the greater parental control under self-governing status gave the school a distinctive ethos and spirit and made it more responsive to parental wishes, and that these factors led to more effective and efficient education as well as increased parental choice in the locality, amounted to 'convictions' for the purposes of A2P1. The parents held at most no more than individual opinions relating to the governance of the school and their views had 'nothing of the nature of the convictions which were exemplified, for instance, in *Kjeldsen, Campbell and Cosans* or

---

[144] *Ibid*, per Rix LJ, at para [82].

[145] *Ibid*, per Buxton LJ, at para [84].

[146] For a detailed analysis, see H Cullen, '*R (Williamson) v Secretary of State for Education and Employment*—Accommodation of Religion in Education' (2004) CFLQ 231–242.

[147] 2002 SLT 1296, Extra Division.

[148] *Ibid*, para [26].

Valsamis' (all noted above).[149] In any event, as in *Kjeldsen*, the parents had an alternative as regards their children's education: here they could send their children to a private and independently governed school instead.[150]

School uniform

The wearing of religious dress to school has generated the occasional dispute over the years but has now come before the courts as a matter of fundamental right (under Article 9 and A2P1) in *Begum*.[151] A school's uniform policy formulated in consultation with local Muslim community representatives, permitted pupils to wear the shalwar kameeze (headscarf) but not jilbab (long cloak) to school. The claimant, a Muslim, argued that she had been excluded from school by the policy's application. Richards J held the policy to be justified under Article 9(2) for the 'protection of the rights and freedom of others,' including the protection of pupils from pressure from others to wear the jilbab (incidentally, one of the factors which influenced policy makers in France to introduce the controversial ban there on the wearing of forms of conspicious religious dress to school[152]). He said that the policy had a legitimate aim, including 'the inculcation of a sense of community identity' and 'the proper running of a multi-cultural, multi faith secular school'[153] (pupils came from 21 different ethnic groups, and Hindu, Sikh and Muslim pupils wore the shalwar kameeze). He found it 'a reasoned, balanced, proportionate policy.'[154] The judge concluded that the girl had not been excluded or that, if she had been, it was not on the grounds of her religious belief but rather her refusal to accept the uniform policy.[155] He also held that her right to education had not been denied, a factor being the possibility of transferring to a different school; but in any event he felt that she had a choice about compliance with the school's policy on uniform.[156] This judgment is narrowly focused on the particular circumstances of the case and yet, like *Williamson* (above), does offer some potential insights as to how courts might in future cases approach the determination of fundamentalist minority rights claims in the context of education.

---

[149] *Ibid*, para [30].

[150] *Ibid*, para [34].

[151] *R (Begum) v Head Teacher and Governors of Denbigh High School* [2004] ELR 374, [2004] EWHC 1389 (Admin). See also *Sahin v Turkey* (Application no. 4474/94) [2004] ELR 520, where the ECtHR found a ban on religious dress at a Turkish university to be compatible with the Convention.

[152] Loi 2004-228 du 15 mars 2004 (Journal official du 17 mars 2004, p 5190). See further D. Meuret, 'School Choice and its Regulation in France', in PJ Wolf and S Macedo (eds), *Educating Citizens. International Perspectives on Civic Values and School Choice* (Washington DC, Brookings Institution Press, 2004), 238–267, p 257.

[153] *Begum*, above n 151, para [90].

[154] *Ibid*, para [91]

[155] *Ibid*, para [74].

[156] *Ibid*, paras [102] and [103].

Special Educational Needs

The contribution of the HRA in the often contentious area of special educational needs (SEN) and provision has been limited by the effect of the Strasbourg case law referred to above, notably the decisions in *Simpson* and *Belgian Linguistics*. As was noted, it upholds the state's discretion concerning the use of resources in the meeting of educational needs generally, to the extent that the state is not required to guarantee any particular type of provision; parents' views need to be considered but will not generally prevail in a conflict situation; and there is doubt over whether a preference for a particular form of education could ever give to a 'philosophical conviction'.

In *T v Special Educational Needs Tribunal and Wiltshire County Council*[157] the parents mounted a philosophical convictions challenge under A2P1 when contesting the LEA's arrangements for the education of their autistic child. They wanted the LEA to fund a Lovaas programme at home. Richards J said that the parents' preference for this particular form of education fell 'far short of a philosophical conviction.'[158] It will clearly be easier to argue religious convictions than those which are related to the more vague notion of philosophical convictions.[159] But even so, the authorities will more often than not be able to justify their decision legally with reference to resource constraints, not least in view of the UK's reservation (which was noted in *Simpson*).

Some children with SEN are educated in residential special schools. In one case the parents argued that a boarding placement for their severely hearing-impaired child, aged 13, who had communication difficulties, would amount to an unjustifiable interference with their family life for the purposes of Article 8.[160] The tribunal had approved the placement, which was favoured by the LEA despite the significant expense involved. Sullivan J said that Article 8 was not engaged, because the tribunal's decision did not compel attendance at a boarding school: the parents could make alternative arrangements of their own (albeit at their own expense). In any event, the judge considered that in view of the child's complex needs and the fact that no other suitable provision had been identified, such interference would be justified under the terms of Article 8(2).

---

[157] [2002] ELR 704, QBD.

[158] *Ibid*, para [39](iii).

[159] But in one case Collins J rejected an argument that the tribunal had failed to take proper account of the parents' preference for a Catholic school placement for their child, contrary to their religious convictions, because the point had not been argued before the tribunal itself: *S v London Borough of Hackney and the Special Educational Needs Tribunal* [2001] EWHC Admin 572, [2002] ELR 45.

[160] *CB v London Borough of Merton and Special Educational Needs Tribunal*, [2002] EWHC 877 (Admin), [2002] ELR 441.

Education Rights of Asylum Applicants

The Court of Appeal rejected an appeal by a Polish couple who had been denied asylum and had argued that by having to return to Poland their 14-year-old daughter's excellent educational progress would be so damaged that her right to education under the Convention would be denied.[161] The parents said that on her return she would need to resume her education where she had left it at the age of eight and would not catch up. The Court held that the Secretary of State had to consider the educational implications of any asylum decision but was not obliged to take a view on whether the Convention right under A2P1 was infringed. In any event, in the Court's view Poland had a well-developed education system and it was not enough simply to say that the girl would receive a better education in the UK. There was a right to a 'minimum standard' of education but once again the Court did not attempt to define what that meant for the purposes of A2P1.

Negligence

In *X (Minors) v Bedfordshire CC*[162] the House of Lords recognised that educational psychologists and teachers could owe a duty of care at common law in the performance of their professional duties and that local education authorities could be vicariously liable for breaches. That position was affirmed by the Lords in *Phelps v Hillingdon LBC*,[163] where the Court held that it would be wrong to strike out the negligence claims (relating to failures in the diagnosis of dyslexia); but in both decisions the court left open the question as to the direct liability of the LEA. Detailed consideration of arguments based around a denial of Article 6[164] due to striking out of the action, although raised by counsel, was considered unnecessary.

One of the difficulties faced by claimants, such as those who allege fault in respect of their undiagnosed dyslexia, is the limitation period for actions.[165] In a recent education case the court confirmed that a limitation period of three years (applicable because the dyslexia cases have been held to involve personal injury (see *Phelps* above)) was not in itself incompatible with Article 6.[166]

---

[161] *Holub and Holub v Secretary of State for the Home Department* [2001] ELR 401.

[162] [1995] 2 AC 633.

[163] [2000] 3 WLR 776.

[164] Referring to *Osman v UK* [1999] 1 FLR 193 and *Z and Others v UK* (No 29392/95) 10 September 1999.

[165] Under the Limitation Act 1980.

[166] *Rowe v Kingston upon Hull City Council and Essex County Council* [2003] EWCA Civ 128, [2003] ELR 771 referring to the judgment of the Court of Human Rights in *Stubbings v UK* [1996] 23 EHRR 213.

THE IMPACT OF THE HUMAN RIGHTS ACT 1998 ON
EDUCATIONAL POLICY AND PRACTICE

In assessing the extent to which recent policy and legislation have advanced
human rights in this field and, in particular, whether the nature of the reforms
introduced and the duties, powers and structures set in place are likely to support the Convention rights of parents, it is proposed to give particular attention
to the two most recent Acts, the Special Educational Needs and Disability Act
2001 and the much longer Education Act 2002.[167] Earlier legislation and policy
was critically reviewed by the UN's Special Rapporteur,[168] encompassing discussion of the UN Convention on the Rights of the Child, whose implementation in the UK has been the subject of separate international monitoring.[169] The
Rapporteur saw the beginnings of a rights-based approach to educational policy, constituting a 'cultural shift'. As noted above, in respect of children, she
expressed concern about their merely vicarious enjoyment of the rights vested in
their parents consequent on the legal relationship between the parents and the
school.[170] Children have no independent rights over such matters as withdrawal
from religious education or collective worship, withdrawal from sex education
and choice of school, all of which reside in the parents. They still have no
independent rights of appeal in the context of school exclusion or decisions concerning special educational needs.

While A2P1 is clearly concerned with a right focused on the child, it is tied by
its second sentence to the right of the parent concerning the provision made in
furtherance of it. As Jane Fortin points out, although the cases such as *Kjeldsen*
brought under the Convention are concerned with aspects of the education of
the child, they are 'in reality, complaints about infringements of the parents'
own strong philosophical convictions.'[171] It remains to be seen whether the
domestic courts, perhaps influenced by the UN Convention and accepting the
cultural trend towards the acknowledgment of children's independent interests,
will give greater recognition to the independent rights of children to and in
respect of education.[172] There are few signs of this to date. Education legislation
is, however, belatedly beginning to give some cognisance to the rights of the

---

[167] The 2002 Act confers wide-ranging legislative powers. On delegated legislation, see D Squires,
'Challenging Subordinate Legislation under the Human Rights Act' [2000] *European Human Rights
Law Review* 116.

[168] Above n 40.

[169] Committee on the Rights of the Child, *Concluding Observations of the Committee on the
Rights of the Child: United Kingdom*, CRC/C/15/Add 34 (Geneva, Centre for Human Rights,1995);
Committee on the Rights of the Child, *Concluding Observations of the Committee on the Rights of
the Child: United Kingdom*, CRC/C/15/Add 188 (Geneva, Centre for Human Rights, 2002).

[170] Above n 40, para 90.

[171] J Fortin, above n 40, at 55.

[172] Fortin (*ibid*, at p 63) is pessimistic, on the basis of the ECtHR's approach to date and the fact
that the HRA affords opportunities for parents to pursue their own rights 'at the expense of those
of their children'.

child as expressed in the UN Convention. There is the power of a school's governing body to invite a child to sign the home-school agreement between parent and school[173] and a greater acknowledgement of the need to enable children's views to be taken into account more generally, as illustrated by the provision in the Education Act 2002 section 176 for consultation by LEAs and school governing bodies with pupils 'in connection with the taking of decisions affecting them.'[174] This provision reflects the general duty of in Article 12 of the UN Convention to enable the child to have an opportunity to express his or her views 'freely in all matters affecting the child' and for them to be 'given due weight' in accordance with the child's age and maturity. Opportunities have also been extended for children to attend and have their views taken into account in relation to SEN matters generally (through the inclusion of more detailed guidance on pupil participation in the SEN Code of Practice[175] which LEAs and school are required to take into account)[176] and in the context of SEN appeal cases and disability discrimination complaints,[177] although they do not have their own appeal/complaint rights. While only pupils aged 18-plus have an independent appeal right concerning school exclusion,[178] the official guidance (to which the LEA and appeal body must have regard), now advises that a younger child should also be heard unless the parent disagrees; and the participation of an alleged victim of the other's misdeeds is also contemplated.[179] The recent Green Paper on children, which covers a range of education (and other) issues, *Every Child Matters*,[180] has been issued for consultation in a version directed at children and young people themselves.

The 2001 and 2002 Acts have strengthened education rights in general. The 2001 Act, for example, extends the Disability Discrimination Act 1995 to schools (including maintained nursery schools) and further and higher education institutions.[181] The right to education of disabled children and their freedom from discrimination on the grounds of disability are thereby promoted. The 2002 Act arguably supports the right to education itself by seeking to improve basic educational structures to improve standards, including a new 'foundation stage' (for ages 3–5) in the national curriculum, wider powers of

[173] SSFA 1998, ss 110(5), but only if he or she is of sufficient understanding, and only as indication that he acknowledges and accepts the school's expectations of its pupils (*ibid*).

[174] See DfES, *Pupil Participation Guidance: Working Together and Giving Children and Young People a Say* DfES 0134/2004 (London, DfES, 2004).

[175] DfES, *Special Educational Needs Code of Practice* (London, DfES, 2001), part 3.

[176] Education Act 1996, s 313(2).

[177] See the Special Educational Needs Tribunal Regs 2001 (SI 2001 No 600), Regs 9, 13, 30; the Special Educational Needs and Disability Tribunal (General Provisions and Disability Claims Procedure) Regs 2002 (SI 2002 No 1985), Regs 9 and 30.

[178] Education (Pupil Exclusion and Appeals) (Maintained Schools) (England) Regulations 2002 (SI 2002 No 3178).

[179] DfES, *Improving Behaviour and Attendance: Guidance on exclusion from schools and pupil referral units* (www.teachernet.gov.uk), paras 6.3–6.5.

[180] Chief Secretary to the Treasury Cm 5860 (London, TSO, 2003).

[181] Part 2 of the Act. For a review, see T Linden, 'Disability Discrimination in Education: the New Law' [2002] *Education Law* 82–88.

intervention by the authorities in respect of under-performing schools and a framework for specification of standards in independent schools. (Such initiatives can be undermined by poor teaching, however, as illustrated by a recent Ofsted report on the impact of the Government's national literacy and numeracy projects in primary schools[182]; Ofsted found that only around 50 per cent of lessons in English and mathematics were good). It also sets in place better systems to support families and communities in the context of education, such as through a duty on school governing bodies and LEAs to promote the welfare of pupils, a broadening of the system of allowances for children who stay on at school and a new requirement for LEAs to specify the arrangements for travel expenses for sixth-formers. Individual parental views on the matter of their children's education are not given greater weight, however; but there is parent governor representation on the new local admission forums. The Act also extends appeal rights to include admission to a school sixth form (although again it is the parents' right exclusively)[183] and introduces a general right of complaint about a school.[184]

Government policy has also promoted the collective rights of parents through the policy of supporting more faith-based schools. The School Standards and Framework Act 1998 made it easier for such schools to be established as state schools and the 2001 Green Paper on schools noted that 'for the first time, Muslim, Sikh and Greek Orthodox schools have been brought inside the state system' and that the Government was 'ready to discuss with other community or privately-run schools the conditions on which they might enter the publicly provided sector.'[185] Government policy aimed at promoting greater inclusion and tackling barriers to education, namely truancy and exclusion from school,[186] is supporting the right to education of all children but particularly those from disadvantaged groups such as black Caribbean boys, whose educational attainment levels are lower than other groups and whose exclusion rates are higher, as noted above.[187] Other initiatives include a drive to eliminate bullying in schools.[188] Pupils are also being made more aware of their basic rights (and responsibilities) through the introduction of 'citizenship' as a foundation subject within the national curriculum in England during the third key stage (ages 11–14).[189]

In the area of sex education, amendments made by the Learning and Skills Act 2000 require governing bodies and head teachers to have regard to guidance

---

[182] Ofsted, *The national literacy and numeracy strategies and the primary curriculum* (HMI 1973) (London, Ofsted, 2003). One in eight lessons were classed as unsatisfactory.

[183] See 2002 Act, Sch 4, para 8.

[184] *Ibid*, s 29.

[185] DfES, *Schools: Building on Success* Cm 5050 (London, TSO, 2001) para 4.18.

[186] See, eg, the new measure for enforcing parental responsibility in the Anti-social Behaviour Act 2003, Part 3.

[187] For the Government's overview of progress, see *Every Child Matters* above n 180, paras 2.11–2.19.

[188] DfES, *Bullying: Don't suffer in silence* (London, DfES, 2002); Ofsted, *Bullying: effective action in secondary schools* (London, Ofsted, 2003).

[189] Education Act 2002, s 84(3).

issued by the Secretary of State aimed at securing that pupils learn about 'the nature of marriage and its importance for family life and the upbringing of children.'[190] The law already required that sex education should be 'given in such a manner as to encourage . . . pupils to have due regard to moral considerations and the value of family life.'[191] The new duties make for a more doctrinaire approach, posing a greater threat to teachers' freedom of expression (for Article 10 purposes). Yet there are sufficient grounds to restrict this freedom—the legal prescription and 'the protection of health or morals' objective noted above, plus the fact that the promotion of family life may not be considered disproportionate, especially given the parents' statutory right to withdraw the child from sex education[192] (thus probably avoiding any conflict with A2P1). The emphasis on family life and marriage could, however, be considered to pay insufficient regard to modern pluralistic society, where many children are brought up by unmarried couples, including some gay or lesbian couples. The recent repeal of 'section 28',[193] the provision under which local authorities were banned from promoting the teaching of homosexuality as a 'pretended family relationship', is nonetheless an important symbolic advance in the recognition of the legitimacy of same-sex relationships (symbolic, because the legislation was of unproven practical significance). Nonetheless, the fact that the official guidance on sex and relationship education must aim to protect children from 'teaching and materials which are inappropriate having regard to the age and the religious and cultural background of the pupils concerned'[194] could well mean that lessons for ethnically diverse classes such as are found in many urban schools might end up paying insufficient attention to issues such as homosexuality, sexual intercourse outside the context of marriage, and contraception.

Finally, turning to higher education, the Article 6 compatibility of the university visitor system for dealing with complaints by students and other members in most pre-1992 universities has been questioned, because of possible lack of independence or impartiality. However, no successful challenge on that basis has been yet come to judgment; and the *Hanuman* decision of the ECtHR (above) raises doubts about whether the courts would regard civil rights as being determined by the visitor, at least where students are concerned. Indeed in the recent case of *Varma*, Collins J rejected such a contention and held that such a decision by the university visitor confirming that the student failed his degree was too remote from the exercise of a judicial function.[195] By contrast, in a recent case where a person who was in dispute with a university over whether she had been engaged as a research associate petitioned the university visitor,

---

[190] Education Act 1996, s 403(1A), inserted by the Learning and Skills Act 2000, s 148.

[191] Education Act 1996, s 403(1).

[192] D Feldman, *Civil Liberties and Human Rights in England and Wales* (2nd edn, Oxford, Oxford University Press, 2002) 790.

[193] In fact, s 2A Local Government Act 1986, inserted by s 28 Local Government Act 1988, but repealed by s 122 Local Government Act 2003 in November 2003.

[194] Above n 190.

[195] *R (Varma) v HRH The Duke of Kent* [2004] EWHC 1705 (Admin), at para 25.

the Court entertained (but dismissed) an Article 6 argument not about the visitor's jurisdiction but rather the length of time the visitor took to resolve the complaint (14 months).[196] In that case civil rights were at issue, because the complainant claimed to have a post with the university.[197] So far as students are concerned, the Government has acknowledged the need for them to have a 'fair, open, and transparent means of redress' and in 2003 announced plans for establishing by statute a new office of 'independent adjudicator' for student complaints.[198] The new Office of the Independent Adjudicator for Higher Education (OIAHE) was established initially on a non-statutory footing and many universities accepted its jurisdiction on a voluntary basis from the end of March 2004. One of the less contentious aspects of the recent Higher Education Act 2004 is its provision for such an independent complaints jurisdiction, which will replace the visitor's jurisdiction over student complaints.

The Government's extension of the financial support measures for students prior to the Bill's second reading in January 2004 was aimed at reassuring both the public and rebel Labour MPs that the Bill would assist rather than hinder the Government's policy aim of promoting widened access to higher education,[199] despite the increase in fee limits. From a human rights perspective, it is ironic that the Court of Appeal recently held that the provision of student support is not a necessary part of A2P1: the current arrangements for student loans were considered to be 'a facilitator of education but they are one stage removed from the education itself,' so that the absence of support (in this case for a student in his late fifties, who was above the age limit of 55 for a student loan) might 'make it more difficult for a student to avail himself of his Article 2 [of P1] rights but they are not so closely related as to prevent him from doing so.'[200] This meant that the student had no recourse under Article 14 in respect of age discrimination.[201]

---

[196]   *R (Mohtasham) v Visitor, King's College London* [2004] ELR 29.

[197]   In *Varma* (above n 189) Collins J said (at paras 25–26) that an employment case would fall within the scope of Article 6 and so the non-justiciability of visitors' decisions on such matters (per the decision of the House of Lords in *R v Lord President of the Privy Council ex p Page* [1993] AC 682) should be considered in the light of the Article.

[198]   Department for Education and Skills, *The Future of Higher Education* (Cm 5735, 2003) paras 4.11–4.12.

[199]   See Department for Education and Skills, *Widening Participation in Higher Education* (DfES, 2003); and, more generally, DfES, *The future of higher education, ibid.*

[200]   *Douglas v North Tyneside*, above n 4, at para 57 (per Scott Baker LJ).

[201]   *Ibid*, para 59, where Scott Baker LJ said: '[A]lthough the tentacles of Art 14 stretch to the field of higher education they do not, as a matter of course stretch to funding for it. If the funding arrangements had been specifically designed to discriminate against a particular category of person that might have been a different matter, for then the arrangements could be said to be necessarily concerned with the right to education. But that was not the case. The funding arrangements are not within the right.'

CONCLUSION

By the date of the full implementation of the HRA in 2000, the education system had already been subjected to two decades of intensifying and wide-ranging regulation, making it unlikely that LEAs and schools noticed much overall change in the legal environment when the Act came into force. In any event, court judgments to date have shown education legislation and structures to be basically compliant with the Act and broadly to reflect the kind of relationship between the state and the individual that was envisaged by the Convention, including the UK's reservation to the second sentence of A2P1. The latitude given by the ECHR to the state over the management of public resources and the pursuance of collective goals in this sphere of activity has been confirmed by the UK judges, mindful of their duty to construe Convention rights in the light of the Strasbourg jurisprudence[202] and treading cautiously in these early years post-incorporation. Few lessons have been handed down to ministers by the courts. The extension of state funding to more minority religious groups' schools has limited any potential claims based on Article 14 (with A2P1), but even here the Strasbourg case law was unlikely to be helpful to those with complaints. The potential of Article 14 as applied to any aspect of educational provision that appears discriminatory is yet to be fully realised in this field. Another key provision, Article 6, may prove of little value unless the right to education becomes recognised as a 'civil right'. But, in any event, any unfairness within the appellate process is challengeable via ordinary principles of judicial review, which indeed has increased potential now that most of the appeal structures and procedures are laid down in regulations rather than primary legislation.[203] Articles 8 and 10 have not had much impact either, because the kinds of interference with the rights and freedoms they encompass have been shown to be legally justified within the terms of the Articles themselves and to have been proportional.

But while, from a purely legal perspective, the HRA has not had a significant impact on education thus far, it has contributed to a general cultural shift. Human rights have entered the political vocabulary and are increasing referred to in debates about education policy, although in this context the more detailed commitments contained in the UN Convention on the Rights of the Child[204] have probably had greater impact than the ECHR.[205] The Government is learning that an increased sensitivity to human rights in education is necessary, as is arguably reflected in its commitment[206] to ensure that all children excluded from school receive full-time educational provision (even though there is still no

[202] HRA 1998, s 2.
[203] This was in furtherance of one of the avowed objectives of the 2002 Act, namely to modernise education law by making it easier to amend and update.
[204] See especially Arts 28 and 29 on education and Art 23 on disability.
[205] See Fortin, above n 40 and N Harris, 'School Standards and Framework Bill' in R Hodgkin (ed), *Child Impact Statements 1997/98* (London, National Children's Bureau, 1999) 134–47.
[206] See *Every Child Matters*, above n 180, para 2.13.

firm statutory duty to that effect)[207] and the inclusion, in the new regulations on discrimination on the grounds of religion and belief, of discrimination against students or applicants to further and higher education.[208] Yet more could be done. The UN's Special Rapporteur also expressed concern about the potential impact of tuition fees on the right to education of university students (and that was before the Government published proposals to permit increased fees). Having already raised questions about educational access for the children of Gypsy and Traveller families (who have recently been found by Ofsted to be still not well served by the education system, despite some improvement),[209] she would doubtless also be alarmed at the arrangements under the Nationality, Immigration and Asylum Act 2002[210] whereby children of asylum seekers might be educated in accommodation centres and not have access to school. Other threats to human rights in education will be highlighted over time. There is no room for complacency.

[207] See Education Act 1996, s 19 and Department for Education and Skills, *Improving Behaviour and Attendance: Guidance on Exclusion for Schools and Pupil Referral Units* (London, DfES, 2004).

[208] Employment Equality (Religion or Belief) Regulations 2003 (SI 2003/1660), reg 20.

[209] Ofsted, *Provision and support for Traveller pupils* (HMI 455) (London, Ofsted, 2003). Attendance and attainment levels among Traveller children are below those of all other ethnic minorities. Many LEAs lack a coherent approach. The exclusion statistics (above n 118, chart 3) shows that the permanent exclusion rates for Gypsy/Roma pupils is as high as for Black Carribean pupils, while pupils from families classed as Travellers of Irish Descent have the highest rate among all ethnic groups.

[210] Ss 36 and 37 (not brought into force to date).

7

Older People

TESSA HARDING

THE SIGNIFICANCE OF THE HUMAN RIGHTS ACT

FOR THE FIRST time in domestic law, the Human Rights Act 1998 (HRA) lays down the basic rights which are common to all individuals and makes explicit fundamental ethical standards concerning how individuals must be treated by the state and its agents. Spelling out individual rights has two significant consequences. First, it changes the balance of power between the individual and the state. As the Joint Committee on Human Rights (JCHR)[1] has pointed out, human rights are not something that is conferred by the state and can be taken away by the state. They are an inherent entitlement, 'an affirmation of the equal dignity and worth' of each person, of which each person should be aware. The individual has a clear entitlement in law to be treated in a particular way, and the Act gives individuals right of redress should their human rights be violated.

Secondly, the HRA asserts the *equal* dignity and worth of each person, regardless of their individual characteristics, status or circumstances, and thereby challenges the ageism and age discrimination that are so deeply rooted in public attitudes to and services for older people.

Unlike some other forms of discrimination, discrimination on grounds of age is not unlawful in the UK. While the European Directive on Equal Treatment[2] will ban age discrimination in employment and training by 2006, there are no proposals at present to extend legislation to cover goods and services. In the absence of such anti-discrimination measures, there is little protection for older people with regard to their access to goods and services or the quality of those: older people can still be treated less favourably than others, and they have no

---

[1] Joint Committee on Human Rights, *The Case for a Human Rights Commission* 2002–03 (6th Report, HL 67-I, HC 489-1, vol I para 7, 19 March 2003).
[2] Council Dir 2000/78/EC.

legal right of redress. Article 14 of the European Convention on Human Rights (ECHR), which requires that everyone should have equal access to Convention rights irrespective of their race, religion, sex or other status, is thus important: it at least ensures that the fundamental rights and freedoms should be assured for older people as for other citizens.

Moreover, the HRA places a clear responsibility on public bodies: it makes it unlawful for a public authority 'to act in a way which is incompatible with a convention right'.[3] It goes further and requires something more proactive than mere compliance—it imposes on the state a positive duty to secure the effective protection and promotion of human rights for all its citizens. This is no longer just about securing standards for public services, which may or may not be met, but about recognition of and respect for people's inalienable rights. To fail to meet a standard is unfortunate and may merit a rap across the knuckles—but to violate someone's human rights is a failure of a different order and is wholly unacceptable.

The impact of such a change in the duties of the state should be profound: it should entail a fundamental shift of perspective by those who provide services. There should be a more equal relationship between the provider and recipient of public services. Older people should be able to be confident that they will be treated with dignity and with a proper recognition of their worth.

There is however as yet little evidence that this shift in culture is happening. Three reports published since the Act was passed have drawn the same conclusion. One considers the impact of the HRA on a number of disadvantaged groups,[4] the second looks specifically at the circumstances of older people,[5] and the third, from the Audit Commission,[6] considers the extent to which public services have responded to the Act. All indicate that the Act has failed so far to make any significant impact on the lives of ordinary people or on the culture of those who provide services.

THE CIRCUMSTANCES OF THE OLDER POPULATION

It is worth reminding ourselves about the circumstances of older people in the UK at the beginning of the twenty-first century. In 2001, there were 9.4 million people aged 65 and over in the UK (an increase of just over 50 per cent since 1961). Older people make up a fifth of the population and that proportion is rising (due partly to people living longer and partly to falling birth rates). Just

---

[3] HRA, s 6.

[4] J Watson, *Something for Everyone: the Impact of the Human Rights Act and the need for a Human Rights Commission* (London, British Institute of Human Rights, 2002).

[5] T Harding and J Gould, *Memorandum on Older People and Human Rights* (London, Help the Aged, 2003).

[6] Audit Commission, *Human Rights: Improving public service delivery* (Audit Commission, London, 2003) 7.

over a million people are aged 85 and over (more than three times as many as in 1961)[7] and this is the fastest growing segment of the population.

The older population is very diverse: it spans four decades and two generations. It includes people with widely differing histories, experience and aspirations, different working lives and skills, family relationships, educational attainment, ethnicity, sexuality, religious belief and financial security. Women outnumber men, because they tend to live longer. The great majority of older people are healthy (two-thirds rate their health as either good or very good), independent and well able to take care of themselves (and quite often others as well), and most consider that their quality of life is good.[8] Chronological age per se, it seems, is not a problem; but some of the social and economic conditions that older people experience do create problems.

About a third of older people are on incomes at or below income support level; a further third have modest additional incomes, taking them just a little over the income support threshold; and a third (mostly men and married couples) are more comfortably off. Very low incomes are an issue for 1.3 million people (nearly a quarter of single pensioners and 8 per cent of pensioner couples) who rely on the state retirement pension and state benefits alone.[9] A significant number of people, especially women and those in advanced old age, are eligible for income-related benefits but do not claim them; £2 billion of these benefits remain unclaimed each year.[10] So a significant number of older people are living well below the poverty line. One study of older people in deprived areas found that

> more than one in ten older people find it difficult to manage on their current incomes—almost half of older people in poverty say they have gone without buying clothes in the previous year, and fifteen per cent of this group have gone without buying food on occasion.[11]

Older women are much more likely to be multiply deprived than older men. The figures are also much higher for ethnic minorities, who may not have had the opportunity to build up savings or pension entitlements: 'Almost eight out of ten older Somali people and seven out of ten older Pakistani people are living in poverty.'[12] Moreover, poverty in old age is almost inevitably long term; replacing expensive household items, making a major purchase or taking a holiday are pipedreams for a substantial proportion of the older population.

[7] Office for National Statistics *Social trends 33* (2003 edition) 30 January 2003.

[8] A Bowling, *Adding Quality to Quantity: older people's views on their quality of life and its enhancement* (Growing Older programme Findings, University of Sheffield, 2002).

[9] Joseph Rowntree Foundation, *Monitoring poverty and social exclusion 2002* (12 December 2002).

[10] Department for Work and Pensions, *Income Related Benefits: estimates of take-up for 2000–2001* (2003).

[11] T Scharf *et al*, *Growing Older in Socially Deprived Areas: social exclusion in later life* (London, Help the Aged, 2003) 4.

[12] *Ibid*, at 5.

Mobility is crucial. Lack of mobility creates problems for significant numbers of older people, making it difficult to lead a normal life, look after oneself and keep up with friends and social activities. Absence of local amenities such as shops, post offices, GP and other health services and social clubs and community centres exacerbates the situation and makes it more difficult to maintain the social relationships that are so important to quality of life. Car ownership is low relative to the general population: only just over half of pensioner households have a car compared with 80 per cent of other households, and access to a car is especially limited among older women and those living alone. Half of all older people, more women than men, use public transport, but 12 per cent do not because of poor health or disability.[13] Moreover, public transport may be unavailable, fail to go to the right place at the right time, or be inaccessible, unreliable, unaffordable or unusable for other reasons.

Housing conditions and the neighbourhood in which people live are other critical factors. Over two-thirds of people over 65 own their own home (roughly the same proportion as for the population as a whole), over a quarter are in social housing and 5 per cent in privately rented housing.[14] Less than 5 per cent live in care homes. However, low incomes make it difficult to repair and maintain owner occupied housing and to ensure a warm home. Nearly a third of older people live in homes that do not meet the English House Condition Survey criterion of 'a reasonable level of thermal comfort'. Poorly heated and insulated homes result in major health problems and high mortality in the winter months—the number of avoidable deaths related to cold weather has been between twenty three and fifty thousand each year over the last five years.[15]

Crime and the fear of crime are also major issues for many older people, and a significant proportion avoid going out at night as a result. While most research indicates that older people are less likely to be victims of crime than other groups, one recent study found that fear of crime was indeed justified in some particularly deprived urban areas, where 40 per cent of older people had been the victim of one or more type of crime in the previous two years, including break-ins, vandalism, theft and assault.[16] Moreover, the consequences of crime for older people can be devastating, economically, psychologically and physically: being knocked to the ground or having your house broken into is unpleasant at any age, but for older people it sends a powerful message of physical and social vulnerability and can signal the end to independence.

The health of older people is on the whole good—three quarters of those over 65 describe their health as either good or fairly good and only a quarter as not good. However, 60 per cent also report a long-standing illness, with two-thirds

[13] Office for National Statistics, *People aged 65 and over: results from the General Household Survey* (June 2003).

[14] *Ibid.*

[15] Help the Aged, *Winter deaths campaign 2003: top ten facts* (2003).

[16] Scharf *et al* above n 11, at 5.

of those saying this limits them in some way.[17] Nearly a third of older people have difficulties with their eyesight and just over a third with their hearing. This apparent contradiction perhaps reflects people's expectation that they will have some health problems as they get older and their capacity to adapt to and accept this as a normal part of ageing. Many older people themselves look after others, usually their spouses, parents or other relatives, and this can be an extremely demanding role. It has been estimated that between a third and a half of all care for older people is provided by other older people.[18]

So what makes for quality of life in old age? Until recently, definitions of quality of life were in the hands of the medical experts, researchers and professionals whose job it is to study older people and their needs. That has begun to change: the ESRC 'Growing Older' research programme, based at the University of Sheffield, has been examining quality of life from a wide range of different perspectives, with an emphasis on what older people themselves have to say on the subject. The overall outcome is a remarkably positive and optimistic view of older age; and a much deeper and more nuanced understanding of what matters to older people. One study[19] asked nearly a thousand people over 65 for their definitions of what makes for quality of life. They identified:

— Having good social relationships with family, friends and neighbours.
— Having social roles and participating in social and voluntary activities, plus other activities/hobbies performed alone.
— Having good health and functional ability.
— Living in a good home and neighbourhood.
— Having a positive outlook and psychological well-being.
— Having an adequate income.
— Maintaining independence and control over one's life.

While income and health are clearly important factors, it is also clear that other less tangible factors, like social relationships, participation and autonomy, are also central to our sense of quality of life.

The final aspiration—of 'maintaining independence and control over one's life'—hints at the fear of loss of control that attends advanced old age, and it is here that the HRA should function as a countermeasure to ensure the continuing dignity and self-determination of older people.

AGEISM AND AGE DISCRIMINATION

One major burden on the older population is the prevalence of ageism and age discrimination in our society. Older people are essentially seen as 'different', of lesser value ('not economically active') and excluded from the mainstream of

---

[17] Office for National Statistics, above n 13.
[18] A Milne, E Hatzidimitriadou, C Chyssanthopolou, and T Owen, *Caring in later life: reviewing the role of older carers* (London, Help the Aged/Tizard Centre University of Kent, 2001).
[19] A Bowling, above n 8.

life. They are assumed to be 'retired'—non-participants, 'a burden' on the young, and a drain on the nation's resources. These profoundly negative perceptions result in a deep sense of exclusion for many older people who are made to feel that they are no longer of use or value to the world they live in.

Margaret Simey, who has been active in local politics and community life in Liverpool well into her nineties, expresses this powerfully:

> One thing is for certain: older people like myself are almost universally aware of the fact that we are now regarded as being different, simply by virtue of our age. We are a problem, a burden, dependent, objects of pity, denied any role in the management of the common affairs of the community we live in. . . . What is it like to be thus excluded from all that makes life worth living? I experienced a new sense of loneliness, not because I lack company but because I am shut out. . . . We simply don't belong. Like balloons filled with gas but cut off from any anchorage, we float aimlessly, futile, without purpose . . . It is the denial of our need to belong, to have the security of a recognised place in society, however insignificant, that is so demeaning, so demoralising . . . I believe that the need to belong to some group larger than ourselves is a fundamental human necessity that is, and always has been, the glue that binds a community together. None of us can go it alone; we must have a context, a structure, a social framework in which we have a slot. To deny us that, to throw us out as useless, is to deny that most fundamental need.[20]

The assertion of equal dignity and worth in the HRA is a positive and welcome challenge to such disenfranchisement in old age. But it is set against a history of entrenched social attitudes. As Sandra Fredman and Sarah Spencer point out, deep-seated inequalities on grounds of age are widely accepted as natural or even appropriate.[21] Age discrimination is so deeply entrenched and so much part of the fabric of social attitudes that we may not even recognise it when we see it.

Indeed, chronological age has come to be seen as a defining factor and an acceptable basis for social policy. The use of specific ages for essentially progressive social policies, such as the state pension and the concept of retirement, has resulted in strong demarcation lines in the way we see ourselves and in the way we are seen by others. But distinctions based on age are essentially arbitrary—an artificial social construct. As individuals, we do not change much from day to day, yet a single birthday can dictate whether or not we have a job, which benefit we are entitled to, or what kind of social care we get. In spite of their arbitrary nature, distinctions based on age have been carried through into social policy and the way we organise public services. As a result, age discrimination is found throughout social policy and public services, and in the private sector too—in education, health and social care, in transport planning and provision, in social security policy, in insurance and in a myriad of other fields.[22]

---

[20] M Simey, 'Foreword' in *Age Discrimination in Public Policy: a review of evidence* (London, Help the Aged, 2002).

[21] S Fredman and S Spencer (eds), *Age as an Equality Issue: Legal and Policy Perspectives* (Oxford, Hart Publishing, 2003).

[22] Help the Aged, *Age discrimination in Public Policy: a review of evidence* , above n 20.

Until recently, older people, like disabled people, were seen almost solely in terms of the demands they were likely to make on the health and care systems. Their continuing stake in the rest of society—in transport systems, cultural, educational and recreational activities, their actual and potential contribution to the community—was largely overlooked. They were excluded both from the mainstream of life and the considerations of policy makers.

As it became clear that the demographic picture was changing fast, with most people now living well beyond the age of 65 and increasing numbers surviving into extreme old age, politicians and opinion formers responded first with alarm at the potential expense of supporting a large older population with a diminishing proportion of workers. Headlines about the 'time-bomb' of an ageing population and a 'grey tide' of older people, rather than celebrating significant social progress, implied a threat to the majority, while denying the equal citizenship of older people.

Subsequently, and increasingly, more thoughtful responses have emerged, such as policies on 'active ageing' and strategies that aim to respond to and plan positively for an ageing population: the Cabinet Office's 'Winning the Generation Game',[23] the European Directive on Equal Treatment and, more recently, the Welsh Assembly's 'Strategy for Older People'[24] are all examples of this trend. Older people themselves have increasingly claimed their right to be heard: senior citizens forums, made up of older people and with broad agendas of their own, have sought to influence local policy and practice.[25] The 'Better Government for Older People' programme has sought to ensure that local authorities and other public bodies engage directly with older people and recognise their interests across the whole range of local services.[26]

THE IMPACT OF AGE DISCRIMINATION

It is only very recently that researchers have begun to examine the nature and prevalence of age discrimination, but already it is clear that much current social policy assumes that, after a certain age, people can be treated differently and often less favourably. For example:

— The 2001 census failed to ask those over 75 about their educational attainments or their transport needs, as though this information was of no interest to planners and policy makers.

— Older people face higher insurance premiums for car insurance, they may find it extremely difficult to rent a car and may be denied active roles as volunteers in their own communities due to lack of insurance cover.[27]

[23] Cabinet Office, *Winning the Generation Game* (2000).
[24] Welsh Assembly, *Government Strategy for Older People* (2003).
[25] *Senior Citizens Forums—a voice for older people* (London, Help the Aged, 2002).
[26] Better Government for Older People, *All our futures* (May 2000).
[27] D Sinclair, *Consultation paper on Insurance and Age Discrimination* (London, Help the Aged, Jan 2004, unpublished draft).

— There is an age barrier built into disability benefits: someone who becomes disabled before the age of 65 is entitled to Disability Living Allowance, which includes a mobility component—extra money to enable disabled people to be mobile and live full and active lives. People who become disabled after the age of 65 receive Attendance Allowance instead, which makes no provision for mobility.[28]

— The focus of education policy has been on young people and vocational training to the virtual exclusion of older adults, their interests and their potential. Modern Apprenticeships stop at the age of 30 and those over 55 are not eligible for student loans. People over 50 make up fewer than 10 per cent of those engaged in formal learning, in spite of demographic change and the rapidly changing nature of the job market.[29]

— In the NHS, there has been widespread discrimination, in which age has often been used as a means of rationing scarce resources. Older patients may not be offered treatment options (for stroke or coronary care, for example) that would be automatically available to younger people. There are large disparities between the resources and professional expertise available to 'adult' mental health services and mental health services for older people. Research studies show that older people often wait longer for treatment in accident and emergency departments and may have difficulty accessing specialist care.[30]

— Social services have traditionally had age-based services, with lower funding per head and lower expectations about what older people are entitled to expect from the service, compared with younger adults. A rationing process reserves cash limited resources for those in the most acute need; and preventive services (which are intended to meet needs early and to stave off dependency) are in short supply.[31]

Further in-depth analysis is beginning to emerge with regard to certain policy fields, for example in *Age as an Equality Issue*, which includes chapters on employment, education, and health and social care by experts in those fields.[32] But in most fields, little positive action has as yet been taken to begin to address the issue.

In the health service and in social care, however, efforts are being made to tackle age discrimination. The National Service Framework for Older People,[33] published in March 2001 (and applying only to England), announced itself as 'the first ever comprehensive strategy to ensure fair, high quality, integrated

---

[28] M Howard, 'Age Discrimination in Social Security' in *Age Discrimination in Public Policy: a review of evidence*, above n 20.

[29] J Soulsby, 'Age discrimination in Education' in *ibid*.

[30] E Roberts, 'Age discrimination in Health' in *ibid*.

[31] M Henwood, 'Age discrimination in social services' in *ibid*.

[32] S Fredman and S Spencer, above n 21.

[33] Department of Health, *National Service Framework for Older People* (2001).

health and social care services for older people.' It set out eight standards, the first of which is to 'root out' age discrimination in health and social care:

> NHS services will be provided, regardless of age, on the basis of clinical need alone. Social care services will not use age in their eligibility criteria or policies, to restrict access to available services.

The second standard is equally important. It aims to ensure that 'NHS and social care services treat older people as individuals and enable them to make choices about their own care . . .' This makes clear that older people and their carers should receive person-centred care and services which respect them as individuals and which are arranged around their needs. Respect and dignity and the need to enable older people to make their own informed decisions echo some of the human rights principles enshrined in the Human Rights Act.

In social care, following the National Service Framework and subsequent guidance, services now need to be allocated on the basis of individual need,[34] without regard to the age of the person concerned. But without additional funding to bring services for older people up to the quantity and quality of those for younger adults, it is far from clear how that can be achieved.

Shortly after the National Service Framework for Older People was published, the Kings Fund undertook a study[35] of a hundred managers across health and social care, to find out how much they felt age discrimination was affecting their services. Three-quarters of the respondents believed that age discrimination existed in their local area, particularly in social services:

> [Age discrimination] is very noticeable when assessing the needs of younger persons . . . 'Do they have a social life?' and so on. For older people we take a much more basic view.[36]
>
> The limit (of spending) for younger disabled people is much higher . . . because residential costs are higher. The market for older people is more 'pile 'em high, sell 'em cheap.' But also, there's a notion that it's more important to keep a young person at home.[37]
>
> There isn't enough chiropody or rehabilitation. If you want any physical refurbishment done to your home, like stair rails, you can wait a very long time.[38]
>
> The medical director of an NHS trust felt that discrimination was more tangible in the way people were treated after admission. 'People are very well managed in the first few days.' But after initial treatment, she felt that doctors were quick to discharge older patients to residential care, without much thought of the long term outcomes for the patient or their wishes.[39]

---

[34] Department of Health, *Fair Access to Care Services* (2002).

[35] E Roberts, J Robinson, and L Seymour, *Old Habits Die Hard: tackling age discrimination in health and social care* (London, Kings Fund, 2002).

[36] Director of Social Services, *ibid*, p 11.

[37] Head of Older People's Strategy, *ibid*, at 11.

[38] Head of Primary Care PCT, *ibid*, at 19.

[39] *Ibid*, at 19.

Another in-depth study carried out by the University of Leicester in 2002[40] examined the policies and practices in six local authority social services departments and found similar concerns:

> Officers in authorities with lower overall funding or the least political support were more likely to raise anxieties about the quality of care they could provide. Lower staffing ratios, lower quality of services overall; services which were unable to stretch beyond meeting the most basic personal and social needs of older people; and the need to make a relatively small amount of money stretch to a large population in need were all mentioned in [four of the six authorities studied].

More recently still, the Commission for Health Improvement's (CH1) 2003 report on *Emerging Themes—Services for Older People*[41] revealed clear disquiet about the standards of hospital services for older people. This study collated material from seventeen clinical governance reviews over the six months between August 2002 and February 2003, examining stroke services and those for fractured neck of femur (FNOF), both of which are common among older patients. While the language of the Commission is measured and restrained, and it is careful to give examples of good practice, there is no mistaking the message:

> Some reports raise particular concerns about privacy and dignity in relation to vulnerable elderly people. In at least two acute trusts where the review focused on stroke services, CHI was concerned that arrangements for feeding patients were not adequate. Some environments were inadequate for appropriate stroke care and particularly rehabilitation. Many clinical governance reviews raise concerns about a lack of a cohesive approach to care of the elderly across and between organisations in the local health economy, for both stroke and FNOF. As a consequence older people are most likely to suffer from delayed and poorly managed discharge to the care of community services. In some acute trusts there are concerns that care is not organised so that older people have access to the specialist care they need.

All these studies indicate not only that services for older people lag behind expected standards for the population as a whole, but that their quality is such that human rights may well be routinely at risk.

THE IMPLICATIONS FOR HUMAN RIGHTS

Older people become particularly vulnerable to human rights violations at the point in their lives when, because of physical or mental ill health or frailty, they become dependent on the care of others. 'Abuse is a violation of an individual's human and civil rights by any other person.'[42] It is usually classified under six

---

[40] S Katbamna, G Martin and G Parker, *Nothing personal: rationing social care for older people* (London, Help the Aged, 2002).

[41] Commission for Health Improvement, *Emerging Themes—Services for Older People* (March 2003).

[42] Department of Health and Home Office, *No Secrets: guidance on developing and implementing multi-agency policies and procedures to protect vulnerable adults from abuse* (London, 2003).

headings: physical; psychological; financial; sexual abuse; neglect or acts of omission (such as ignoring medical needs or failing to provide proper nutrition); and discriminatory abuse (such as racist or sexist slurs or harassment).

Violation of the human rights of older people can probably best be understood by considering three categories: abuse by individuals; violations resulting from the culture of an organisation or institution which allows (or even expects) abusive practices; and systemic violations, where the very policies and systems established to meet the needs and uphold the dignity of older people fail to do so.

Abuse by Individuals

In some instances older people may be subject to abuse by individuals acting alone. Abusers may be members of their own family—rarely the primary carer who provides day-to-day hands-on care, more often a member of the extended family.[43] Older people can also experience abuse from neighbours who harass them or vandalise their property, from private landlords,[44] and from 'bogus callers' (eg people purporting to read meters who steal) and 'rogue traders' (people offering a service who harass or overcharge).[45] Sometimes, however, abuse may be perpetrated by paid workers whose job it is to provide day-to-day care in people's own homes, or by members of staff in residential homes, hospitals and other health care settings.

In 2000, Action on Elder Abuse published a study of over 1400 calls made to its confidential helpline between 1997 and 1999.[46] Three-quarters of such calls concerned abuse in people's own homes (including sheltered housing), while a quarter of the calls concerned abuse in institutional settings—hospitals, nursing homes or residential homes. (This is a disproportionately large number, since only 5 per cent of older people live in institutional settings.)

A great deal of attention has been devoted in recent years to identifying children at risk of abuse and developing appropriate responses which safeguard the child. New responses to domestic violence have also been developed, with stronger action to protect the victim and help them rebuild their lives. There is no comparable level of awareness or action with regard to older people; and nobody knows the real incidence of elder abuse, as it tends to be hidden and goes unreported. When older people themselves speak out, like children and abused women before them, they may not be believed, and friends and neighbours may feel helpless to intervene.

[43] G Fitzgerald, *Memorandum on Elder Abuse: evidence to the Health Select Committee* (London, Action on Elder Abuse, November 2003).

[44] N Carlton *et al*, *The harassment and abuse of older people in the private rented sector* (Bristol, The Policy Press, 2003).

[45] Help the Aged, *Senior Safety campaign* (2003).

[46] Action on Elder Abuse, *Listening is not enough* (London, AEA, 2000).

Much of what *is* reported concerns abuse perpetrated by strangers—the person who has been mugged for their pension or been tricked out of their savings (this is similar to the 'stranger danger' about which children are warned). However, it is likely that the majority of elder abuse, as with child abuse, goes on within the home and from people who are known to the victim. The Community and District Nursing Association found that, in a survey of 5000 senior nurses, 88 per cent had witnessed elder abuse, often from a family member. Less than half of them had had specific training to deal with the problem and few knew what to do or where to go for help.[47]

The Department of Health and the Home Office have recently issued joint guidance on developing and implementing multi-agency policies and procedures to protect vulnerable adults, including older people, from abuse. In this guidance, a wide range of agencies, including health workers, the police and social services, have a responsibility to identify instances of abuse and to act to protect the individual concerned. But it is clear that much more needs to be done. Greater public awareness is needed. Older people and their friends and neighbours need to know where to go for help, and access to independent advocates to offer support and help them rebuild their lives and their confidence. All staff who visit older people in their own homes or are employed in other care settings, whether nurses, GPs or care workers, should be suitable as individuals and aware of their responsibilities with regard to human rights. Employers and professional bodies have a responsibility to vet staff and ensure that all those employed to look after older people (it is only very recently that checks with the Criminal Records Bureau have been required). Multi-agency training on elder abuse, and what to do about it, should be standard practice. In short, elder abuse needs to come out of the closet and become a public and political priority.

The Culture of Institutions

Sometimes, however, abuse of human rights may not be the action of rogue individuals but may be tolerated and sustained by institutional culture. The usual moral safeguards against harmful behaviour break down and behaviour which violates people's human rights becomes the norm.

There are numerous examples of poor treatment of older people in hospital wards, which can be severe enough to constitute inhuman or degrading treatment, and which can put lives at risk. Help the Aged's 'Dignity on the Ward' campaign uncovered over 1,300 cases of varying degrees of abuse and neglect in hospital care over a two-year period to 2001, some of which were undoubtedly life threatening, and most of which concerned inhuman and degrading treatment. Indeed, inhuman and degrading treatment can become an

---

[47] http//www.elderabuse.org.uk/mainpages/whatsnew.htm#nurses

everyday experience. The following are quotations from letters received by the 'Dignity on the Ward' campaign[48]:

> A nurse unceremoniously lifted her shift garment they had put on her and exposed her completely in front of my son and I. It seemed terrible to me for her to be treated in such an undignified and humiliating manner.
>
> Every day without fail and regardless of my time of arrival I had to change my father as all his clothes were permanently soaked in urine.
>
> She was most upset because she kept on asking for a bedpan and no one arrived, or on many occasions, arrived too late and she wet herself. She was both embarrassed and hurt at the reaction she got to having wet the bed. She ended up with no dignity at all.
>
> Her meal would be on the tray cold and hardly touched. More often than not her teeth would be on the locker at the other side of the bed, well away from the chair on which she was sitting. At no time was she encouraged to eat, the food was not cut into bite-size pieces and no person seemed to be responsible to see that the patients received nourishment.

At times, such a culture can be directly life threatening. One woman recounted her experience to Help the Aged's 'Campaign for Age Equality': she tells of being admitted to hospital following an asthma attack and referred to a non-specialist ward 'known locally as the chamber of horrors.' She was denied access to a nebuliser at the required times, the drip bag was allowed to run dry and the oxygen ran out. She suffered a respiratory arrest and had to be resuscitated. At that point she was transferred to the coronary ward and then the chest ward, where the treatment was excellent and the 'ages were varied and quite a few of them had asthma like me':

> My daughter asked the consultant why, whenever she had been admitted to hospital with an asthma attack, she had always gone to the decent ward, even though she had never been as bad as me. He said people were living longer and they could not cope . . . The thought of ever going into hospital again still scares me.[49]

'Do not resuscitate' notices placed on the records of older patients without their consent, which caused an outcry in the press in 2001, clearly reflect assumptions by medical staff about the quality of life of older people and violates their right to life. More recently, the Commission for Health Improvement published a damning report of an investigation following allegations of physical and emotional abuse of patients by care staff at a mental health unit for older people run by Manchester Mental Health and Social Care Trust:

> This is the third investigation by the health watchdog into the care of vulnerable older people, leading to concerns about standards of care for these people nationally. . . . The care of older people nationally is very concerning.[50]

---

[48] *Dignity on the Ward*. Selected quotes from letters received from older people and their relatives and carers (London, Help the Aged, 2000, unpublished).

[49] T Harding and M Felton, *Everyday age discrimination: an analysis of case studies from Help the Aged's Age Equality campaign* (London, Help the Aged, 2004).

[50] http://www.chi.nhs.uk/eng/news/2003/sep/14.shtml

Care homes are another form of institution in which a culture of denial of human rights can arise and the unthinkable can become normal. Older people may be routinely ignored when they call for help, or fed their breakfast while seated on the commode to save staff time.[51] 'The rules' may impinge on residents' freedom of movement and older people may be bullied within a culture of oppression. Cleaning may be inadequate, leading to unpleasant and smelly surroundings, and one inquiry found that the medical needs of residents were being ignored and they were required to share commodes:

> The caller found out yesterday that her mother is being abused in the care home where she lives. Her mother is malnourished and was taken to hospital yesterday because one of her toe nails is missing. As she is not mobile she could not have knocked herself. A care worker accompanied them to hospital and told the caller about all the abuse in the home, residents not being fed, not being taken to the toilet etc. One man has died and his wife is complaining, so the home is now under investigation.[52]

Lack of suitably qualified staff in care homes can put the lives of older people at serious risk:

> An inquest in Eastbourne in October 2002 found that an elderly woman with Alzheimer's' disease died of dehydration after a week in a care home, because no-one understood that she needed help with drinking and eating. In another case in north London, a man with dementia was taken off medication for his heart condition when he went into a care home, in spite of detailed instructions left by his wife. Instead Temazepam (a short-acting sedative) was administered. His health deteriorated rapidly and he died a few weeks later.[53]

New standards have been introduced for care homes and a new system of inspection has been put in place under the auspices of the Commission for Social Care Inspection. However, inspections are only required twice a year, one announced and one unannounced. While all homes are required to have a complaints system, it can be difficult for residents or their relatives to complain to unreceptive staff or managers. In one case relatives had to be extremely persistent in voicing their concerns and it took many months for action to be taken on serious allegations of poor standards and abusive practice.[54]

It is clear that much more active steps are needed to ensure that 'closed cultures' do not develop in institutions like care homes or hospital wards. Residents, patients and their relatives and friends need ready access to independent advocates whose job it is to uphold their human rights. Staff need to be encouraged to uphold high standards and to speak out when they see bad practice. Managers need to take responsibility for setting those standards and ensuring they are met. And there needs to be active intervention by the law when

---

[51] J Watson, above n 4.
[52] SeniorLine, February 2003.
[53] T Harding and J Gould, above n 5.
[54] Lynde House Relatives Support Group, *Lynde House Independent Investigation* (South West London Health Authority, May 2002).

human rights are violated, whether or not an individual chooses to take action. It will be crucial that the proposed Commission for Equality and Human Rights can act independently on behalf of those whose human rights are at risk in areas where there is cause for concern.

Private Providers

A further issue arises with care homes: under the HRA, the state has a positive duty to secure the effective protection of human rights. 'Public Authorities have an obligation not only to avoid violating the rights of those in their care, or whom they serve, but also to have regard to their wider and more positive duty to "secure for everyone the rights and freedoms" which the HRA and the other instruments define.'[55] However, many previously 'public functions' are now carried out by the private or voluntary sectors. With regard to care homes for older people, by March 2001, the independent sector provided 92 per cent of all homes and 85 per cent of places in care homes.[56] Increasingly, domiciliary care in people's own homes is also provided by the private and voluntary sectors, rather than directly by local authorities.

In March 2002, the Court of Appeal decided that the activities carried out by a private care provider did not constitute a public function[57] and so those in such homes (whether they are paid for by the local authority or whether they pay themselves) did not have the protection of the Human Rights Act. In England alone, therefore, about 355,000 older people are without any guarantee that their fundamental human rights will be protected and without recourse to legal remedies for human rights violations. This is clearly an extremely worrying situation, and the JCHR has published a report on this legal loophole, which leaves many of the most vulnerable older people unprotected. In the meantime, the increasing provision by the private and voluntary sectors resulting from the closure of local authority facilities and the sale of local authority homes makes the HRA virtually redundant for many of those who need it most.

Systemic Abuse of Human Rights

Systemic violations of human rights, while less intimate and personal, are in some ways even more disturbing than abuse perpetrated by individuals or condoned by institutional culture. Rather than the one-off individual who commits a crime against an older person, or the one bad ward or care home, older

---

[55] Joint Committee on Human Rights, *The Case for a Human Rights Commission* 6th Report, para 5.

[56] Community Care Statistics 2001, http//www.doh.gov.uk/public/sb0129.htm

[57] *R (Callin and Heather) v Leonard Cheshire Foundation* [2002] EWCA Civ 366.

people's human rights are put at risk by the very system charged with upholding them.

Poor quality services and difficulty in accessing services impact heavily on the human rights of older people. Older people may be living in deteriorating circumstances, in dirty homes they cannot clean or heat properly, unable to manage their washing or cooking and unable to move freely around in their own homes. They have to be in severe need of help before they become eligible for an assessment of their needs and the provision of services. Even when they do meet these tough criteria, help may be delayed for months, or they may end up having to pay for it themselves. Many older people and their relatives go round and round the system trying to get the help they need and being frustrated at all turns. In order to qualify for social care from a local authority, older people have to meet certain eligibility criteria. These have become increasingly strict year by year, as local authorities have attempted to manage their budgets in the face of rising demand and the growth in the numbers of very old people. As a consequence, many people who are finding it difficult to manage aspects of their daily lives get little or no help. The following case studies are from Help the Aged's free advice line, SeniorLine:

> The caller has asked social services for help with providing household adaptations and equipment for his mother who is nearly 100. They have asked for information about what she needs but say it will be at least eight months until she can be assessed, and the equipment will not be provided before then. (SeniorLine, April 2003).
>
> The caller is 77-years-old and needs grab rails to help her get around her home. So far she has waited a year for the rails to be fitted but she has no idea when the work will be carried out and mobility is becoming more of a problem. She is afraid she may not be able to remain in her home much longer without this help. (SeniorLine, May 2003).

Scarcity of resources to provide adequate support also results in a failure to take steps to maintain the psychological and emotional integrity of older people. Older people often live in circumstances where their capacity to pursue their interests or to maintain any social or recreational life beyond the four walls of their home is frustrated by the lack of services to support such life enhancing activities. It is hardly surprising that the incidence of depression among older people who need help to live a normal life is very high.

There can be little doubt that many older people in these circumstances are experiencing inhuman and degrading treatment and a severe loss of human dignity. The HRA is being contravened by the omission of those services which would enable older people to retain their dignity and self-respect in the face of increasing physical or mental ill health. It is quite possible that people die as a result of lack of care and attention. There is no system for monitoring how many people die in their homes or following emergency admission to hospital because they have been denied an assessment or a service they were assessed as needing. The kind of inquiry that is undertaken when a child dies, seeking to establish 'what went wrong' with the services that were supposed to protect the rights and well-being of that child, rarely happens with older people. Nor are inquests often held, as the death of older people is rarely considered unusual.

When people have had an assessment, do meet the criteria and do qualify for help, the social services department has a legal duty to supply the relevant services. Nevertheless, the person may not necessarily receive them. Funding panels are established which review individual cases and allocate the available resources. Such panels are unlawful but unfortunately commonplace. Individual cases are settled to avoid threatened litigation, but the practice continues.[58] Individuals then find themselves unable to access the services they have been assessed as needing. In both of the examples below, the right to respect for private and family life (Article 8 of the ECHR) would seem to have been overlooked:

> The caller rang some months ago for advice about paying for residential care as her husband was in hospital and had been assessed as requiring residential care. He is still in hospital which is not a suitable environment for him. His case keeps coming before the funding panel but keeps being refused. The latest letter from social services said the delay was due to severe funding difficulties caused by the number of people requiring residential care. (SeniorLine, May 2003).
>
> A 92-year-old woman was in a residential home until she had an unsuccessful operation just over a year ago. She was then assessed by the hospital social worker as needing nursing home care. For a year, social services paid £500 of the full weekly cost of the nursing home, with the woman's daughter paying the additional £25. However, social services have now told the daughter that they will only pay £385, their usual rate, so the woman will have to move. She is partially sighted and deaf. The present home takes time to understand her, unlike the previous residential home where she was abused when she could not understand. There has been no reassessment of the woman's needs and her daughter is concerned that another move would be detrimental to her mother's health. (SeniorLine, April 2003).

The right to respect for one's private and family life is also frequently infringed by the widespread practice of requiring older people to leave their homes when the cost to the local authority of maintaining them at home would be greater than the cost of a residential place. While major efforts are often made to enable younger people to remain independent and to live in their own homes, the same is not true of older people, who may be allowed only a limited amount of support at home before it is decided that 'the time for residential care has come.' Particularly emotive stories arise occasionally concerning older couples who are forced to separate against their will, because one of them needs more care than can be provided at home. In one case in Oxfordshire (November 2002), an older couple was placed in two different homes, though this was soon rectified when exposed in the press. In Portsmouth (August 2003), a couple who had been married for 61 years were placed in homes five miles apart because they had different needs: she had advancing dementia and he was physically disabled and in

---

[58] T Harding and J Gould, above n 5.

a wheelchair, and a home suitable for them both could not be found. They agreed to this, on condition an adapted taxi would be supplied five days a week to enable the man to spend the day with his wife. However that arrangement broke down when resources became tight. An outcry in the press ensued.

It is clear that sheer financial pressure on local authority budgets can result in situations where the human rights of older people are at risk. The closure of care homes is one field where the HRA has been used to try to protect human rights. Care homes close for a number of reasons: they may not meet the standards required and not be amenable to alteration; they may not be financially viable; or the home owner may decide to sell the home for business reasons. Residents, by definition sufficiently ill or disabled to need round the clock care, have no tenancy rights and can be asked to leave at any time. The impact of closure on the residents is of course profound: not only do they lose the home they expected to be in for the rest of their lives, but they lose their friends and familiar staff as well. Their right to private and family life is certainly at issue. The research into the effect of home closures shows that older people's well-being, their health and indeed their lives are at risk unless the greatest care is taken in making the move.[59] In two cases in 2003, those of Violet Townsend in Gloucestershire and Winifred Humphrey in Hastings, both of whom were moved from their care home at short notice and without their consent, the person concerned died within two or three weeks of being moved.

One inquiry into the proposed closure of a local authority care home in Plymouth[60] (Granby Way) interviewed each of the affected residents and subsequently issued a set of guidelines for good practice in closing homes, involving careful consideration of the needs and desires of each resident. In those cases, where the court has upheld a decision to close the home, it has largely been because the local authority concerned had taken all reasonable measures to inform and involve the residents and has therefore minimised the risk to their lives. Individual human rights suffer in a system which is both under-funded and under pressure; and older people are at particular risk because the services intended for their use already start from a lower base line. Older people thus habitually suffer discrimination (contrary to Article 14) in the enjoyment of their human rights.

MAKING A REALITY OF HUMAN RIGHTS FOR OLDER PEOPLE

When the whole system operates *as if* older people had no rights, it is not surprising that older people themselves do not know they have them and do not feel

[59] Dr David Jolley, *Report to the High Court of Justice Queen's Bench Division* CO/2278/2002 *Lancashire Care Association and Others and Lancashire County Council* (2002).

[60] J Clarke, A Stevenson and B Parrott, *Report and Findings of the Extraordinary Complaints Panel; Granby Way Residential Care Home for Older People* (Plymouth City Council and Nicola Mackintosh Solicitors, 2002).

able to exercise them. It is clear that much stronger action is needed if the HRA is to become meaningful for older people and they are to benefit from it. There is an urgent need for more proactive intervention. The only way that older people can make use of the HRA at present is through litigation. For the vast majority, that is not a realistic option. No matter what their experience, older people who suffer abuse rarely make formal complaints, and are very unlikely to instigate legal action. Evidence from the Action on Elder Abuse helpline shows that:

> many relatives were phoning to discover what could be done to help a victim who could not contact the helpline themselves—for example, because they lived in a care home and had no access (or no private access) to a phone or they had dementia or another disorder which meant that they had communication difficulties.[61]

The Dignity on the Ward campaign received over 1,300 complaints from members of the public. These ranged in severity from dirty wards and lack of respect, to abusive treatment and downright neglect. The great majority of those complaints came from relatives or friends of the abused person, and often only after that person had died. It was very common for the older person not only to remain silent, but to plead with relatives 'not to make a fuss,' while relatives themselves often felt that to complain would only put the person concerned at even greater risk.[62] Making a complaint is a confrontational act which requires energy, courage and conviction. Older people who have been abused, and who may be literally dependent on those about whom they wish to complain, are very unlikely to take on such a daunting commitment. Not all older people have relatives watching over their welfare, and not all relatives have the knowledge to challenge professional practice and the opportunity to assert their views. Furthermore, individual litigation on a case-by-case basis is a slow, uncertain and unpredictable way to enforce the law to protect older people from highly distressing situations. It is also very expensive. More urgent and proactive measures need to be taken.

If the Human Rights Act is to become meaningful to older people, the need for a human rights commission is therefore paramount. The Government has announced its intention of establishing a Commission for Equality and Human Rights by October 2006. The new commission will need a full range of powers of education, promotion, inquiry and enforcement to ensure that the HRA becomes meaningful and effective in those situations where older people's rights are most at risk. The commission will need to take a number of proactive measures.

---

[61] Action on Elder Abuse, above n 46.

[62] J Ellis, *Failing Older People: flaws in the NHS complaints procedure* (London, Help the Aged, 1999).

Empowerment of Older People

Older people and their relatives and friends need to know that they have rights which must be respected and what those rights are. A high profile public information initiative is therefore needed, backed up by a system of local independent advocates, to whom older people and their relatives can turn for clarification or at times of difficulty or distress. Older people need someone who is at their side and on their side and who can be trusted.

Promoting a Human Rights Culture

The commission should have a duty to promote human rights and to ensure that those responsible for providing services understand their responsibilities under the Act and put them into practice. Education, advice and guidance needs be provided to all those responsible for running services for older people in both the public and private sectors. Respect for human rights and the worth and dignity of each individual needs to become the bedrock of the training of all health and care professionals and of the culture of all agencies that carry responsibility for vulnerable people.

   The commission should also ensure that the regulatory bodies charged with monitoring standards in public services, such as the Commission for Social Care Inspection, make human rights the cornerstone of those standards and keep these in the forefront of the inspection process. Inspections of services should be frequent and rigorous and ensure that older people and their friends and relatives can talk in confidence to inspectors, who need to be trained to watch and listen for warning signs. All staff working with vulnerable adults, like those working with children, should be checked for their previous criminal record, and managers held to account for the behaviour of staff members. Audits of local authorities and health trusts should examine service systems to ensure these are not failing those who come to them for help.

Enforcement

The commission should ensure support for those whose human rights have been violated, either through mediation or through supporting or acting on behalf of victims. In cases where individuals are not able or willing to take legal action in their own right, for example, because of mental incapacity, the commission should be able to take action on their behalf. A local advocacy office in each area, linked to the commission, would ensure that support was available at the grass roots where it is needed and had a human face.

Inquiries

Further, a human rights commission should have the power to undertake inquiries, call for evidence and make recommendations to government in situations where there is cause for concern. Two examples illustrate the kinds of issues that the commission might wish to address. One is the position of residents when care homes close. The 'extraordinary complaints panel' that was established to examine the proposed closure of Granby Way in Plymouth[63] upheld the residents' complaints that the decision to close their home did not take account of the threat to their right to life, of the need to protect them from inhuman and degrading treatment and the duty to respect their private and family life. The panel concluded, 'Growing old is not an illness, and people's age must not be used as a justification for restricting their rights in any way.' It appended to its report draft guidelines for local authorities when considering the closure of a care home which place responsibility for safeguarding older people's human rights at the heart of the process. These go further than the courts have thus far gone and are an example of the kind of action that could be undertaken by the commission.

There are also areas where the application of the HRA is not straightforward and rights may be in conflict. These difficult ethical areas require investigation and clarification. For example, the use of restraints is not uncommon in some care settings. Restraints may be physical, taking the form of locked doors or chairs placed in such a way that the person sitting in them cannot rise or move elsewhere. They may be chemical and take the form of drugs which have a calming or sedative effect. Or they may be electronic and take the form of 'tags' which enable people to be tracked when they leave a particular building or environment.[64] At what point do these practices violate human rights? Is the covert administration of medication acceptable where such action is deemed to be in the patient's best interests, as guidance from one of the professional nursing bodies has suggested? The application of human rights dimensions to these practices requires urgent and independent consideration by a human rights commission.

CONCLUSION

With the kinds of powers outlined, the Commission for Equality and Human Rights should be in a real position to ensure that the HRA becomes a meaningful and effective instrument to safeguard older people. However, for older people to become truly equal citizens, the new commission will also need to

[63] J Clarke, A Stevenson and B Parrott, *Report and Findings of the Extraordinary Complaints Panel: Granby Way Care Home for Older People* (Plymouth City Council, 2002).

[64] C Bewley, *Tagging—a technology for care services?* Briefing paper from a joint working group of Age Concern England, Alzheimers' Society, Counsel and Care, Help the Aged, Mind, Public Law Project and Values into Action, London 1998.

address the discrimination that older people face in so many aspects of their daily lives. Forthcoming legislation to ban age discrimination will only address employment and training, not the wider aspects of discrimination that older people experience. Spencer and Fredman argue that this limitation means that 'the Government is giving older people far less protection from discrimination than that provided to victims of discrimination on grounds of race, gender or disability.'[65] A far more positive approach would be to outlaw age discrimination wherever it is found and to require public bodies to promote equality as a whole, for older people as for other groups in society.

It is only once older people truly come in from the cold and are treated as full and equal members of society that the underlying culture that condones the abuse of their human rights will begin to change.

[65] S Spencer and S Fredman, *Age Equality Comes of Age: Delivering Change for Older People* (London, IPPR, 2003) 96.

8

The Human Rights Act 1998 and Disabled People: A Right to be Human?

ANNA LAWSON

INTRODUCTION

THE PROMOTION OF human rights among disabled people is, not surprisingly, at the forefront of the international disability movement. This is powerfully expressed in the opening words of the Madrid Declaration, signed by over 400 participants at the European Congress on Disability in March 2002:

> Disability is a human rights issue. Disabled people are entitled to the same human rights as all other citizens. . . . In order to achieve this goal, all communities should celebrate the diversity within their communities and seek to ensure that disabled people can enjoy the full range of human rights: civil, political, social, economical and cultural as acknowledged by the different international Conventions, the EU Treaty and in the different national constitutions.

A UN convention on the rights of disabled people now seems likely to materialise soon. Disability, however, has not always been regarded as a human rights issue. It has been treated as a medical problem calling for medical solutions in the cure of the individuals concerned and responses from welfare or charitable organisations. Conceiving it as a human rights issue focuses attention instead on the physical, social, attitudinal, legal and other barriers which prevent disabled people participating in the life of their communities.[1] In the language of the social model of disability, developed from within the disability movement

---

[1] See further, T Degener, 'Disabled Persons and Human Rights: The Legal Framework' in T Degener and Y Koster-Dreese (eds), *Human Rights and Disabled Persons: Essays and Relevant Human Rights Instruments* (Dordrecht/Boston/London, Martinus Nijhoff, 1995) 9–11.

itself,[2] people who have physical, sensory, intellectual or other impairments are disabled by the societal barriers erected against them.

The exclusion and poverty experienced by disabled people throughout the world was documented in Liandro Despouiy's 1991 report, commissioned by the UN.[3] He observed that[4]:

> [Disabled] persons frequently live in deplorable conditions, owing to the presence of physical and social barriers, which prevent their integration and full participation in the community. As a result, millions of children and adults throughout the world are segregated and deprived of virtually all their rights, and lead a wretched, marginal life.

The problem has not disappeared. Current, and often shocking, accounts of the human rights abuses endured by disabled people throughout the world have been catalogued by Disability Awareness in Action. In the words of Richard Light, who manages this database,[5] 'We require and merit tangible acknowledgement of our humanity, something that is routinely denied and suppressed.'

Disabled people in the UK are not exempt from such marginalisation. The Disability Discrimination Act 1995 (DDA) was prompted, in part, by startling accounts of the levels of discrimination and deprivation experienced by British disabled people in all aspects of their lives.[6] Though the DDA can be expected to bring about gradual improvements, significant inequalities remain.[7]

How, then, has the Human Rights Act 1998 (HRA)—which allows rights under the European Convention on Human Rights 1950 (ECHR) to be enforced directly in our domestic courts—affected disabled people? A comprehensive answer to this question would not be confined to an analysis of case law alone. It would also consider the ways in which the lives of disabled people have been affected by changes in the way public authorities operate as a result of the Act. Such an investigation is beyond the scope of this chapter. Here, I will simply attempt to assess the implications of some of the recent case law which has particular relevance to disabled people. People with mental health difficulties will often be regarded as disabled and, therefore, there is an inevitable overlap between this chapter and that on mental health. In order to keep this to a minimum, issues which have arisen primarily in the context of mental health or intellectual impairment will not be considered here. Before turning to issues

---

[2] The social model is also evident in the *UN Standard Rules on Equalisation of Opportunities for Disabled People (1993)*, for discussion of which see B Lindqvist, 'Standard Rules in the Disability Field: A New UN instrument' in T Degener and Y Koster-Dreese *ibid*, at 63.

[3] *Human Rights Studies Series*, No 6, Centre for Human Rights (Geneva, United Nations publications, sales no E.92.XIV.4).

[4] *Ibid.*

[5] 'Disability and Human Rights: The Persistent Oxymoron—UN Efforts to Resolve the Conundrum' in A Lawson and C Gooding (eds), *Disability Rights in Europe: From Theory to Practice* (Oxford, Hart Publishing, 2005).

[6] See especially, C Barnes, *Disabled People in Britain and Discrimination: A Case for Anti-Discrimination Legislation* (London, Hurst & Co, 1991).

[7] See, eg, the statistics provided in R Daw, *The Impact of the Human Rights Act on Disabled People* (London, Disability Rights Commission and Royal National Institute for Deaf People, 2000) 7–10.

which have arisen in the context of particular articles of the ECHR, the relationship between the HRA and the DDA will be outlined.

A ROLE FOR THE HUMAN RIGHTS ACT BEYOND THAT OF THE DISABILITY DISCRIMINATION ACT (DDA)?

The DDA prohibits unjustified discrimination against disabled people in relation to areas such as employment, the provision of goods, facilities and services, housing and education. Unlike the HRA, it applies to private individuals and bodies as well as many public authorities.[8] Consequently, a lay person might well wonder whether the HRA will have any effect beyond that already achieved by the DDA.

Article 14 of the ECHR[9] does prohibit discrimination against people on grounds of 'other status' (which includes disability).[10] The scope of Article 14, however, is limited in a number of respects.[11] First, though it does not require the discrimination concerned to amount to an actual breach of another convention right, it does require it to amount to an interference with the enjoyment of such a right.[12] Thus, public authorities may well discriminate against a person under the DDA in a way which does not amount to an interference with a convention right and therefore does not infringe Article 14. Secondly, concepts of indirect discrimination have been slow to emerge from the Article 14 cases[13] and, as yet, there is no clear indication that Article 14 will be interpreted so as to require public authorities to make reasonable adjustments for disabled people—a requirement imposed in most areas of the DDA. This, however, may change after *Thlimmenos v Greece*,[14] where it was held that Article 14 had been breached by a state's unjustified failure (in the context of religion) to treat differently persons whose circumstances were materially different. There is also the possibility that Article 8 rights will be developed so as to require the removal of barriers which would otherwise prevent disabled people from the full enjoyment of their private and family life.[15]

---

[8] The number of public authorities covered by the DDA would be increased by cl 4 of the Draft Disability Discrimination Bill (published on 3 December 2003).

[9] For fuller discussions of Art 14 in the context of disability, see R Daw, above n 7, at 33–37 and L Clements and J Read, *Disabled People and European Human Rights: A Review of the Implications of the 1998 Human Rights Act for Disabled Children and Adults in the UK* (Bristol, The Policy Press, 2003) 25. See also, more generally, A McColgan, 'Human Rights and Equality: Article 14 in the Courts' (a paper delivered at the University of Leeds, Human Rights Research Unit Seminar Series, 5 December 2003).

[10] See eg *Botta v Italy* Series A no 66 (1998) EHRR 241.

[11] Protocol 12 to the ECHR, which would confer a free-standing right to be free from discrimination, has not been ratified by the UK. See generally R Wintemute, 'Within the ambit: how big is the "gap" in Article 14 European Convention on Human Rights? Part 1' [2004] EHRLR 366 and 'Filling the Article 14 "Gap": Government ratification and judicial control of Protocol No 12 ECHR, Part 2' [2004] EHRLR 484.

[12] Thus the claim failed in *Botta v Italy*. See below nn 64–68 and accompanying text.

[13] See A McColgan, 'Principles of Equality and Protection from Discrimination in International Human Rights Law' (2003) 2 *European Human Rights Law Review* 157, 168–70.

[14] Application no 34369/97 (2001) 31 EHRR 15.

[15] See further below pp 146–9.

There will, then, be many situations in which the DDA provides a better refuge for a disabled person than the HRA. There will be many others, however, in which the HRA will be available where the DDA will not or in which it represents the preferable alternative. Claimants under Article 14 are unlikely to have to show that they can leap through all the hoops required to comply with the definition of a disabled person under Part 1 of the DDA. Further, it may well be more difficult for public authorities to justify discriminatory treatment under Article 14 than it would be under the DDA. Finally, while the DDA is confined to the prohibition of discrimination, the HRA is broader. Disabled people will be able to argue that their convention rights have been infringed without the need to show that they have been treated less favourably than a suitable comparitor without their impairment. In some instances these rights will be infringed where public authorities fail to take positive measures to protect or otherwise support them.

ARTICLE 2: THE RIGHT TO LIFE

General

There are many ways in which Article 2 might affect disabled people. Here, though, just two issues will be explored—first, the effect of Article 2 on the use of 'Do Not Resuscitate' orders[16] and, second, the question of whether Article 2 confers a right to die on disabled people.

Do Not Resuscitate Orders

According to the official guidance on the use of 'Do Not Resuscitate' orders (DNR) in the UK,[17] it is appropriate to consider such an order,

> where successful cardiopulmonary resuscitation is likely to be followed by a length and quality of life which would not be acceptable to the patient.

It also states that the responsibility for a decision not to resuscitate lies with the relevant consultant but that it should be made,

---

[16] Issues relating to the withdrawal of food and water from hospital patients unable to give consent will not be considered here but see GT Laurie and JK Mason, 'Negative Treatment of Vulnerable Patients: Euthanasia by Any Other Name?' [2000] *Juridical Review* 159; J Keown, 'Restoring moral and intellectual shape to the law after *Bland*' (1997) 113 *Law Quarterly Review* 481; and C Gooding, 'The Application of the ECHR in British Courts in Relation to Disability Issues' (a paper delivered at the Global Themes in Disability Law—The Context for Irish Law Reform Conference, Human Rights Commission, Law Society of Ireland and National Disability Authority, Dublin, 13 September 2003).

[17] Guidelines drawn up by the British Medical Association and the Royal College of Nursing in conjunction with the Resuscitation Council, March 1993, para 1c.

after appropriate consultation and consideration of all aspects of the patient's condition, the perspectives of other members of the medical and nursing team, the patient and with due regard to patient confidentiality.[18]

There has long been serious concern amongst disabled people and their families that DNR decisions may be made on the basis of false assumptions that the quality of their life would be unacceptable to them. This is not surprising given accounts such as the following[19]:

A company director with spinal muscular atrophy, who is a qualified solicitor, was admitted to hospital with a chest infection. To her horror she found that a doctor had placed a 'Do Not Resuscitate' notice on her medical notes because it was considered that her quality of life did not warrant such intervention.

Referring to phrases used to describe the deaths of disabled people such as 'blessed relief' and 'altruistic filicide', one disabled activist has made the following observation[20]:

There can be no more robust authority for my contention that our humanity is denied than this discursive conflation of charity with murder.

In the recent case of *Glass v UK*,[21] the European Court of Human Rights (ECtHR) had to decide, among other questions, whether Article 2 was infringed by a doctor's decision to issue a DNR order in respect of a 'severely mentally and physically disabled' child who had been admitted to hospital because of respiratory tract infections. The child's mother had not been informed of the notice, to which she was vehemently opposed. The case culminated in a violent assault on the medical staff by other family members which enabled her to reach her son, whom she successfully resuscitated. He recovered from his infection and returned home with his mother. The Court ruled that the claim was inadmissible under Article 2 as it had not been argued that the primary motivation of the doctors had been to kill or shorten the life of the child. They claimed to have been acting on the basis of his best interests. Even if their decisions had, in fact, been errors of professional judgment, there would be no breach of Article 2 if the state had 'made adequate provision for securing high professional standards among health professionals and the protection of the lives of patients' which, it considered, the UK had done. The Court also ruled the complaint inadmissible under Article 14 on the grounds that there was no evidence that the doctors had taken the view that, because of the child's impairments, his quality of life would be lower than that of a non-disabled person. The fact that his

disability was undoubtedly a relevant factor in assessing clinically his chances of survival and determining the treatment which was considered the most appropriate in the circumstances was unimportant.

---

[18] *Ibid*, para 3. The desirability of involving the patient in these decisions is also stressed in 'Resuscitation Policy' (HSC Circular 2000/028).

[19] *From Exclusion to Inclusion* (Disability Rights Task Force 1999), paras 10.13–10.15, 187.

[20] R Light, above n 5.

[21] Application no 61827/00, 18 March 2003.

The decision in *Glass* indicates that disabled people and their families who believe, but have no concrete proof, that decisions not to resuscitate have been based on assumptions about poor quality of life resulting from disability will have little chance of mounting successful challenges under Articles 2 or 14.[22] Redress may well be available, however, in those cases where there is evidence that the decision was primarily motivated by a desire to shorten life or by the belief that the patient's disability itself rendered their life not worth living. This would represent an important step towards full recognition of the inherent and equal value of the lives of disabled people. In practice, however, such recognition will feel like little more than a deceptive mirage to disabled people unable to challenge the unspoken, and perhaps even unconscious, assumptions of medical staff.

The issue of inappropriate DNR orders has recently attracted considerable publicity. In *R v Portsmouth Hospital ex parte Wyatt*[23] the parents of a severely disabled baby objected to the decision of doctors to impose such a notice on their child. Hedley J, however, ruled that such an order was in the best interests of the child and that therefore the parents' wishes should not be determinative.

A Right to Die?

Under UK law, a person of full mental capacity may refuse treatment, even if this has the consequence of shortening their life. Further, since the Suicide Act 1961, it has not been unlawful to commit suicide. To assist another to do so, however, remains a criminal offence.[24]

The implications of this legal framework for disabled people who have full mental capacity and choose to die but are unable to do so unassisted because of their impairments burst upon public consciousness in the case of *Pretty v UK*.[25] Dianne Pretty, who had motor neurone disease which had resulted in paralysis from the neck down, was physically unable to commit suicide. She wished to die in order to spare herself the final stages of the disease which were 'exceedingly distressing and undignified'.[26] Her husband was willing to assist her but she would not accept his help in the absence of an assurance from the DPP that he would not subsequently be prosecuted for assisting suicide. Mrs Pretty sought judicial review of the DPP's refusal to grant this assurance—a case which, having been defeated in the House of Lords, eventually reached the ECtHR.

The Court held that[27]:

---

[22] In *Glass*, however, claims that Art 8 had been breached by the way in which the decisions had been made (without the knowledge or consent of the mother) were held to be admissible and the case eventually succeeded on this basis (see App no 61827/00 (9 March 2004).

[23] [2004] EWHC 2247 (7 October 2004). See, for further discussion of 'best interests', *R v General Medical Council ex parte Burke* [2004] EWHC 1879, concerning the withdrawal of food and water provided through artificial means to a terminally ill patient.

[24] Section 2(1).

[25] Application no 2346/02 (2002) 35 EHRR 1.

[26] *Ibid*, para 8.

[27] Above n 25, at para 39.

Article 2 cannot, without a distortion of language, be interpreted as conferring the diametrically opposite right, namely a right to die; nor can it create a right to self-determination in the sense of conferring on an individual the entitlement to choose death rather than life.

Article 2 concerned simply the protection of life, regardless of its quality or the wishes of individuals not to have it. Though Mrs Pretty argued that her inability to choose to die infringed other Articles, she was not successful. Her argument under Article 14, that UK law discriminated between those who were physically capable of committing suicide and those who were not by treating them in the same way despite material differences in their circumstances, failed on the grounds that:

> to seek to build into the law an exemption for those judged to be incapable of committing suicide would seriously undermine the protection of life which the 1961 Act was intended to safeguard and greatly increase the risk of abuse.[28]

Thus, any claim of discrimination on grounds of disability would be defeated by an objective and reasonable justification.

It is difficult to disagree with Lord Bingham's observation that,[29] 'No-one of ordinary sensitivity could be unmoved by the frightening ordeal which faces Mrs Dianne Pretty.' No doubt, many people facing similar ordeals will feel frustrated and betrayed by the approach adopted by the ECtHR. For many others, however, including many disabled people, there will be relief that the Court was not prepared to enter into the question of whether life below a certain quality is worthy of protection.

No treatment of recent developments relating to disabled people and a right to die would be complete without some reference to *Re B*[30]—a case decided within months of *Pretty* but not on the basis of the HRA. Ms B, a 43-year-old woman who had become tetraplegic following a sudden illness, having spent a year in an intensive care unit, applied to the Court for a ruling that her ventilator should be switched off with the inevitable consequence of bringing about her death. The Court of Appeal granted this ruling because it found Ms B to have full mental capacity and, therefore, to be entitled to make her own decisions about the continuation of treatment. It summarily dismissed the argument advanced by the NHS Trust (whose staff were reluctant to turn off the ventilator) that she lacked the information on which to base these decisions as she had not yet experienced rehabilitative treatment and was, therefore, unaware of its potential benefits. To hold that consent to the withdrawal of treatment could not be 'informed' until a patient had undergone a rehabilitation programme, according to Butler-Sloss LJ,[31] would be to deny that patient the choice of whether or not to submit to such a programme. A report in *The Times*,

---

[28] Above n 25, at para 89.
[29] Quoted above n 25, at para 14.
[30] [2002] EWHC 449.
[31] *Ibid*, para 63.

welcoming the decision, commented that,[32] 'There was hardly a person in the courtroom who did not hope that she would be allowed relief from her living death'. Within the disability community, however, the decision in *Re B* has caused concern.[33] First, it has been criticised for brushing aside too readily the informed consent argument. Though Ms B felt that her ventilator-dependent life was 'worse than being dead,'[34] such feelings are not uncommon among newly disabled people who do subsequently develop a strong attachment to life.[35] One ventilator-dependent American activist has attributed the unwillingness of many to face such a life to the need to spend it in an institution despite the fact that, given adequate funding, life in the community would be entirely possible. In his words, 'It's not the respirator. It's the money.'[36] Secondly, it has been argued that the decision is based, at least in part, on unfounded assumptions about the reduced value of life to people with severe impairments. These assumptions result in a greater willingness to find mental capacity in a suicidal disabled person than in a suicidal person without any impairments:

> Most 'able bodied' people attempting suicide are assumed to be acting irrationally. The irrationality of disabled people desiring euthanasia or stopping essential life-sustaining treatment is not usually questioned in the same way.[37]

Pretty, then, rules that the ECHR, and consequently the HRA, confers no right to die upon us whether or not we are disabled. *Re B*, however, demonstrates that we do have a right to refuse life-sustaining medical treatment, provided we are judged to have sufficient mental competence. There is, as Butler-Sloss LJ recognised, a danger that a 'benevolent paternalism' might deny disabled people the same right to personal autonomy in this regard as that given to others.[38] However, there is also a danger—perhaps a greater one—that unexpressed, or even unacknowledged, assumptions about quality of life with impairments will deny disabled people the same chance to live (albeit contrary to their express wishes of the moment) as that granted to others.

---

[32] V Grove, 'Ms B Smiles as she Wins the Right to Die' *The Times*, 23 March 2002.

[33] For powerful arguments advanced by people with impairments similar to those of Ms B, see I Bassnet, 'Will to Live Wins Over Right to Die' *The Observer*, 24 March 2002; and D Coleman and S Drake, 'The Law, Death and Medical Ethics: A Disability Perspective from the US on the case of Ms B' (2002) 28 *Journal of Medical Ethics* 240.

[34] [2002] EWHC 449 at para 78 per Butler-Sloss LJ.

[35] See *ibid* at paras 59–62 for an account of the evidence of Mr G, one of the medical experts, who estimated that it would generally take two years for a person to gain the experience and perspective required to adjust psychologically to life with the types of impairments in question.

[36] E Roberts, quoted in D Fleischer and F Zames, 'The Disability Rights Movement: From Charity to Confrontation' (Philadelphia, Temple University Press, 2001), 146. See also MA Priestley, *Disability: A Life Course Approach* (Cambridge, Polity Press, 2003), 173–74.

[37] I Bassnet, 'Will to Live Wins Over Right to Die' above n 33.

[38] [2002] EWHC 449 at para 94.

ARTICLE 3

Article 3 imposes both a negative obligation on a state to refrain from inflicting torture or inhuman and degrading treatment on its subjects and a positive obligation to guard against their becoming the victims of such treatment at the hands of others.[39] It has been held to impose a positive duty on states to take measures to protect vulnerable adults and children from physical abuse.[40] It requires states to provide an adequate level of medical care to prisoners and others in its care.[41] Further, it requires states not to extradite people who need a certain level of medical treatment, care and support to a country in which it will not be available.[42] While issues such as these have obvious relevance to disabled people, they will not be explored in detail here. I will, instead, focus on the implications of *Price v UK*[43] and the extent to which they might extend beyond the prison context.

Adel Price had spent three nights in prison for contempt of court, having refused to answer questions in debt recovery proceedings in the county court. She was four limb deficient and had kidney problems. She was refused permission to take the battery charger for her wheelchair to prison; she had to spend the first night in a cell which was dangerously cold for her and contained a bed she was unable to use; she had to be assisted in using the toilet by male staff (having been left sitting on the toilet for three hours, on one occasion, until she gave up hope of being assisted by a woman); and, at the end of her sentence, she required catheterisation due to lack of fluid and to urine retention caused by difficulties in using the toilet facilities.

The UK's argument that Ms Price had not established the minimum level of severity of ill-treatment required for 'degrading treatment' under Article 3 was rejected. The ECtHR held that whether this standard had been reached depended on

> all the circumstances of the case, such as the duration of the treatment, its physical and mental effects and, in some cases, the sex, age and state of health of the victim.[44]

---

[39] See generally, M Nowak and W Suntinger, 'The Rights of Disabled People not to be subjected to Torture, Inhuman and Degrading Treatment or Punishment' in T Degener and Y Koster-Dreese (eds), above n 1, at 117.

[40] See *Z et al v UK* Application no 29392/95 (2002) 34 EHRR 97 and *In Re F* [2000] 3 CCLR 210.

[41] See, eg, *McGlinchey v UK* Application no 50390/99, 29 April 2003, which concerned the failure of a UK prison to provide adequate medical care to a prisoner who had asthma and severe heroin withdrawal symptoms resulting in her death. See also *Keenan v UK* Application No 27229/95 (2001) 33 EHRR 38 which concerned the adequacy of medical support provided to a mentally ill prisoner.

[42] *D v UK* Series A no 37 (1997) 24 EHRR 423 which concerned the extradition of a man in the last stages of AIDS from the UK to St Kitts.

[43] Application no 33394/96 (2002) 34 EHRR 1285.

[44] *Ibid*, para 24. See also *A v UK* Application no 25599/94 [1999] 27 EHRR 611 at para 20.

In light of all the circumstances in *Price*, this level had been attained, even though there had been no positive intention to humiliate or debase.[45]

The precise implications of *Price* for disabled people are, as yet, unclear. The decision might herald a greater emphasis on the responsibilities of states to take into consideration, and to minimise or remove, the disabling effects of policies, practices and structures. The concurring judgment of Judge Greve lends particular support to this view. In her view:

> In a civilised country like the United Kingdom, society considers it not only appropriate but a basic humane concern to try to improve and compensate for the disabilities faced by a person in the applicant's situation. In my opinion, these compensatory measures come to form part of the disabled person's physical integrity.

This approach has obvious implications for the obligations of states in relation to disabled people, not only under Article 3 but also under Article 8—a point accepted by Munby J in *R v East Sussex CC ex parte A and B*.[46] In addition, Judge Greve made it clear that, in her view, Article 14 would be infringed in a case such as *Price* on the basis that a state had discriminated against a disabled person by treating them in the same way as others despite a material difference in their circumstances.

Price, however, was interpreted restrictively, at least in relation to Article 3, in *Bernard v Enfield LBC*.[47] There Sullivan J held that the minimum level of severity for degrading treatment had not been attained by Mrs Bernard. Due to the council's failure to provide her with suitable accommodation, she had lived for 20 months in a house not accessible to her. Because she was unable to use her wheelchair in the house, she had to spend much of her time in a shower chair which caused her pain. Because she was unable to reach the bathroom without help, she soiled herself several times each day. She attempted to reduce this problem by drinking less, which exacerbated her diabetes. Because the kitchen was inaccessible, she was unable to cook for herself and her family. She was unable to answer the door or leave the house independently.

Though Mrs Bernard succeeded on other grounds, her failure to establish a breach of Article 3 will be disappointing to some.[48] Sullivan J, who was mindful of the unqualified nature of Article 3,[49] took the view that[50] 'The cases concerned with prisoners' rights . . . must be treated with great caution outside the prison gates.' Although there had been no intention to humiliate or debase

---

[45] Though such an intention is an important factor in establishing an Art 3 case, it is not always essential—*Peers v Greece* Application no 28524/95 (2001) 33 EHRR 51. See generally S Foster, 'Inhuman and Degrading Prison Conditions' [2001] 151 *New Law Journal* 1222.

[46] High Court (Admin) CO/4843/2001 18 February 2003 at para 93.

[47] [2002] EWHC 449.

[48] See M Nowak and W Suntinger, above n 39, at 117, 119 for a suggestion that failure to design a public transport system in such a way as to ensure that disabled people would not need to travel in humiliating conditions might infringe Art 3. See also R Daw, above n 7, at 55–56 for suggested scenarios in which deficient community care might infringe Art 3.

[49] [2002] EWHC 449 at para 23.

[50] *Ibid*, para 28.

Ms Price, there had been a deliberate intention to place her in custody. The deplorable circumstances in which Mrs Bernard had had to live were, by contrast, brought about entirely through neglect and were not deliberately inflicted upon her.[51] This reasoning is not entirely convincing. In *Bernard*, the council had selected the inappropriate house in which the Bernards were to live and, to that extent, made a deliberate decision to impose the conditions complained of on Mrs Bernard. The crucial factor may be that prisoners, unlike tenants, are subjected against their will to regimes controlled in every detail by others. On this basis, *Price* would apply equally to other institutions in which disabled people might be confined, such as psychiatric wards. Outside the institutional context, however, it would seem to be extremely difficult to establish a breach of Article 3 without proof of a positive intention to humiliate or debase. The effects of such a limitation, however, will be significantly mitigated by the possibility of redress under Article 8 (as occurred in *Bernard* itself). It remains to be seen whether this approach will also be adopted by the ECtHR.

ARTICLE 8

General

The implications for disabled people of the right to respect for one's private and family life, one's home and correspondence have already received some judicial scrutiny and are likely to continue to do so. The fact that the article is qualified in nature means that it is relatively easy to establish an interference with a protected right but that disputes often centre around whether such alleged infringements are justified under Article 8(2). Given the consequent width of Article 8, it is particularly difficult to give it comprehensive coverage in a work such as this. Some of the important developments for disabled people will be considered below under two broad headings—'family life' and 'private life and the right to personal integrity'.[52]

Family Life

The ECtHR has recognised that, where a family plays an important role in supporting a disabled person, imposing a separation between them will require particularly strong justification. Thus, in *Nasri v France*,[53] the deportation of a man who was unable to hear or to speak or to use sign language would have

---

[51] [2002] EWHC 449 at para 29.
[52] Many important issues have arisen primarily in the context of people with mental or intellectual impairments and these will not be considered here.
[53] Series A no 324 (1995) 21 EHRR 458.

resulted in an unjustified infringement of Article 8. The only people with whom he was able to communicate were his family and deporting him would have resulted in his total social isolation.

Article 8 will also be infringed where a public authority fails, unjustifiably, to provide a disabled person with the support necessary to allow them to participate fully in the life of their family. This was one of the grounds on which Mrs Bernard, and also her husband, succeeded in *Bernard v Enfield LBC*.[54] Because the council neglected to provide them with accessible accommodation, they and their six children lived, for 20 months, in adverse conditions which affected the whole family. Mr Bernard, as carer, was not able to leave the house for any length of time and developed back injuries as a result of having to lift his wife so regularly. Mrs Bernard was denied the means of caring for her children and, instead, was forced to adopt a completely dependent role. The couple had no privacy, having to sleep in the sitting room with their two youngest children. Sullivan J used his power under section 8 HRA to award substantial damages to the Bernards in respect of the infringement of their rights to a private and family life.

Private Life and the Right to Personal Integrity

The ECtHR has given the concept of private life a wide interpretation which includes the notion of physical and psychological integrity. This was expressed as follows in *Botta v Italy*[55]:

> Private life, in the Court's view, includes a person's physical and psychological integrity; the guarantee afforded by Article 8 of the Convention is primarily intended to ensure the development, without outside interference, of the personality of each individual in his relations with other human beings.

Thus, a state has been held liable for failing to take adequate steps to protect a disabled woman from rape—rape constituting a violation of her personal integrity.[56] It has also been accepted that excessive delay in the provision of medical care, which a state is required to provide, might found a claim under Article 8 if it creates a serious risk of injury to the health (and, thereby, to the physical or psychological integrity) of the claimant.[57]

Notions of personal integrity also formed a significant part of the ruling in *Bernard v Enfield LBC*.[58] It was held there that the conditions in which Mrs Bernard lived violated her physical and psychological integrity and thus

---

[54] [2002] EWHC 449.
[55] Series A no 66 (1998) EHRR 241 at para 32. See also *Niemietz v Germany* series A no 251-B (1992) 16 EHRR 97.
[56] *X and Y v Netherlands* Series A no 91 at 11 (1986) 8 EHRR 235.
[57] *Passannante v Italy* Application no 32647/96 (1998) 26 EHRR CD 153.
[58] [2002] EWHC 449.

amounted to a breach of her right to respect for her private life. According to Sullivan J[59]:

> Suitably adapted accommodation would not merely have facilitated the normal incidence of family life . . . it would also have secured her 'physical and psychological integrity'. She would no longer have been house-bound, confined to a shower chair for most of the day, lacking privacy in the most undignified of circumstances, but would have been able to operate again as part of her family and as a person in her own right rather than being a burden, wholly dependent on the rest of her family. In short it would have restored her dignity as a human being.

'Human dignity' was identified by Munby J in *R v East Sussex CC ex parte A and B*[60] as one of two particularly important concepts embraced by the notion of physical and psychological integrity. It is a value, he considered, which underlies the ECHR as a whole as well as the European Charter on Fundamental Rights and much of our domestic law. In his words[61]:

> True it is that the phrase is not used in the Convention but it is surely immanent in Article 8, indeed in almost every one of the Convention's provisions. The recognition and protection of human dignity is one of the core values—in truth *the* core value— of our society and, indeed, of all the societies which are part of the European family of nations and which have embraced the principles of the Convention. It is a core value of the common law, long pre-dating the Convention and the Charter. The invocation of the dignity of the patient in the form of declaration habitually used when the court is exercising its inherent declaratory jurisdiction in relation to the gravely ill or dying is not some meaningless incantation designed to comfort the living or to assuage the consciences of those involved in making life and death decisions: it is a solemn affirmation of the law's and of society's recognition of our humanity and of human dignity as something fundamental.

The second important concept Munby J considered to be embraced by the notion of physical and psychological integrity in the context of disabled people was the right of such people to participate in the life of their community and to have access to essential economic and social activities and to an appropriate range of recreational and cultural activities.[62]

The *East Sussex* case involved a challenge to the council's blanket ban on the manual lifting of disabled people. A and B were two sisters in their twenties who lived at home with their parents and who received significant support from the council. They had physical impairments which meant that they had to be lifted (eg in and out of bed or the bath). Without manual lifting it would have been impossible (largely due to the lack of appropriate facilities or mechanical lifting devices) for the sisters to go shopping, swimming or horse riding—activities which were important to them. Munby J held that their Article 8 rights were engaged, both by reason of their dignity interest and also their participation or

---

[59] *Ibid*, para 33.
[60] High Court (Admin) CO/4843/2001, 18 February 2003, para 85.
[61] *Ibid*, para 86.
[62] *Ibid*, para 99.

autonomy interest. Whether Article 8 had been infringed would depend on a balancing exercise between the interests of the sisters and those of the carers (made relevant by virtue of Article 8(2)). In his view, a blanket ban on manual lifting would not be justified under Article 8. This decision will be welcomed by many disabled people condemned by 'no lifting' policies to the confines of their homes and other buildings known to have appropriate mechanical lifting devices or to endure such indignities as wearing nappies in public places (to avoid the need for them to be lifted onto toilets).[63]

The extent to which states are required to take positive steps to remove barriers preventing disabled people from participating in the society around them was explored in *Botta v Italy*[64] itself. There, Mr Botta (a wheelchair user) claimed that, in failing adequately to enforce laws requiring private beaches to provide physical access for disabled people, the state had not complied with its obligation to respect his private life and to allow him to develop his personality. The physical barriers to accessing the beaches in question rendered him unable to enjoy a 'normal social life' and 'to participate in the life of the community.'[65] The ECtHR accepted that compliance with Article 8 would sometimes require a state to adopt 'measures designed to secure respect for private life even in the sphere of the relations of individuals between themselves.'[66] Such an obligation would arise where there was a 'direct and immediate link between the measures sought by an applicant and the latter's private and/or family life.'[67] There was, however, no such direct and immediate link in *Botta*—the right claimed there concerning 'interpersonal relations of such broad and indeterminate scope that there can be no conceivable direct link.'[68]

Though the actual claim in *Botta* failed, as Clements and Read explain:[69]

> The judgement is important since the Court accepted that unreasonable barriers (physical or otherwise) might violate a disabled person's rights under Article 8. In each case an assessment will be required, establishing whether the consequences for the applicant are so serious as to invoke a positive obligation.

To date, the cases in which a positive duty to take steps to protect Article 8 rights have largely, though not exclusively,[70] concerned a substantial risk of harm to the health or safety of the applicant.[71] No direct and immediate link

---

[63] See generally C Gooding, above n 16.

[64] Series A no 66 (1998) EHRR 241.

[65] *Ibid*, para 27.

[66] *Ibid*, para 33.

[67] *Ibid*, para 34.

[68] *Ibid*, at 55.

[69] Above n 9, at 64.

[70] *Airey v Ireland* Series A no 32 (1979) 2 EHRR 305 concerned a state's failure to provide legal aid for separation proceedings and, thereby, deny access to court.

[71] *X and Y v the Netherlands* Series A no 91, concerning the failure of the state to provide adequate protection to a disabled woman who was raped; and *Guerra et al v Italy* Series A no 64 (1998) 26 EHRR 357, concerning the failure of a state adequately to explain and communicate the risks of living in an area affected by pollution from a local factory. See further *Botta v Italy* Series A no 66 (1998) 26 EHRR 241 para 34.

was found in *Zehlanova and Zehnal v the Czech Republic*,[72] where a disabled person challenged the failure of the state to enforce laws requiring public buildings (including the post office, swimming pool and police station) to be made accessible. Though the buildings were in the town in which the applicant lived, the Court considered that there was insufficient evidence as to their everyday use by the applicant to establish the necessary link. In *Sentges v the Netherlands*,[73] however, the ECtHR was prepared to assume the existence of a direct and immediate link but rejected the complaint on the ground that states had a wide margin of appreciation and were required to weigh the needs of a particular individual against the interests of the rest of the community. There, the applicant challenged the state's refusal to supply him with a robotic arm which would have significantly reduced his otherwise total dependence on assistance from carers and thereby enabled him to have a more independent social life.

Thus, while it is possible that *Botta* will be expanded,[74] it seems likely that if harm to one's social life is ever to qualify that harm will have to be extremely severe and will then need to be balanced against the interests of the community at large. Where the action required can be categorised as a service offered to the public, and where the disabled person concerned can satisfy the DDA's definition of disability, the DDA is likely to remain a much stronger tool. In other cases, however, the *Botta* reasoning might well prove useful.

ARTICLE 6

This Article has been said to have 'great potential to assist disabled people in both criminal and civil cases.'[75] The specific guarantees relating to criminal proceedings, listed in Article 6(3), are likely to prove particularly significant— especially as they apply from the moment of arrest and therefore cover treatment in police stations. The extra protection conferred on disabled people during trials by the Youth Justice and Criminal Evidence Act 1999[76] was, no doubt, prompted partly by the increased emphasis on the human rights of disabled people brought about by the enactment of the HRA and the DDA. The same motivating factor seems likely to underlie the extensive guidance on the treatment of disabled people in court provided by the Judicial Studies Board.[77]

---

[72] Application no 38621/97, 14 May 2002.

[73] Application no 27677/02, 8 July 2003.

[74] See further O De Schutter, 'Reasonable Accommodations and Positive Obligations in the European Convention on Human Rights' in A Lawson and C Gooding (eds), above n 5.

[75] R Daw , above n 7, at 72.

[76] See ss 19–21, which confer a right to speak through an intermediary, to use communications devices and, in some circumstances, to give evidence through live-link.

[77] Equality Before the Courts 2002 (http://www.jsboard.co.uk/etad/ebtc/mf_00.htm). This builds upon the advice initially contained in the *Equal Treatment Bench Book*, published in autumn 2000.

Article 6 came to the assistance of a disabled person in *R v Isleworth Crown Court (ex parte King)*.[78] There, Mr King sought judicial review of a decision to reject his appeal against a conviction for an offence under the Housing Act 1985. A stroke three years before the appeal had rendered him unable to walk, talk or write. Though he had slowly recovered these functions, his concentration, memory and clarity of thought and expression were still significantly impaired, particularly when he was tired or stressed. Mr King was tired by the time his case was heard, it having been delayed for five hours, and his stress and anxiety when presenting his argument were exacerbated by the evident irritation and impatience with which he was treated by the judge. In quashing the decision, the High Court emphasised the importance of the advice provided by the Judicial Studies Board—according to which situations such as the one at issue would not have arisen[79]—and the fact that the procedural safeguards recommended in that advice were reinforced by the requirements of Article 6.[80]

Two Strasbourg cases concerning Article 6 and its implications for disabled people are less encouraging. In *Malone v UK*,[81] a woman who had rheumatoid arthritis and used a wheelchair complained that the possession proceedings brought against her were heard in inaccessible courts in London and not transferred to a court with appropriate access in Grimsby where she then lived. In order to attend court, she had had to leave home at 4.30 am; travel nearly 1000 kilometres (including the return trip), which caused so much pain that, following one journey, she had had to spend four days in bed; be carried by court officials up the steps to, and within, the court building; and suffered extreme discomfort as a result of the inaccessible toilet facilities—a problem intensified by the fact that, on one occasion, she had had to wait for nearly six hours before her case was heard. The Commission ruled Ms Malone's case inadmissible because she had failed to take adequate steps to bring her requirements to the attention of the court. She had not applied for a transfer until the case had been listed for London.

Malone is, as Clements and Read observe, 'an unsatisfactory decision'.[82] While disabled people should be expected to inform relevant authorities of their requirements, this should not absolve those authorities of all responsibility when, as in *Malone*, the disability is known to them and the consequences of failure to act will be serious for the disabled person. 'Equal treatment' they observe 'is not a special dispensation available only if booked in advance.'[83]

Another disappointing decision is *Stanford v UK*.[84] There, a man who was being tried for rape had a hearing impairment which prevented him from hear-

---

[78] [2001] *Administrative Court Digest* 289.
[79] The advice had actually been published a year after the case concerned.
[80] [2001] *Administrative Court Digest* 289, at 291.
[81] Application no 25290/94, 28 Feb 1996.
[82] Above n 9, at 45.
[83] *Ibid.*
[84] Series A no 282.

ing the testimony of the victim. He complained about this to his prison guard and also to his solicitor but his lawyers decided, for tactical reasons and contrary to the wishes of their client, not to mention this to the judge. When he challenged the proceedings under Article 6, it was accepted that the right of an accused to participate effectively in a trial, conferred by that Article, included 'not only his right to be present, but also to hear and follow the proceedings.'[85] According to the ECtHR, however, Article 6 had not been infringed because the accused had not brought his hearing difficulty to the attention of the trial judge. Though he had mentioned it to his guard and his solicitor, they were not court officials and, therefore, the court was not at fault. This suggests that Mr Stanford would have been better advised to shout the details of his problems directly to the judge, rather than mentioning them discretely to those near him—not an obvious tactic and not one likely to have endeared him to the jury.

The goods and services provisions of Part III of the DDA now apply to lawyers and courts. There is therefore some overlap with Article 6. The latter is, in some respects, broader—applying, for instance, to the treatment of disabled people in police stations after arrest and not requiring the strict DDA definition of disability to be established. Interestingly, the HRA might have implications for the way in which DDA cases themselves are conducted and reported. Rowena Daw has argued that the right to respect for private life may require the adoption of more restrictive publishing practices in DDA cases, at least in relation to the names and medical details of claimants.[86] She has also suggested that it might require the introduction of measures permitting the restriction of public access to the hearing of DDA cases which involve examination of personal details about a claimant's disability[87] and warned that, should such examinations prove unnecessarily intrusive, they might themselves fall foul of Article 8.[88]

CONCLUSION

Clements and Read have drawn attention to the very small number of cases brought under the HRA by disabled people.[89] It would clearly be naive to treat this as an indication that the rights of disabled people are not being infringed or that, even if they are, disabled people are happy to accept such infringements.

---

[85] *Ibid*, para 26.

[86] R Daw, above n 7, at 86. See also *Z v Finland* Application no 22009/93 (1998) 25 EHRR 371 where it was held that the publication of the identity of the wife of an Aids sufferer in a legal report amounted to a breach of her Art 8 rights.

[87] Above n 7, at 71. Though there is provision for this in relation to employment (ss 62 and 63 DDA), there is none in relation to Part III cases, which come before the county or sheriff courts rather than employment tribunals.

[88] Above n 7, at 82.

[89] L Clements and J Read, above n 9, at ch 4. See also L Clements, 'The Dog that didn't Bark: The Issue of Access to Rights under the ECHR by Disabled People' in A Lawson and C Gooding (eds), above n 5.

Clements and Read suggest that the explanation is to be found in major access barriers. These are not confined to those arising in the course of legal proceedings, with which Article 6 and also the DDA might help. For many disabled people, the path to justice under the HRA is barred well before they reach the courtroom.

Ignorance of the existence of the HRA, or of its relevance to them, will bar the claims of many disabled people.[90] For others, the lack of appropriate advocacy arrangements may be the obstacle.[91] Another extremely important deterrent against making complaints and bringing legal actions is fear of the repercussions—particularly when those challenged provide one with some vital service.[92] Further, it should not be forgotten that mounting a legal action is a stressful process, requiring considerable mental (and often physical) stamina. Many disabled people have limited energy which they would prefer to invest elsewhere. Finally, even where legal aid may be available,[93] fear of financial consequences is likely to be an important deterrent to many disabled people.

These barriers are made still more difficult to surmount by the lack of support available to disabled people contemplating bringing an HRA case. Though the DRC has power to support individual cases under the DDA, it has no such power to support a disabled person bringing a case under the HRA. This is a point of concern to the DRC, which has urged the Government to extend its enforcement powers accordingly.[94] It is important that this type of difficulty should be avoided in any unified Commission for Equality and Human Rights.[95] As the anticipated date for the creation of such a commission is late 2006, there is still an urgent need for the requested extension of the DRC's powers.

Though there may have been only a small number of disability related ECHR cases, the importance of such cases as there have been should not be underestimated. They are certainly not universally positive, as the above discussion has demonstrated. Nevertheless, what is beginning to emerge from them is the notion that disabled people are human beings whose lives are not to be regarded as less valuable than those of others and who have a right (albeit a qualified right under Article 8) to be treated with dignity and respect. The extent to which this message is being heard and understood by public authorities is beyond the scope of this chapter. If it is understood, the lives of disabled people will undoubtedly improve. There is a concern, however, that some public authorities will instead

---

[90] See L Clements, 'The Human Rights Act: A New Equity or a new Opiate? Reinventing Justice or Repackaging State Control?' (1999) 26 *Journal of Law and Society* 72 for criticism of the low priority given by the Government to publicising the HRA.

[91] See L Clements and J Read, above n 9, at 71–72.

[92] See K Simons, *I'm Not Complaining, But . . .* (York, Joseph Rowntree Foundation, 1995).

[93] See L Clements, above n 90 at 77–79 for criticism of recent restrictions on the availability of legal aid.

[94] *Disability Equality: Making it Happen* (London, DRC, 2003) 83–84.

[95] *Fairness for All: A New Commission for Equality and Human Rights* (White Paper) (London, Department of Trade and Industry, 12 May 2004).

respond to the HRA in a defensive, formalistic way which will have little or no benefit for disabled people. It is one thing for an organisation seriously to review its policy and practice with the essence of the HRA in mind. It is quite another matter for it to set about a Strasbourg-proofing exercise.[96] The proposed introduction of a positive duty on public authorities to promote equality for disabled people[97] is, therefore, very welcome.

The idea that there is a right to be valued as a human being and treated with dignity is a message which will be warmly welcomed by disabled people. It is a message which, despite its goals, the DDA has struggled to send.[98] While the rights conferred by the DDA are in many respects stronger than those conferred by the HRA, the need to begin a case by explaining the medical details of one's impairment and the ways in which it limits one's day-to-day life often results in an experience which is humiliating, embarrassing, frustrating and far from dignified. The number of cases in which this type of investigation is required would be significantly reduced if entitlement to a state disability benefit were accepted as proof of a disability, as recommended by the DRC.[99]

Before concluding it is worth turning again to the words of the report which perhaps marked the beginning of the official international recognition of disability as a human rights issue[100]:

> It might appear elementary to point out that persons with disabilities are human beings—as human as, and usually even more human than, the rest. The daily effort to overcome impediments and the discriminatory treatment they regularly receive usually provides them with special personality features, the most obvious and common of which are integrity, perseverance, and a deep spirit of comprehension and patience in the face of a lack of understanding and intolerance. However, this last feature should not lead us to overlook the fact that as subjects of law they enjoy all the legal attributes inherent in human beings and hold specific rights in addition. In a word, persons with disabilities, as persons like ourselves, have the right to live with us and as we do.

While the main thrust of these words is to be welcomed, many disabled people would feel the need to point out that we are not more human. Neither are we less so. We are simply human, like everybody else. The great appeal of the HRA lies in the fact that it confers rights upon us all just because of our humanity. As Aart Hendriks has observed, 'human rights law starts from the assumption that *all* human beings are equal in respect of their dignity.'[101] The impact of the HRA on the lives of disabled people will, in large part, depend on the extent to which

---

[96] L Clements and J Read, above n 9, at 95.

[97] Draft Disability Discrimination Bill (published on 3 December 2003) cl 8.

[98] The revised code of practice on Part III does contain several explicit references to the need to respect the dignity of disabled people—see *Rights of Access: Goods, Facilities, Services and Premises* (London, Disability Rights Commission, 2002) paras 4.33 and 5.38.

[99] *Disability Equality: Making it Happen* (London, Disability Rights Commission, 2003), 64.

[100] Above n 3, at paras 6–7.

[101] 'The Significance of Equality and Non-discrimination for the Protection of the Rights and the Dignity of Disabled Persons' in T Degener and Y Koster-Dreese (eds), above n 1, at 46 (my emphasis).

it can make this assumption a concrete reality. Only when this occurs will disabled people have the chance to lead ordinary lives within their chosen communities. It, like the anticipated UN convention on the rights of disabled people, 'will ultimately be judged on whether it reaches into small places—all the places where people ordinarily live, work and interact.'[102]

In conclusion, it has been shown here that there is scope for improving and strengthening the operation of both the DDA and the HRA. Together, however, they constitute an extremely important milestone on the road to a society in which disabled people are able to participate fully and in which they are treated with the same dignity and respect as are the rest of the population. While it is reassuring to feel that we are finally travelling in this direction, it should be remembered that there is a great deal of work still to be done and a very long way still to go. After all, '[t]here is no state on the planet that can afford to be complacent about disabled people's human rights.'[103]

---

[102] G Quinn, 'On the Occasion of the United Nations Day of Disabled People' (a speech delivered at the UN, New York, 3 December 2003).
[103] R Light, above n 5.

9

The Emperor's New Clothes?
The Impact of the Human Rights Act
1998 on Mental Health Care

CAMILLA PARKER

INTRODUCTION

FIRST IMPRESSIONS SUGGEST that the introduction of the Human Rights Act 1998 (HRA) has made a significant and positive impact on mental health care.[1] Closer inspection reveals, however, that such an impression is misleading or, at best, premature. By facilitating greater opportunities for legal challenge, the HRA has broadened the scope of judicial scrutiny of aspects of mental health practice such as detention, compulsory treatment and seclusion; but to date its impact on the planning and provision of mental health care, and ultimately the experience of those receiving mental health services ('service users'), is less clear. Furthermore, the Government's current proposals for reforming the Mental Health Act 1983 (MHA),[2] far from providing greater protection of the rights of people with mental health problems, pose a serious threat to them.[3]

The Audit Commission describes the cultural change that the HRA was intended to bring about:

---

[1] This chapter focuses on the provision of mental health services, primarily in-patient provision. It covers law and policy relevant to England as at early 2004. Readers will be aware that there were two significant developments in late 2004, namely the revised draft Mental Health Bill (published September 2004) and the European Court of Human Rights' decision in *HL v UK* (2004) 7 CCLR 498 (ECtHR). While both of these are likely to have a major influence on future mental health law, policy and practice they do not detract from the general comments made in this chapter about the current situation.

[2] Department of Health, *Draft Mental Health Bill* (Cm 5538-1, June 2002). Note: the revised draft Mental Health Bill was published in September 2004 (Cm 6305-1).

[3] See, eg, The Mental Health Alliance, *Briefing on Proposed Mental Health Act Reform* (August 2002).

... service decisions would be made with reference to basic rights, such as the right to privacy and family life, the right to a fair hearing and the right not to suffer degrading treatment. The Government expected that public service decision-makers would work within a human rights framework. Managers would have a clear understanding of their obligations under the Act and carefully balance an individual's rights against those of the wider community when making their decisions.[4]

The development of such a culture of respect for human rights is crucial in the field of mental health. Not only is this an area in which individuals can be subject to compulsory powers such as detention and treatment without consent, thereby threatening their 'dignity and autonomy and their related human rights including their liberty and physical integrity,'[5] but they can also be subjected to severe prejudice and discrimination.[6] Although the experience of using services is thought to be critical to an individual's recovery,[7] as discussed below, reports highlight the poor quality of services and the lack of involvement of service users in their care planning.[8]

THE HUMAN RIGHTS ACT 1998 AND MENTAL HEALTH LAW

One in four people have mental health problems at some point in their lives.[9] Mind estimates that at least a million people have significant mental health problems at any one time.[10] While many people can live in the community with varying degrees of support, some may at times of crisis be admitted to hospital, often having been detained under the MHA 1983. This Act provides for the circumstances in which individuals can be admitted to hospital against their wishes and treated for their mental disorder without their consent.

Part II of the MHA includes the 'civil admission' procedures for the compulsory admission of individuals to hospital for treatment for their mental disorder. The application for admission is usually made by an Approved Social Worker (ASW)— a social worker with specialist training and experience in working with people with mental disorder—which must be supported by the recommendations of two doctors. Save for emergencies,[11] all three professionals must assess the person's mental health and decide whether the conditions for detention exist. The Mental

---

[4] Audit Commission, *Human Rights: Improving public service delivery* (Audit Commission, London, 2003) para 1.

[5] Joint Committee on Human Rights, *Draft Mental Health Bill* 2001–02 (25th Report, HL 181, HC 1294, 11th November 2002) para 5.

[6] See, eg, J Read and S Baker, *Not Just Sticks and Stones: A survey of the Stigma, Taboos and Discrimination Experienced by People with Mental Health Problem* (Mind, 1996).

[7] Commission for Health Improvement (CHI), *What CHI has found in: mental heath trusts, sector report,* 18 December 2003, at 4.

[8] See 'The Human Rights Act 1998 and Mental Health Care', below.

[9] See eg, above n 7, at 4.

[10] Mind, Memorandum to the Joint Committee on Human Rights, *The Case for a Human Rights Commission* 2002–03 (6th Report, vol II) Ev 341.

[11] S 4 provides that where admission is of urgent necessity, an application for admission for assessment may be made without obtaining a second medical recommendation.

Health Act Commission (MHAC), the statutory body responsible for overseeing the implementation of the MHA in relation to detained patients, states that the use of civil compulsion has roughly doubled during the lifetime of the MHA.[12]

Part III of the MHA provides courts with the power to order that a person be detained in hospital, for example where a person has been convicted of an imprisonable offence.[13] Since the introduction of the HRA, there has been a wealth of case law in relation to the implementation and interpretation of the MHA.[14] Some of the key issues arising from these cases are discussed below.

Ensuring Compliance with the European Convention on Human Rights

Article 5 (the Right to Liberty): Detention and Discharge

The '. . . lawful detention of . . . persons of unsound mind . . .' is included in the exhaustive list of limited circumstances in which detention may be justified under Article 5 (the right to liberty) of the European Convention on Human Rights (ECHR). Accordingly, this provision is of direct relevance to the powers and procedures for compulsory admission to, and subsequent discharge from, hospital under the MHA. ECHR case law[15] has established that, save in emergencies, the following three minimum conditions have to be satisfied in order for detention, on the basis of 'unsound mind', to be lawful:

— A true mental disorder must be established before a competent authority on the basis of objective medical expertise.
— The mental disorder must be of a kind or degree warranting compulsory confinement.
— The validity of continued confinement depends on the persistence of such a mental disorder.

Article 5(4) provides that individuals who have been detained are entitled 'to take proceedings' to decide on the lawfulness of their detention and be released if 'the detention is not lawful'. The MHA provides for this review to be undertaken by Mental Health Review Tribunals (MHRTs). These are three-member panels consisting of a lawyer, a doctor and a 'lay person', who are independent of the hospital where the person is detained and have the power to discharge patients from detention. Individuals who are detained under the MHA have the right to apply to MHRTs to seek to be discharged from detention.[16]

---

[12] Mental Health Act Commission, 10th Biennial Report 2001–2003, *Placed Amongst Strangers—Twenty years of the Mental Health Act 1983 and future prospects for psychiatric compulsion* (London, TSO, 2003) para 8.25 (MHAC).

[13] S 37, MHA.

[14] See MHAC ch 3.

[15] *Winterwerp v The Netherlands* (1979) 2 EHHR 387.

[16] The right to apply to a MHRT does not apply to the 'short term' powers such as emergency admission under s 4 and the 'holding' powers under s 5.

Unsurprisingly, Article 5 has been the focus of a number of legal challenges in relation to the MHA and the role of MHRTs.[17] One of the most significant is *H v Mental Health Review Tribunal, North East London Region and the Secretary of State for the Department of Health*.[18] The Court of Appeal held that the MHA was incompatible with the ECHR as the burden was placed upon the patient to prove that the conditions for detention no longer existed in order to ensure discharge from detention. Accordingly, the Court of Appeal issued a declaration of incompatibility and in response to this, the Government issued regulations amending the MHA so that MHRTs are now required to direct the patient's discharge if they are not satisfied that the conditions for detention continue to exist.[19]

Article 8 (the Right to Private and Family Life) and the 'Nearest Relative'

The MHA contains a list of individuals (for example, spouses, children, parents and siblings) who can be the person's 'nearest relative'. The identity of the 'nearest relative' will depend on the person's current personal circumstances. The 'nearest relative' has various powers under the MHA. For example, in certain circumstances he or she can object to the person's compulsory admission.[20] Where the person has been detained under the civil admission powers, the 'nearest relative' must be informed about the detention.

Despite the 'nearest relative's' pivotal role in relation to compulsory admission and access to otherwise confidential information, individuals can neither choose, nor seek to replace, him or her. This was held to be in breach of the right to private life under Article 8 of the ECHR in *JT v The United Kingdom*.[21] The case was settled with the UK Government agreeing to amend the MHA so that individuals would be able to apply to the Court to have the 'nearest relative' replaced. The Government's failure to introduce such measures was criticised by the High Court.[22] The court considered that there was no justification for the delay in making the appropriate amendments to the MHA and issued a declaration of incompatibility.

However, more concrete change has been achieved in the provisions concerning the identity of the 'nearest relative', with the High Court issuing a consent order confirming that in the light of the HRA, the MHA should be read so that it accommodates same-sex partners.[23]

---

[17] See MHAC paras 3.9–3.19 for summary of cases relating to MHRTs.
[18] [2001] EWCA Civ 415.
[19] Mental Health Act 1983 (Remedial) Order 2001 SI No 3712.
[20] See s 11(4) MHA.
[21] *JT v UK* (1998) [2000] 1 FLR 909.
[22] [2003] EWHC 1094 (Admin).
[23] *R (SSG and Liverpool City Council) v Secretary of State for the Department of Health* (2002) 5 CCLR 639.

GREATER SCRUTINY OF THE USE OF THE MENTAL HEALTH ACT: COMPULSORY TREATMENT

Compulsory Treatment Decisions

The MHA provides for the circumstances in which detained patients can be given treatment for mental disorder without their consent.[24] It makes specific provision for the administration of medication and electro-convulsive therapy (ECT).[25] The doctor in charge of the patient's care (the 'responsible medical officer'—'RMO') can authorise the administration of medication without the person's consent for up to three months (starting from the time that medication is first given during the period of detention). Thereafter, such treatment can only be given with the patient's consent or if a Second Opinion Appointed Doctor (SOAD) has authorised such treatment. This 'three month rule' does not apply to ECT. It can only be given with the patient's consent or if a SOAD has authorised such treatment. In either case (whether the proposed treatment is ECT or medication), the SOAD must consider whether, having regard to the likelihood of the treatment alleviating or preventing a deterioration of the patient's condition, the treatment should be given.

Changes to the Practice of SOADs

As a result of recent case law, changes have been introduced to the practice of SOADs. They must reach an independent view as to the desirability and propriety of the treatment proposed by the RMO.[26] When SOADs authorise treatment to be given without the patient's consent, they are also required to give written reasons for their decision to the RMO who must give these reasons to the patient, unless such disclosure would be likely to cause serious harm to the physical or mental health of the patient or any other person.[27]

Human Rights and Treatment without Consent

More fundamentally, the Court of Appeal has confirmed that 'the decision to impose treatment without consent upon a protesting patient' may breach that individual's rights under Article 3 (freedom from torture, inhuman or degrading

---

[24] See Part IV of the MHA. The compulsory treatment provisions do not apply to individuals who are detained under the short-term detention powers such as s 4 (emergency admission)—s 56.

[25] S 58 MHA.

[26] *R v Responsible Medical Officer Broadmoor Hospital and Anor, ex parte Wilkinson* [2001] EWCA Civ 1545.

[27] *R v Feggetter and Mental Health Act Commission, ex parte Wooder* [2002] EWCA Civ 554.

treatment or punishment) and Article 8 (right to private life), thereby meriting judicial scrutiny of the propriety of the treatment proposed.[28] It is now established, in the light of the European Court's judgment in *Herczegfalvy v Austria*,[29] that in deciding whether treatment should be given in the absence of consent, consideration must be given to whether the proposed treatment is in the patient's best interests and has been convincingly shown to be medically necessary.[30]

Following these rulings, the human rights implications of compulsory treatment were examined in detail in *R (PS) v Responsible Medical Officer, Dr G and Second Opinion Appointed Doctor, Dr W*.[31] The court was asked to decide whether treatment could be given to a patient (PS) who was refusing the proposed treatment and had the capacity to make such a decision. The court considered that the proposed treatment could only be given:

> if that proposed treatment satisfies the 'best interests test' and additionally it does not interfere with the claimant's rights under Articles 3, 8, and 14.

The court concluded that the administration of the proposed treatment (medication) would not violate PS's rights despite his competent refusal. However, in reaching its decision, the court gave detailed consideration to a range of issues including the consequences of PS not receiving the medication, the expected benefits of the medication and its possible side effects. In assessing whether Article 8 had been breached, it was assumed that the compulsory treatment of an individual who had capacity to refuse such treatment would breach Article 8 unless it was justified under Article 8(2). A key factor was whether the treatment would be in PS's 'best interests'. The court concluded that both stages of the 'best interests test' were met. In the light of the expert opinions supporting the proposed treatment, the court was satisfied that this accorded with 'responsible and competent professional opinion.' The second part of the test—that the proposed treatment was the 'single best option'—was also met. This was because the treatment was likely to alleviate or prevent a deterioration of PS's condition, there was no less invasive treatment and it was necessary for the treatment to be given to PS.

Compulsory treatment raises important issues such as respect for the individual's autonomy and physical integrity. Accordingly, this is an area in which further legal challenges are likely to be brought. Although finding against PS, the principles outlined by the court as a basis for deciding whether treatment can be given without the patient's consent, together with the Court of Appeal's ruling on the importance of complying with the Code (see below), provide scope for further judicial scrutiny.

---

[28] See Hale LJ, above n 26, at para 83.
[29] (1992) 15 EHRR 437.
[30] *R (N) v Dr M, A Health Authority and Dr O* [2003] 1 MHLR, 157; [2002] EWCA Civ 1789.
[31] [2003] EWHC 2335 (Admin).

CLARIFICATION OF THE STATUS OF THE CODE OF PRACTICE TO THE MENTAL HEALTH ACT

The Court of Appeal's judgment in *Munjaz v Mersey Care NHS Trust*[32] ('the seclusion case') was significant due to its findings on the use of seclusion and the status of the Code of Practice to the Mental Health Act 1983 (the Code).[33] The Code is issued under section 118 of the MHA and is intended to provide guidance to mental health professionals on the implementation of the MHA. Although seclusion is not referred to in the MHA, guidance on the use of seclusion is included in the Code, which describes seclusion as:

> . . . the supervised confinement of a patient in a room, which may be locked to protect others from significant harm. Its sole aim is to contain severely disturbed behaviour which is likely to cause harm to others.[34]

While holding that the use of seclusion can be lawful, the Court of Appeal stressed that there are limits to the use of such a power; whether seclusion is used for treatment or control, the criterion must be one of 'reasonable necessity'. The Court of Appeal considered that seclusion was capable of breaching Articles 3 and 8, thus making the arguments for according the Code a greater status more compelling:

> Where there is a risk that agents of the state will treat its patients in a way which contravenes Article 3, the state should take steps to avoid this through the publication of a Code of Practice which its agents are obliged to follow unless they have good reason to depart from it. Where there is an interference with the rights protected by Article 8, the requirement of legality is met through adherence to a Code of Practice again unless there is good reason to depart from it. The same will apply where the Code deals with the deprivation of liberty within the meaning of Article 5.[35]

Although this case concerned the use of seclusion, the Court of Appeal's ruling on the status of the Code has wider implications. This has been confirmed by the Department of Health:

> Although the declaration granted by the Court regarding the status of the Code was limited to those parts of the Code that covered seclusion, the Department takes the view that the Court's analysis of the legal status of the Code is applicable to all aspects of it.[36]

This is significant as the Code provides guidance to mental health professionals on the implementation of the MHA, such as: the roles and responsibilities of those undertaking a mental health assessment (to ascertain whether a person

---

[32] [2003] ECWA Civ 1036.
[33] Department of Health and Welsh Office (London, The Stationery Office, March 1999).
[34] Para 19.16.
[35] Para 74.
[36] Chief Executive's Bulletin, Issue 187, September 2003.

needs to be detained in hospital under the MHA); the procedures to be followed in relation to the compulsory treatment provisions; and the information which must be given to detained patients. In addition, the Code covers areas which are not included in the MHA, but which are relevant to the care and treatment of detained patients, such as preparation for their aftercare and rights to receive visitors. In the light of the Court of Appeal's comments on the importance of the Code of Practice in protecting the human rights of those who are detained, it is likely that there will be future challenges concerning non-compliance with the Code.

THE HUMAN RIGHTS ACT 1998 AND MENTAL HEALTH CARE

There have been major developments in mental health policy over the past five years or so, with the Government stating that greater priority needed to be given to the development and modernisation of mental health care.[37] The Department of Health's *National Service Framework for Mental Health Modern Standards and Service Models* (NSF for Mental Health),[38] published in 1999, set out standards and targets to be met by local services in planning and delivering mental health care, with *The NHS Plan*[39] (a ten-year programme of reform for the NHS, published in 2000) including further specific targets for mental health. In addition, a series of government announcements promised extra funding to finance the implementation of these initiatives.[40]

Despite these positive beginnings, recent reports portray a rather bleak picture of current mental health care. Serious concerns have been raised about the adequacy of the funding for mental health services. A survey undertaken on behalf of the Royal College of Psychiatrists found that in real terms the available funding for many NHS Trusts has decreased.[41] A survey carried out by the Sainsbury Centre for Mental Health concluded that despite its status as a priority service the share of mental health in NHS and social care budgets is falling and that mental health continues to be a 'Cinderella service'. The Commission for Health Improvement, the statutory body responsible for monitoring patient care within the NHS, has recently published a report on mental health[42] which expresses similar concerns:

[37] Department of Health, *Modernising Mental Health Services: Safe, Sound and Supportive* (December 1998).

[38] Department of Health, London.

[39] Department of Health, *The NHS Plan: A Plan for Investment, A Plan for Reform* (London, The Stationery Office, 2000).

[40] Eg, in December 1997 Frank Dobson, then Secretary of State, stated that an extra £700 million would be found over the next three years for health and social services to invest in the better treatment and care of mental illness.

[41] Paul Lelliott, *Change in the funding of English Adult Mental Health Care Providers Between 2001/2002 and 2002/2003*, July 2003.

[42] CHI, above n 7.

Despite a broad consensus about mental health policy, wide engagement with that agenda and evidence of innovation and change, there is a considerable dissatisfaction and frustration in the mental health sector that the priority accorded to mental health is not always reflected in practice. Commissioning and performance priorities remain focused on the acute healthcare sector . . . The resource allocated for service developments have not always found their way into services.[43]

In this context it is perhaps not surprising that recent reports have highlighted major concerns about the quality of mental health services.

Poor Quality of In-patient Provision

Environment and Services

In June 2002, the Sainsbury Centre for Mental Health (SCMH) published a briefing which highlighted a range of problems facing acute in-patient care, including poor quality and often frightening environments (especially for women), lack of privacy, staffing problems (such as low morale and inadequate training) and a lack of meaningful or therapeutic activities for service users. While welcoming the Government's guidance on 'Mental Health Policy Implementation Guide: Adult Acute Inpatient Care Provision'[44] which set out an action plan for acute inpatient provision, SCMH stressed the need to develop realistic plans to deliver in-patient care that is therapeutic and supports recovery:

> Unless we develop and implement such plans, nationally and locally, we will see an increasing cycle of decline in acute mental health care with increasing user dissatisfaction, incidents and inquiries and the loss of high quality staff—all despite the best efforts of committed staff. The situation is little short of a crisis and has to be addressed now. In some instances the quality of care is so poor as to amount to a basic denial of human rights.[45]

The Commission for Health Improvement's (CHI) recent report on mental health confirms such findings[46] and lists a range of concerns about the environment in some NHS Trusts, particularly where care is provided in old Victorian buildings. These include mixed-sex wards with shared bathroom facilities, poor security between dormitories, lack of privacy for making phone calls or receiving visitors and the lack of child friendly visiting areas. CHI emphasises that it found a great deal of good practice in its reviews and that across the sector there are committed and dedicated staff. However, it also found that staff and service users 'too often work in environments that are unacceptable' and factors such

---

[43] *Ibid*, at 8.
[44] 30 April 2002, Department of Health.
[45] *An Executive Briefing on adult acute inpatient care for people with mental health problems* (SCMH, June 2002).
[46] See 20–21.

as isolation of services, closed cultures, poor clinical leadership and supervision 'have caused the neglect of patients.'[47]

Service User Perspective

Service users reported to both CHI and the Kings Fund's Mental Health Inquiry 2003, which examined mental health services in London, that they do not have access to fresh air due to either insufficient staff escorts or because of unsafe external environments,[48] they feel bored on in-patient wards, the range and quality of activities are limited, especially in the evening and at weekends, and there are also limited treatment options and complementary therapies.[49] Violence on the wards is also a common concern, with service users reporting incidents of aggression and violence by staff towards patients and vice versa.[50]

Care of Older People

Both CHI[51] and the MHAC highlight concerns about the poor quality of care for older people in in-patient care.[52] In a separate report into older age services in the Manchester region, following allegations of physical and emotional abuse of patients by staff on Rowan ward (a ward for older people with mental health problems) CHI concluded:

> The Rowan ward service has many of the known risk factors for abuse: a poor and institutionalised environment, low staffing levels, high use of bank and agency staff, little staff development, poor supervision, a lack of knowledge of incident reporting, closed ward culture and weak management at ward and locality level.[53]

Care and Treatment of People from Black and Ethnic Minorities[54]

CHI states that most NHS Trusts are struggling to meet the demands of black and ethnic minority communities, 'even when they are a majority population.'[55] The problems identified included not meeting dietary requirements and lack of

---

[47] See 9.
[48] R Levenson *et al*, *London's State of Mind* (London, Kings Fund, 2002) 77; CHI above n 7, at 21. See also the MHAC's Biennial Report, 9.29–9.33 and 12.46.
[49] CHI above n 7, at 21.
[50] Kings Fund above n 48, at 78.
[51] Above n 7, at 22.
[52] Above n 48, at 15.9.
[53] CHI, *Investigation into matters arising from care on Rowan Ward, Manchester Mental Health & Social Care Trust* (September 2003).
[54] This is an area in which steps are being taken to address issues of concern. See, eg, the Department of Health's *Delivering Race Equality: A Framework for Action, Mental Health Services, Consultation Document* (October 2003) and the National Institute for Mental Health in England, *Engaging and Changing: Developing Effective Policy for the Care and Treatment of Black and Minority Ethnic Detained Patients* (October 2003).
[55] Above n 7, at 22.

interpreters with the necessary training and experience for interpreting on behalf of mental health service users. The MHAC highlights the over-representation of black and minority ethnic patients among the detained population. It comments that in relation to issues such as translation and interpretation, there have been few significant overall improvements in black and minority ethnic patients' experiences of mental health services since these concerns were raised in its First Biennial Report (twenty years ago).[56] While reports of poor quality of care cannot be taken as representative of all services across the country it is clear that there are significant problems which need to be urgently addressed.

Problems in Accessing Services

The linchpin for mental health care is the Care Programme Approach (CPA) which was introduced in 1991.[57] It applies to all adults of working age who are in contact with specialist services (similar principles apply to care planning for older people). The key elements of the CPA are the assessment of an individual's health and social care needs; as a result of that assessment, a care plan should be agreed and then implemented, monitored and reviewed.[58] Health and social care agencies are expected to work together to provide a holistic service.

However, CHI's recent report notes that although the CPA was introduced over twelve years ago, there are still problems with its implementation: in particular large numbers of users are not being placed on the CPA or allocated a care plan and co-ordinator.[59] Furthermore, CHI has found that services for service users in crisis are underdeveloped. *The NHS Plan* included a target of creating 335 'crisis resolution teams' (intended to provide support to people in crisis within the community, thereby avoiding admission to hospital) which, by 2004, would be available to service users at any time. However, CHI has found crisis resolution services to be limited and 'service users commonly report problems in accessing out of hours services or the ability to contact someone out of hours.'[60] In some areas, service users and carers reported to CHI on the difficulties in arranging admission to hospital—feeling that they have to wait until their situation reaches crisis point before they can be admitted. The concern that people have to reach crisis point before receiving help and support has been frequently highlighted by mental health organisations. For example, in 1999 the National Schizophrenia Fellowship (now Rethink) carried out a survey in which

---

[56] Paras 16.8–16.9.
[57] See HC(90)23/LASSL(90)11 for the Department of Health's 1990 guidance. The CPA was revised by *Effective Care Co-ordination in Mental Health Services—Modernising the Care Programme Approach* (Department of Health, October 1999).
[58] Paras 3.2.7 and 3.2.8.
[59] Above n 7, at 28.
[60] Above n 7, at 19.

over one in three of the respondents (35 per cent) stated that they had been turned away when seeking help and one in four (25 per cent) were refused help when they sought hospital admission.[61] The report added:

> There are countless cases of people speaking from their experience of desperately seeking help and struggling to obtain modern treatments and support, only to be turned away. As a result their condition deteriorated until crisis was reached, and then they were often detained against their will in traumatic conditions.[62]

Rethink's survey, 'Just One Percent—the experience of people using mental health services' (published in June 2003) found that more than one in four (28 per cent) of the respondents reported being shunned when seeking help.

Where crisis services are in place and working effectively, unnecessary admissions to hospital can be prevented, but as CHI notes, the lack of appropriate community-based services also affects the length of time that the person needs to stay in hospital: 'Problems in accessing services are mirrored by problems discharging users, most commonly because of a lack of supported accommodation.'[63]

Lack of Service User Involvement in Care Planning

Despite clear guidance that service users (and with their consent any relative or friend providing informal support—'carers') should be 'central participants in the process' of their care planning, with a copy of the agreed care plan being given to them,[64] the reality is often very different. CHI found that many service users and their carers have 'little or no input into care plans and some are not even aware that they have one.'[65]

This is supported by the results of Rethink's survey which found that four years after the introduction of the NSF for Mental Health, which expects all service users on the CPA to have a copy of a written care plan and be able to access services 24 hours a day (every day of the year), 48 per cent of service users did not have or could not be sure if they had a care plan, and 19 per cent did not know how to access help out of hours. Rethink comment that it is unlikely that such a large number of individuals do not have a care plan, rather they probably do not realise that they have a care plan. However, this would mean that they are not able to represent their views and needs when the care plan is prepared—thereby undermining a key principle of the CPA.

---

[61] National Schizophrenia Fellowship (NSF), *Better Act Now!* (NSF, 1999).
[62] *Ibid*, at 4.
[63] Above n 7, at 20.
[64] CPA, above n 57, at para 86.
[65] Above n 7, at 27.

Human Rights Implications

All these areas suggest serious human rights violations, and therefore could be susceptible to legal challenge. However, as the following points illustrate, achieving real and sustainable improvement cannot be achieved through litigation alone.

Difficulties in Pursuing Legal Challenges

The poor quality of in-patient care may, for example, breach Article 8 (mixed-sex wards with shared bathroom facilities and the lack of privacy for receiving visits from family members) and Article 3 (where individuals feel frightened and threatened by abuse and/or violence by others on the ward). However, individuals wishing to pursue such legal challenges would need to have access to lawyers with the necessary knowledge and expertise. Whereas individuals who are detained under the MHA must be informed of their right to apply to MHRTs;[66] and also told how to contact a suitably qualified solicitor and that free legal aid may be available,[67] there is no requirement to help individuals who have been admitted into hospital informally (ie, without the use of the MHA) in getting legal advice.

This is of particular concern for those individuals (generally older people with mental health problems and people with severe learning disabilities) who have been admitted to hospital for treatment for their mental disorder informally in the light of the House of Lords' decision in *Bournewood*.[68] The court held that individuals who lack capacity to consent to their admission to hospital for treatment for their mental disorder, but do not object to their admission, can be admitted informally (without the need to use the compulsory admission powers of the MHA). This means that none of the safeguards available to those detained under the MHA apply to such patients. For example, there is no independent review of either their admission to hospital or their treatment and they fall outside the MHAC's remit[69] (the MHAC only covers individuals who are detained under the MHA). Pointing out the lack of overview of the standards of care and treatment for older people and the absence of a body 'with responsibility for considering the human rights aspect of de facto detention',[70] the MHAC recommends that arrangements

> for monitoring the use of compulsion should extend to mentally incapacitated patients receiving psychiatric care and treatment under all circumstances.[71]

---

[66] S 132.

[67] Code of Practice 14.5, c.

[68] *R v Bournewood Community and Mental Health NHS Trust, ex p L* [1999] AC 458. Note: in *HL v UK* (2004) 7 CCLR 498 the ECtHR found that this practice breached Article 5(1) and (4).

[69] Para 15.9.

[70] *Ibid.*

[71] Para 15.10. The recently introduced services to support patients who may wish to complain about their NHS care—PALS (Patient Advisory Liaison Services) and Independent Complaints Advocacy Services (ICAS)—may lead to greater protection for vulnerable patients but the quality of such services is likely to be subject to local variation.

Furthermore, people with mental health problems may be reluctant to seek legal advice due to concerns about the legal costs and the fear of complaining about those responsible for the provision of their care.

Limitations of Individual Legal Challenges

Legal challenges may also be an ineffective means of achieving positive change. This can be illustrated by the courts' response to delays in discharge from hospital due to lack of adequate support in the community. In *Johnson v The United Kingdom*[72] the European Court of Human Rights held that while it is not necessary to discharge immediately and unconditionally a person who no longer suffers from a mental disorder, Article 5(1) would be breached if the discharge was unreasonably delayed. In Mr Johnson's case the delay was due to problems in finding a suitable hostel.

In *IH*[73] the House of Lords held that there had been a violation of the rights of the patient (IH) under Article 5(4). This was because the conditions for discharge which had been set by the MHRT proved impossible to meet; and on the basis of a previous ruling by the House of Lords[74] (before the introduction of the HRA) the MHRT had been precluded from reconsidering this decision. The Lords overturned this ruling and held that where the patient's discharge is delayed because there are problems in meeting the aftercare arrangements required by the MHRT, then the MHRT should reconvene to reconsider the arrangements. However, the court determined that at no stage was IH unlawfully detained. There was a 'categorical difference' between IH's situation and that of Mr Johnson (where the European Court had held that he had been unlawfully detained). This was because in Mr Johnson's case the MHRT had found that he no longer had a mental disorder, this being one of the conditions which must be met in order for a person's detention on the grounds of mental disorder to be lawful.[75] Accordingly, there were no grounds for continuing to detain Johnson; so when the conditions required by the MHRT proved impossible to meet, the only option was to discharge him. Thus, Johnson's detention became unlawful when his discharge was unreasonably delayed. In IH's case however there was no such finding—rather the MHRT had considered that IH could be satisfactorily treated and supervised in the community if its conditions were met. In IH's case therefore, if the conditions proved impossible to meet, he could continue to be lawfully detained.

The House of Lords confirmed that where a MHRT has set out conditions for an individual's aftercare, the duty placed on health and social services author-

---

[72] (1999) 27 EHRR 440.
[73] *R v Secretary of State for the Home Department and another (Respondents) ex parte IH (FC) (Appellant)* [2003] UKHL 58.
[74] *Oxford Regional Mental Health Review Tribunal* [1987] 3 All ER 8.
[75] *Winterwerp v Netherlands* (1979–80) 2 EHRR 387.

ities to provide such aftercare[76] will be met if they use their 'best endeavours' to comply with such conditions. The court also commented that the European Court did not rule on the argument pursued in *Johnson v UK* that it was for the authorities to ensure that a placement in a hostel could be guaranteed.

Thus, to date, the courts have avoided addressing the connection between the necessity to detain an individual in hospital and the level of support available in the community, taking the view that ECHR jurisprudence makes no requirement on states 'to put in place facilities for the treatment in the community of those suffering from mental disorders so as to render it unnecessary to detain them in hospital.'[77] ECHR case law concerning Article 8 may provide scope for future development in this area.[78] For example, the European Court has stated that in some, albeit exceptional, circumstances Article 8 may impose positive obligations

> where the State's failure to adopt measures interferes with that individual's right to personal development and his or her right to establish and maintain relations with other human beings and the outside world.[79]

Potentially this could apply to an individual who has been, or is at risk of being, detained, or continues to be detained, due to inadequate support and/or accommodation in the community.[80] However, even if such arguments are successfully made for the individual complainant, this will not necessarily lead to a governmental decision to take steps (such as additional funding) to increase the availability of community-based provision.

Case Law Needs to be Disseminated to Practitioners

In order for cases to have a real impact, the details of the judgments and their wider implications must be disseminated to all agencies and individuals who are expected to comply with the rulings, in particular front-line staff. The MHAC stresses that the task of government should be to provide authoritative guidance on the law and requirements of good practice relating to the compulsion of psychiatric patients and that such guidance is essential if practitioners are to move beyond a defensive approach to human rights.[81] This is an area in which the MHAC is being increasingly proactive, having published guidance for SOADs and RMOs following the Court of Appeal's ruling that SOADs must provide reasons for their decision to authorise compulsory treatment under the MHA.[82]

---

[76] See s 117 of the MHA—this duty only applies to certain categories of detained patients on their discharge from hospital. See s 117(1).

[77] *R v Secretary of State for Health, ex parte IH* [2003] UKHL para 87.

[78] See *Botta v Italy* (1998) 26 EHRR 241.

[79] *Sentges v The Netherlands* Application no 27677/02, 8 July 2003.

[80] See also *Kutzner v Germany* 46544/99, 26 February 2002 which pointed out that there may be 'positive obligations inherent in an effective "respect" for family life' (para 61).

[81] Paras 2.7 and 2.8.

[82] The guidance can be obtained from MHAC's website www.mhac.trent.nhs.uk. The MHAC is also planning to issue guidance on the status of the Code in the light of the seclusion case and the implications of *PS* (discussed under 'human rights and treatment without consent').

As discussed above, there have been some important developments in case law relating to compulsory treatment under the MHA. Accordingly, this is an area in which guidance and training will be crucial. All mental health practitioners who are involved in the care and treatment of people with mental health problems (but most particularly RMOs), the doctors working under their supervision and nursing staff, should be clear about the implications of these judgments and the requirement to comply with the Code (which includes specific guidance on medical treatment)[83] unless there are good reasons for not doing so. Such training and guidance should highlight that the human rights principles raised in the case law apply to all individuals receiving care and treatment, not just detained patients. For example, although the requirement of written reasons to authorise treatment without the patient's consent relates only to SOAD decisions, it highlights the importance of giving information to patients about their treatment. Issues relating to consent to treatment and the provision of adequate information on the type of treatment proposed, its possible side effects and alternatives to such treatment are of crucial importance to informal patients as well as those who are detained under the MHA. The importance of giving relevant information is underpinned by the Code's definition of 'consent':

> the voluntary and continuing permission of the patient to receive a particular treatment, based on adequate knowledge of the purpose, nature, likely effects and risks of that treatment including the likelihood of its success and any alternatives to it. Permission given under any unfair or undue pressure is not consent.[84]

Despite such a clear definition, the MHAC regularly highlights the failure of doctors to record their discussions with the patient about the proposed treatment; while lack of information about the proposed treatment is a frequent complaint made by service users.[85] The MHAC comments that twenty years after the introduction of the MHA there is greater respect and consideration for patients' consent to treatment and the circumstances in which treatment can be given without consent, but:

> the concerns that we have raised in every Biennial Report regarding the prevalence of poor practice in the assessment of, and subsequent respect for, patient's capacity and consent to treatment continue to be a major feature of many Commission visits.[86]

This clearly needs to be addressed in order to ensure that people are given the necessary information to make informed decisions about their care and treatment. As the case of PS makes clear, the provision of treatment without an individual's consent engages Article 8 and must therefore meet the criteria set out in Article 8(2) in order to be lawful. In deciding whether compulsory treatment is justified consideration needs to be given to questions such as whether there are

---

[83] Chs 15 and 16.
[84] Para 15.13.
[85] See, eg, the Kings Fund, above n 48, at 85–86.
[86] Para 10.1.

treatments which are less invasive and/or are more acceptable to the individual concerned. On this basis, the person should be told why such treatment is being proposed, what the alternatives are and why they would not be appropriate.

TOWARDS A CULTURE OF RESPECT FOR HUMAN RIGHTS?

Proposals for Future Mental Health Legislation

The Government published a draft Mental Health Bill in June 2002. Some aspects of the proposals for reform are welcome, such as the introduction of safeguards for people who lack capacity who are receiving treatment for mental disorder in hospital. However, other provisions, such as powers to compulsorily treat people with mental health problems in the community, have met with widespread opposition. Over 60 organisations have joined the Mental Health Alliance, a coalition which is campaigning to introduce substantial changes to the Government's proposals. The Alliance's members include voluntary organisations, service user groups and professional bodies whose members would be involved in implementing the new legislation.

While acknowledging that the draft Bill would introduce many improved safeguards, the Joint Committee on Human Rights highlighted a number of concerns 'on human rights grounds'. These included the broad criteria for compulsion, the concern that this may lead to the preventive detention of some individuals, particularly those with a diagnosis of personality disorder and insufficient safeguards in the compulsory treatment provisions.[87] Pointing out that the proposals 'disproportionately focus on perceived dangerousness and risk,' the Mental Health Alliance[88] suggests, 'Improvements in community and inpatient services would better alleviate some of the problems that the Government is seeking to address by the use of compulsory powers.'[89]

The Need to Raise Awareness about Human Rights

The Joint Committee on Human Rights (JCHR) concluded in its report *The Case for a Human Rights Commission* that: 'The culture of human rights has yet to be internalised within public authorities or their inspectorates.'[90] The Joint Committee's fears that the momentum to develop such a culture appeared to be slowing (in some areas to a standstill) was confirmed by the Audit Commission's report of its survey of 175 public authorities to examine how they

---

[87] Joint Committee on Human Rights *Draft Mental Health Bill* 25th Report, above n 4, at 32.
[88] See Mental Health Alliance: www.mentalhealthalliance.org.uk.
[89] *Reforming the Mental Health Act: the key issues*, at 2.
[90] Joint Committee on Human Rights, *The Case for a Human Rights Committee* 2002–03 (6th Report, Vol 1, HL 67-I, HC 489-I 19 March 2003), para 95.

had responded to the HRA. *Human Rights: Improving public service delivery* found that the impact of the HRA 'is in danger of stalling'.[91] While the Audit Commission suggests that mental health NHS Trusts are better prepared than other health sector agencies in their approach to the HRA because of developing case law,[92] the MHAC comments that although there is an awareness of the HRA within the health and social services authorities that have powers and duties under the MHA, this may not apply to front-line staff and many authorities adopt a primarily defensive approach to human rights issues.[93]

The lack of awareness of the potential of the HRA to help achieve positive change is not confined to public authorities. A report published by the British Institute for Human Rights, *Something for Everyone*, noted that voluntary organisations had made no serious attempt to use the HRA to create a culture that could in turn lead to systemic change in the provision of services by the public sector.[94] The language of human rights is largely absent in the reports on mental health care discussed in this chapter. For example, despite highlighting major concerns about the mental health services, CHI makes no reference to the HRA. While the Kings Fund report comments in its overview of mental health policy that with the introduction of the HRA 'a human rights perspective on mental health policy and practice is an important development,'[95] neither the findings nor the recommendations make any reference to it. A notable exception is the MHAC, which has made clear that it considers the promotion of a human rights culture in the field of mental health to be a core element of its work.[96] The MHAC's Tenth Biennial Report provides a detailed analysis of the impact of the HRA on mental health law and practice in relation to detained patients. However, the MHAC's remit is limited to safeguarding the interests of individuals who are detained under the MHA.

OPPORTUNITIES FOR CHANGE

Given the concerns raised in reports on current mental health care, and the human rights implications of the proposals for reforming the MHA, there is clearly a pressing need to ensure that respect for human rights becomes integral to mental health law, policy and practice. While legal challenges under the HRA can play an important role in such a process, the development of case law is not enough. Nor can such work wait until the proposed Commission for Equality and Human Rights is established in 2006/07.

---

[91] Audit Commission, para 1.
[92] Para 21.
[93] Para 2.5
[94] J Watson, *Something for Everyone: The Impact of the Human Rights Act and the need for a Human Rights Commission* (London, British Institute of Human Rights, 2002), executive summary.
[95] Above n 48, at 29.
[96] Para 2.3.

If public services are to deliver quality services that meet the needs of individual service users, a human rights perspective must be developed across the spectrum of mental health care. This would mean that when front-line staff make decisions about individuals with mental health problems, they do so by balancing the rights of individuals alongside the rights of any others involved, such as family members and in some cases, members of the public. Where invasive action is necessary, those making such decisions must be confident that any restrictions on individuals' rights can be justified under the HRA. Similarly, the range of agencies involved in the planning and delivery of mental health services should take into account the impact of their decisions on service users, such as the allocation of resources and deciding what services are to be made available and how they are to be delivered.

The Audit Commission's report, which provides some practical examples for public authorities on how they can develop a human rights culture,[97] demonstrates that much can be done to promote the HRA as a positive and useful framework for decision making. Educational programmes such as the BIHR's community outreach work can play a key role in not only ensuring that voluntary organisations and service users are aware of their rights, but can also use the human rights principles to support their work to achieve positive change for people with mental health problems. Failing this, there is a very real risk that the vision of a culture of respect for human rights will not be realised and that the HRA will continue to be seen as the domain of lawyers. As *Something for Everyone* warns:

> Without more attention paid to the promotion of the Human Rights Act and the principles which lie behind it in a way that makes it accessible to lay people the vicious circle of unresponsive public services which lead to challenges cannot be broken.

---

[97] Ch 4.

10

Sexual Orientation and Gender Identity

ROBERT WINTEMUTE*

INTRODUCTION

LESBIAN, GAY AND bisexual ('LGB') individuals, and transsexual[1] individuals, are probably two of the social minorities that have benefited the most from the concept of human rights, and from the gradual strengthening of legal protection of human rights in Europe and the UK. They have been forced to become adept practitioners of human rights law because they are classic examples of minorities that are small (indeed statistically tiny in the case of transsexual individuals) but nonetheless threatening to the heterosexual and non-transsexual majority, and therefore politically unpopular. They have had great difficulty in persuading governments to sponsor the legislative reforms necessary to remove or prohibit discrimination based on sexual orientation (in the case of LGB individuals) or gender identity (in the case of transsexual individuals). Instead, they have often had to invoke human rights principles before courts, and have enjoyed increasing success since 1997. In the remainder of this chapter, I will recall the dismal state of the rights of LGB and transsexual individuals (together, 'LGBT' individuals) in English and Welsh law[2] in 1993, examine the dramatic progress that has been made over the last

* Professor of Human Rights Law, King's College London. Thanks to Mark Bell and Stephen Whittle for their comments on an earlier version. This chapter generally incorporates developments of which I was aware on 2 Dec 2004. I would like to thank the Leverhulme Trust for the award of a Leverhulme Research Fellowship for 2003–04 (which allowed me to write this chapter as part of a larger research project).
    [1] Because space is limited, I will not attempt to consider: (i) other transgendered individuals who live in the social sex role that does not correspond to their birth sex, or across social sex roles, but have no desire to undergo gender reassignment (putting aside any medical or financial constraints); and (ii) intersexed individuals (born with physical characteristics of both sexes).
    [2] I will occasionally include references to the law of Scotland or the law of Northern Ireland.

eleven years, and consider the extent to which the concept of human rights can be given credit for this progress.

Before doing so, I should first explain what the two very distinct phenomena of sexual orientation and gender identity have in common, and what might explain the recent increase in solidarity among LGBT individuals in Europe. The concept of 'sexual orientation' is used to classify individuals as heterosexual, bisexual, lesbian or gay, whereas (one sense of) the concept of 'gender identity' is used to classify individuals as non-transsexual or transsexual. An individual can be a member of the majority with respect to one of these characteristics, both or neither: most individuals are heterosexual and non-transsexual, but some are LGB and non-transsexual, some are heterosexual and transsexual, and some are LGB and transsexual. What sexual orientation discrimination and gender identity discrimination have in common is that they are both 'minority' forms of sex discrimination, which are often not recognised as sex discrimination because they involve what the majority sees as disturbing departures from traditional social sex roles (eg, in the case of a gay man, wishing to marry another man, or in the case of a transsexual woman who was born male, wishing to have her penis surgically removed). LGB individuals and transsexual individuals are therefore both members of 'sex discrimination minorities'.[3] As by far the larger of the two minorities, LGB individuals have a moral duty to speak out on behalf of transsexual individuals.

THE LAW IN ENGLAND AND WALES IN 1993

Looking back to 1993, very little had been done to ensure equal rights and obligations for LGBT individuals in England and Wales. Although sexual activity between men had been legal since 1967, the age of consent to male–male sexual activity was 21 vs. 16 for male–female or female–female sexual activity, sexual activity involving three or more men was illegal, the armed forces actively excluded LGBT personnel, there was no legislation prohibiting discrimination based on sexual orientation or gender identity in employment, and the infamous Section 28 of the Local Government Act 1988 prohibited 'promot[ing] the teaching . . . of the acceptability of homosexuality as a pretended family relationship.' In the case of LGB individuals who formed same-sex partnerships, they could not marry, were denied the rights and obligations of married and unmarried different-sex partners (including succession to the tenancy of a local authority house or flat), and could not adopt each other's children or adopt unrelated children jointly (which was also the case for unmarried different-sex partners).[4]

---

[3] See R Wintemute, 'Recognising New Kinds of Direct Sex Discrimination: Transsexualism, Sexual Orientation and Dress Codes' (1997) 60 *Modern Law Review* 334.

[4] See R Wintemute, 'Sexual Orientation Discrimination' in C McCrudden and G Chambers (eds), *Individual Rights and the Law in Britain* (Oxford, Oxford University Press, 1994) 491–533.

As for transsexual individuals, they could not have the sex on their birth certificates changed after gender reassignment.[5] If they were heterosexual after gender reassignment, they could not marry a person of the sex opposite to their (non-recognised) reassigned sex or (in the case of transsexual men) be treated as the fathers of their non-transsexual female partners' children by donor insemination.[6] However, if they were LGB after gender reassignment, they *could* marry a person of the same sex as their (non-recognised) reassigned sex and (in the case of transsexual women) be treated as the fathers of their non-transsexual female partners' children by donor insemination. Thus, unlike heterosexual transsexual individuals, LGB transsexual individuals were better off *not* having their gender reassignments recognised, as long as sexual orientation discrimination in relation to marriage and donor insemination persisted.

THE LAW IN ENGLAND AND WALES IN 2004

Discrimination in the Criminal Law

Same-Sex Sexual Activity, Expression of Same-Sex Affection, and LGBT Publications

Since 1993, discrimination against same-sex sexual activity in the formulation (as opposed to the enforcement) of the criminal law has gradually been eliminated. The age of consent to male–male sexual activity was lowered first from 21 to 18 in 1994,[7] and then from 18 to 16 in 2000.[8] England and Wales thus finally equalised the age of consent 28 years after the Netherlands and 18 years after France. The reform followed the 1997 report of the European Commission of Human Rights ('ECommHR') in *Sutherland v UK*,[9] finding that the unequal age of consent violated Articles 8 (respect for private life) and 14 (non-discrimination) of the European Convention on Human Rights (ECHR), and required three attempts in Parliament. The first two attempts, in 1998 and 1999, were blocked by the House of Lords,[10] forcing the Government to invoke the Parliament Acts 1911 and 1949 to permit the Bill to Receive Royal Assent on 30 November 2000, without the consent of the House of Lords.

---

[5] See *Cossey v UK* (27 Sept 1990) (ECtHR) (J). Except where a paper-published version is mentioned, every judgment (J), report (R) or admissibility decision (AD) of the European Court (ECtHR) and Commission (ECommHR) of Human Rights cited in this chapter is available at <http://www.echr.coe.int> (HUDOC, tick appropriate box(es) at left, type the applicant's name after Case Title or the application number, Search).

[6] See *X, Y & Z v UK* (22 April 1997) (ECtHR) (J).

[7] Criminal Justice and Public Order Act 1994, ss 143, 145 (s 146 decriminalised male–male sexual activity in the Armed Forces and the Merchant Navy).

[8] Sexual Offences (Amendment) Act 2000.

[9] (1 July 1997) (ECommHR) (R). The Court was not asked to confirm the Commission's opinion in *Sutherland*, but did so later in *L and V v Austria* and *SL v Austria* (9 Jan 2003) (ECtHR) (J).

[10] *Hansard* (HL), 22 July 1998, cols 936–75 (Crime and Disorder Bill), 13 April 1999, cols 647–759 (Sexual Offences (Amendment) Bill).

The November 2000 reform did not address other discriminatory provisions of the criminal law, such as the rule that male–male sexual activity is illegal if 'more than two persons take part or are present.'[11] In July 2000, in *ADT* v *UK*,[12] the European Court of Human Rights ('ECtHR') held that this rule violates Article 8 (respect for private life), meaning that everyone has a right to engage in private group sexual activity (at least where the group consists of three to five consenting adults). The Court did not find it necessary to consider under Article 14 the fact that the rule discriminated by not applying to male–female or female–female sexual activity.

Instead of amending the age of consent Bill, the UK Government chose to link compliance with *ADT* to the comprehensive review of sexual offences that began in January 1999.[13] The review carefully considered the requirements of the European Convention and culminated in the Sexual Offences Act 2003, which received Royal Assent on 20 November 2003. By repealing and replacing most of the Sexual Offences Acts 1956 and 1967, the Act makes the amendment required by *ADT*, and removes all remaining direct sexual orientation discrimination from the criminal law.

The Bill was preceded by a Home Office consultation document entitled *Setting the Boundaries: Reforming the Law on Sex Offences*[14] (published in July 2000 just before *ADT*), which accepted that '[t]he criminal law should not treat people differently on the basis of their sexual orientation,'[15] and recommended the repeal of the 'unnatural offences' of 'buggery' (which includes male–male anal intercourse) and 'gross indecency' (all other male–male sexual activity), as well as the men-only offence of 'solicit[ing] or importun[ing] in a public place for an immoral purpose' (which was applied mainly to male–male soliciting for non-commercial sexual activity).[16] Instead of these directly or indirectly discriminatory offences, the consultation document proposed that 'soliciting by men for the purposes of prostitution . . . [should be regulated] on the same basis as soliciting by women,'[17] and that '[a] new ["gender and sexuality neutral"] public order offence should be created to deal with sexual behaviour that a person knew or should have known was likely to cause distress, alarm or offence to others in a public place.'[18]

The first version of the Bill adopted the consultation document's sexual-orientation-neutral approach (including with regard to prostitution),[19] repealed the offences of 'buggery', 'gross indecency', and 'soliciting for an immoral purpose', and provided for the termination of sex offenders' notification

---

[11] Sexual Offences Act 1967, s 1(2).
[12] (31 July 2000) (ECtHR) (J).
[13] See <http://www.homeoffice.gov.uk/justice/sentencing/sexualoffencesbill/bill_prog,html>
[14] See < http://www.homeoffice.gov.uk/docs/vol1main.pdf>
[15] *Ibid*, at para 6.5.3.
[16] *Ibid*, at paras 6.6.–6.6.17, discussing Sexual Offences Act 1956, ss 12, 13, 32.
[17] *Ibid*, at para 6.6.17.
[18] *Ibid*, at para 8.4.11.
[19] See Sexual Offences Act 2003, sch 1.

requirements for those convicted in the past of consensual 'buggery' or 'gross indecency' that is now legal.[20] However, the Bill's new offence of 'sexual behaviour in a public place', punishable by up to six months' imprisonment, met opposition in the House of Lords. Clause 74 of the first version[21] would have made it an offence for a person to engage in sexual activity 'in a public place' (including 'the common parts of a building containing two or more separate dwellings') or 'not in a dwelling', if he or she 'knows that, or is reckless as to whether, someone (other than a person he [or she] reasonably believes to be a willing observer) will see any part of him [or her] or of another participant.'

Concern that Clause 74 would criminalise sexual activity in the back garden of a house led the Government to drop the clause, and announce that it would rely on the existing common law offence of 'outraging public decency' and on statutory public order offences[22] to regulate same-sex and different-sex 'semi-public sexual activity'.[23] However, Baroness Noakes thought that these offences would often fail to catch male–male sexual activity in public toilets (especially in a cubicle with the door closed), because no third party would have been outraged or offended. She therefore proposed a sexual-orientation-neutral offence of 'sexual activity in a public lavatory', also punishable by up to six months' imprisonment.[24] This was adopted by the Lords, modified slightly by the Commons, and became section 71 of the Act. Its effect is to 'equalise down', by extending the former absolute prohibition of male–male sexual activity in a public lavatory (regardless of the impact on third parties)[25] to male–female and female–female sexual activity.

The elimination of direct (but not necessarily indirect) sexual orientation discrimination in the criminal law by the Sexual Offences Act 2003 is buttressed by sections 3 and 6 of the Human Rights Act 1998 ('HRA'), which preclude discriminatory interpretation by a UK court of neutral common law or statutory offences relating to public decency, public order, prostitution,[26] sado-masochism,[27] obscenity[28] or blasphemy.[29] This means that neutral offences cannot be applied to same-sex conduct (or to publications depicting or describing same-sex conduct), if similar different-sex conduct (or publications) would not give rise to a prosecution or a conviction, and that the sentence following a conviction must be equal. Thus, the 1986 conviction of two men for 'insulting

---

[20] *Ibid*, at sch 4.
[21] See <http://www.publications.parliament.uk/pa/ld200203/ldbills/026/2003026.pdf>
[22] See, eg, Public Order Act 1986, s 5.
[23] See Wintemute, above n 4, at 500–01.
[24] *Hansard* (HL), 19 May 2003, cols 576–88, 9 June 2003, cols 69–74.
[25] Sexual Offences Act 1967, s 1(2).
[26] See *F v Switzerland* (no 11680/85) (10 March 1985) (ECommHR) (AD) (the reasoning on the non-applicability of Art 14 is questionable).
[27] See *Laskey v UK* (19 Feb 1997) (ECtHR) (J), para 47.
[28] See *Scherer v Switzerland* (25 March 1994) (ECtHR) (J), para 26.
[29] See *Wingrove v UK* (25 Nov 1996) (ECtHR) (J); *Gay News Ltd v UK* (no 8710/79) (7 May 1982) (ECommHR) (AD), 28 Dec & Rep 77.

behaviour', consisting of kissing and cuddling at a bus stop at 1.55 am, should no longer be possible.[30]

Anti-LGBT Violence and Incitement to Anti-LGBT Hatred

Although the criminal law no longer discriminates actively against same-sex sexual activity or LGBT individuals, it has done so passively through two major omissions: the absence (until very recently) of legislation on 'hate crimes' against LGBT individuals (providing for a special offence, or a higher penalty for a general offence, where a crime of violence is motivated by hostility to the sexual orientation or gender identity of the victim), and the absence of legislation on 'hate speech' directed at LGBT individuals (which can cause third parties to commit 'hate crimes' against them).

In the United States, 'hate crime' legislation includes sexual orientation in 29 states and the District of Columbia, and gender identity in seven states and DC.[31] In Canada, the federal Criminal Code provides that 'evidence that the offence was motivated by bias, prejudice or hate based on race . . . religion, sex, age, mental or physical disability, sexual orientation, or any other similar factor . . . shall be deemed to be aggravating circumstances'[32] causing the sentence to be increased. In England and Wales, 'racially aggravated' offences were created in 1998,[33] and 'religiously aggravated' offences were added in 2001,[34] but sexual orientation was not covered. This was despite the bombing of the Admiral Duncan gay pub in London on 30 April 1999, which killed three persons and injured over sixty.[35]

The Criminal Justice Act 2003, section 146, partly fills the gap by obliging courts to treat as an aggravating factor in sentencing the fact that '(a) . . . the offender demonstrated towards the victim of the offence hostility based on (i) the sexual orientation (or presumed sexual orientation) of the victim, or . . . (b) that the offence is motivated (wholly or partly) (i) by hostility towards persons who are of a particular sexual orientation.' However, the section, which imposes a similar obligation in relation to disability, corresponds to only part of the existing legislation on race and religion,[36] because it does not create any special offences 'aggravated by reference to sexual orientation.'[37] Nor does it cover gender identity or sex.

The ECtHR considers the prohibition of 'hate speech' a justifiable interference with the Article 10 right to freedom of expression,[38] and legislation

---

[30] See *Masterson v Holden* [1986] 3 All ER 39 (QB Div).
[31] See <http://www.thetaskforce.org/theissues/issue.cfm?issueID=12>
[32] Criminal Code, s 718.2.
[33] Crime and Disorder Act 1998, ss 28–32.
[34] Anti-Terrorism, Crime and Security Act 2001, s 39.
[35] See *The Independent*, 1 May 1999, 1.
[36] Criminal Justice Act 2003, s 145 (formerly Crime and Disorder Act 1998, s 82, then Powers of Criminal Courts (Sentencing) Act 2000, s 153).
[37] Compare Crime and Disorder Act 1998, ss 28–32.
[38] See *Garaudy v France* (7 July 2003) (ECtHR) (AD).

banning incitement to hatred or insults based on sexual orientation has been passed in such European countries as Belgium, Denmark, Iceland, Ireland, Luxembourg, the Netherlands, Norway, Spain, and Sweden,[39] as well as in South Africa[40] and the Australian states of New South Wales, Queensland and Tasmania.[41] The legislation in Queensland also covers gender identity.[42] On 17 September 2003, the House of Commons of Canada's federal Parliament voted to amend the Criminal Code's ban on 'wilfully promot[ing] hatred against any identifiable group,'[43] by adding 'sexual orientation' to the definition of an 'identifiable group' ('any section of the public distinguished by colour, race, religion or ethnic origin').[44] Yet in England and Wales, Part III of the Public Order Act 1986 prohibits only incitement to 'racial hatred', the House of Lords having rejected an attempt to add 'religious hatred' (as in Northern Ireland)[45] through a provision of the Anti-Terrorism, Crime and Security Act 2001.[46]

Legal Recognition and Public Funding of Gender Reassignment

Given that the criminal law has never prohibited gender reassignment expressly, the most fundamental legal issue for transsexual individuals (like decriminalisation of same-sex sexual activity for LGB individuals) has been obtaining the right to have their gender reassignments recognised for all legal purposes, and to have their birth certificates amended to reflect their new legal sex. This battle took over thirty years, from the adoption in 1970 of a rigid common law definition of legal sex as determined by chromosomes,[47] through three unsuccessful challenges in the ECtHR in 1986, 1990 and 1998,[48] to final victory in 2002 in *Christine Goodwin v UK* and *I v UK*.[49] In the 2002 cases, the ECtHR finally lost patience with the UK

---

[39] Belgium, Penal Code, Art 444 (Law of 25 Feb 2003); Denmark, Penal Code, Art 266b (Law of 3 June 1987); Iceland, General Penal Code, s 233a (Act No 135/1996); Ireland, Prohibition of Incitement to Hatred Act, 1989; Luxembourg, Penal Code, Art. 457-1 (Law of 19 July 1997); Netherlands, Penal Code, Arts 137c-d-e (Law of 14 Nov 1991); Norway, Penal Code, para 135a (Law of 8 May 1981); Spain, Penal Code, Art 510 (Organic Law of 23 Nov 1995); Sweden, Penal Code, c 5, Art 5 (SFS 1987:610), c 16, Art 8 (SFS 2002: 800), supplemented by Freedom of the Press Act, c 7, Art 4(11) (SFS 2002: 908), and Freedom of Expression Act, c 5, Art 1 (both part of the Swedish Constitution).

[40] Promotion of Equality and Prevention of Unfair Discrimination Act, No 4 of 2000, ss 1(1)(xxii)(a), 10–11.

[41] New South Wales, Anti-Discrimination Act 1977, ss 49ZS–49ZT (added in 1993) ('homosexuality'); Queensland, Anti-Discrimination Act 1991, s 124A (amended in 2002) ('sexuality', 'gender identity'); Tasmania, Anti-Discrimination Act 1998, s 19 ('sexual orientation').

[42] *Ibid*.

[43] Criminal Code, s 319(2).

[44] *Ibid*, s 318(4). For the final version, see S. C. 2004, c. 14.

[45] Public Order (Northern Ireland) Order 1987, SI 1987, No 463, Art 8.

[46] See *Hansard* (HL), 13 Dec 2001, cols 1449–64. But see Serious Organised Crime and Police Bill, sch 10 (Racial and religious hatred), 24 Nov 2004, HC.

[47] *Corbett v Corbett* [1970] 2 All ER 33 (H Ct).

[48] *Mark Rees v UK* (17 Oct 1986) (ECtHR) (J); *Caroline Cossey v UK* (27 Sept 1990) (ECtHR) (J); *Kristina Sheffield & Rachel Horsham v UK* (30 July 1998) (ECtHR) (J).

[49] (11 July 2002) (ECtHR) (J).

Government's refusal to change the law, and found a violation of Article 8 (respect for private life), by 17 votes to 0. On 27 November 2003, the UK Government introduced in the House of Lords the Bill which became the Gender Recognition Act, and bought UK law into compliance with the Convention.[50]

The Act is more generous than legislation in other jurisdictions, which generally requires surgery to alter sexual organs. Instead, an individual is entitled to a 'gender recognition certificate' based on 'living in the other gender' if he or she '(a) has or has had gender dysphoria [gender identity disorder or transsexualism], (b) has lived in the acquired gender . . . [for] two years . . ., (c) intends to continue to live in the acquired gender until death, and (d) complies with the requirements imposed by . . . section 3.'[51] Requirements under section 3 relate to the evidence that must be supplied to support the application, including reports by a gender dysphoria specialist (a medical doctor or psychologist) and by another specialist or non-specialist medical doctor, but do not include either surgery or use of hormones. Once a 'full gender recognition certificate' has been issued, 'the person's gender becomes for all purposes the acquired gender,'[52] and he or she may apply for an amended birth certificate.[53]

Assuming that a gender reassignment will be legally recognised if performed, the other major issue that arises is whether public or private health insurance must cover the costs of surgery or hormones, which can be prohibitive for many transsexual individuals. In 1999, the Court of Appeal quashed, as 'irrational' under principles of administrative law, a regional health authority's blanket policy of not funding gender reassignment surgery, because the authority did not believe that transsexualism is a treatable illness, viewed the surgery as comparable to cosmetic plastic surgery, and considered psychotherapy equally or more effective.[54] The Court chastised the applicants' counsel for invoking the European Convention.

Yet in 2003, in *van Kück v Germany*,[55] the ECtHR held by 4 votes to 3 that German courts violated Articles 6 (right to a fair hearing) and 8 (respect for private life), by interpreting a health insurance contract between a transsexual woman and a private insurance company as not requiring reimbursement of the cost of the hormones, surgery and other medical treatment related to her gender reassignment, because the treatment was not 'medically necessary'. The German courts took the view, like the English regional health authority, that 'the applicant ought to have had first recourse to . . . an extensive psychotherapy of 50 to 100 sessions,' and that 'gender re-assignment measures could not be expected to cure the applicant's transsexuality.'[56]

---

[50] The Bill received Royal Assent on 1 July 2004. See <http://www.dca.gov.uk/contitution/transsex/index.htm>.

[51] Sections 1(1)(a), 2(1), 25.

[52] Section 9(1).

[53] Section 10, sch 3.

[54] *R v North West Lancashire Health Authority, ex parte A*, [2000] 1 WLR 977 (CA).

[55] (12 June 2003) (ECtHR) (J).

[56] *Ibid*, at paras 16, 22.

The majority of the Strasbourg Court concluded that 'gender identity is one of the most intimate private-life matters of a person. The burden placed on a person in such a situation to prove the medical necessity of treatment, including irreversible surgery, appears therefore disproportionate.'[57] The majority did not decide that the Convention always requires reimbursement of the cost of gender reassignment. Rather, where an existing public or private health insurance plan reimburses the cost of 'medically necessary' treatment, the plan must cover the cost of gender reassignment, even if the usual strict criteria for determining 'medical necessity' do not appear to be satisfied. These criteria must be relaxed in order to respect the transsexual individual's self-determination of their gender identity, and to take into account the lack of scientific certainty in this area.[58] The majority's reasoning suggests they would not permit a blanket exclusion of gender reassignment from health insurance policies, but that they would uphold some objective criteria for determining 'medical necessity' (ie, the transsexual individual's wishes are not always conclusive).

Other Discrimination Against LGBT Individuals

Employment

In 1993, the most promising source of protection for LGBT employees and job applicants appeared to be the Sex Discrimination Act 1975 ('SDA'), given the mainly negative case law under unfair dismissal legislation,[59] and the Supreme Court of Hawaii's decision that the exclusion of same-sex couples from civil marriage is prima facie direct sex discrimination.[60] For transsexual employees and job applicants, the sex discrimination argument succeeded in 1996 in *P v S & Cornwall County Council*,[61] not under the SDA, but under Council Directive 76/207/EEC (the 'Equal Treatment Directive' or 'ETD'). The European Court of Justice ('ECJ') held that the ETD's prohibition of sex discrimination in employment 'precludes dismissal of a transsexual for a reason related to a gender reassignment.'[62]

The Employment Appeal Tribunal had no trouble interpreting 'sex' in the SDA in a way that was consistent with *P*,[63] as European Community law requires (if possible). However, in 1999, the Government chose to give effect to *P* (and narrow its impact) by amending the SDA to add a separate prohibition of discrimination: against persons 'intend[ing] to undergo, . . . undergoing or ha[ving] undergone gender reassignment.'[64] This prohibition is limited to

---

[57] *Ibid*, at paras 56, 82.
[58] See Concurring Opinion of Judge Ress.
[59] See Wintemute, above n 4, at 504–05.
[60] *Baehr v Lewin*, 852 P2d 44 (1993).
[61] Case C-13/94, [1996] ECR I-2143.
[62] *Ibid*, at para 24.
[63] See *Chessington World of Adventures Ltd v Reed* [1997] IRLR 556 (EAT).
[64] SDA, s 2A, inserted by Sex Discrimination (Gender Reassignment) Regulations 1999, SI 1999, No 1102.

employment and vocational training (unlike the SDA's prohibition of sex discrimination), and subject to new exceptions not mentioned in *P*, such as jobs requiring the performance of 'intimate physical searches pursuant to statutory powers.'[65]

The new prohibition also excludes transsexual individuals who do not intend to undergo gender reassignment, which is defined as a process that 'chang[es] physiological or other characteristics of sex.'[66] Such individuals could qualify for 'full gender recognition certificates' under the Gender Recognition Act 2004, yet not be protected by the SDA. They might be covered by 'sex', if the ECJ were to extend *P*, but to remove any doubt, an express prohibition of discrimination based on 'gender identity' (for which there are now precedents)[67] should be added. Regardless of how the legislation is drafted, transsexual individuals will continue to face practical difficulties, especially regarding use of toilets at work,[68] before their gender reassignment is complete, or during the two year period of 'liv[ing] in the acquired gender' before a certificate can be issued under the Gender Recognition Act 2004.

In the case of LGB employees and job applicants, every attempt to invoke the prohibitions of sex discrimination in the SDA, the ETD, or EC Treaty Article 141 has been rejected by UK appellate courts[69] and by the ECJ,[70] incorrectly in my view.[71] However, the ECtHR has provided protection under Article 8 (respect for private life), and would almost certainly do so under Article 8 (private life) combined with Article 14 (non-discrimination). On 27 September 1999, in *Smith and Grady v UK* and *Lustig-Prean and Beckett v UK*,[72] the Court held that the UK armed forces' policy of dismissing all LGB personnel, often after an intrusive investigation into their sexual lives, violated Article 8. The UK complied by suspending the policy the same day, and revising it permanently on 12 January 2000. Because the treatment was unjustifiable even if it were extended (hypothetically) to heterosexual personnel, the Court did not need to

---

[65] SDA, s 7B(2)(a). But see *A v Chief Constable of West Yorkshire* [2004] 1 All ER 145 (HL).

[66] SDA, s 82.

[67] See, eg, Victoria (Australia), Equal Opportunities Act 1995, s 6 (amended in 2000); Northwest Territories (Canada), Human Rights Act, SNWT 2002, c 18, s 5(1).

[68] See *Croft v Royal Mail Group plc*, [2003] IRLR 592 (CA).

[69] See *R v Ministry of Defence, ex parte Smith* (1995), [1996] 1 All ER 257 (CA) (ETD) (3–0); *Smith v Gardner Merchant*, [1998] IRLR 510 (CA) (SDA) (3–0); *Advocate General for Scotland v MacDonald*, [2003] IRLR 512 (HL) (SDA) (5–0), affirming *MacDonald v Ministry of Defence*, [2001] IRLR 431 (Court of Session, Inner House) (2-1, Lord Prosser accepted the argument and dissented), and *Pearce v Mayfield Secondary School*, [2001] IRLR 669 (CA) (3–0, Lady Justice Hale accepted the argument and would have dissented but for the binding precedent of *Gardner Merchant*).

[70] See *Grant v South-West Trains*, Case C-249/96, [1998] ECR I-621 (Art 141), paras 27–28; *D and Sweden v Council*, Joined Cases C-122/99 P, C-125/99 P, [2001] ECR I-4319, para 46 (Art 141).

[71] See Wintemute, above n 3; R Wintemute, 'Sex Discrimination in *MacDonald* and *Pearce*: Why the Law Lords Chose the Wrong Comparators' (2003) 14 *King's College Law Journal* 267.

[72] (27 Sept 1999) (ECtHR) (J).

consider the fact that the policy discriminated by not applying to heterosexual personnel.

Several statements by the ECtHR indicate that it will take differences in treatment based on sexual orientation very seriously, under Article 14 combined with Article 8. In *Smith* and *Lustig-Prean*, the Court made an explicit analogy between sexual orientation discrimination and race discrimination: 'a predisposed bias on the part of a heterosexual majority against a homosexual minority . . . cannot amount to sufficient justification for the interferences with the applicants' rights, any more than similar negative attitudes towards those of a different race, origin or colour.'[73] The Court has also made an implicit analogy between sexual orientation discrimination and religion discrimination,[74] and an explicit analogy between sexual orientation discrimination and sex discrimination: 'Just like differences [in treatment] based on sex, . . . differences [in treatment] based on sexual orientation require particularly serious reasons by way of justification.'[75] Similarly, the Court has said: 'In cases in which the margin of appreciation afforded to member States is narrow, as [is] the position where there is a difference in treatment based on sex or sexual orientation, the principle of proportionality does not merely require that the measure chosen is in principle suited for realising the aim sought. It must also be shown that it was necessary . . . to achieve that aim.'[76]

In view of the Court's case law on sexual orientation discrimination, it seems clear that, since 2 October 2000, it has been possible for LGB individuals (and probably also transsexual individuals) who are employed by (or applying for jobs with) 'public authorities' to use HRA section 6 to enforce their rights under Articles 14 and 8 of the Convention. Even though there is no Convention right to employment, their cases should fall 'within the ambit' of Article 8, allowing them to invoke Article 14, because the discrimination has a coercive effect on their private lives (by providing an incentive not to be LGBT or not to be openly LGBT).[77]

Since 1997, a major reason for the rejection of the sex discrimination argument by the ECJ and by UK appellate courts has been the prospect of a European Community directive on sexual orientation discrimination. The Treaty of Amsterdam's insertion of Article 13 into the EC Treaty created an express competence to 'take appropriate action to combat discrimination based on . . . sexual orientation'. The EC did so on 27 November 2000 by adopting Council Directive 2000/78/EC, which prohibits harassment and direct or indirect discrimination on grounds of sexual orientation in employment, vocational train-

---

[73] *Ibid*, at paras 97 (*Smith*), 90 (*Lustig-Prean*).

[74] Compare *Salgueiro da Silva Mouta v Portugal* (21 Dec 1999) (ECtHR) (J), para 36, with *Hoffmann v Austria* (23 June 1993) (ECtHR) (J), para 36.

[75] See *L and V v Austria, SL v Austria* (9 Jan. 2003) (ECtHR) (J), paras 45 (*L and V*), 37 (*SL*).

[76] See *Karner v Austria* (24 July 2003) (ECtHR) (J), para 41.

[77] Compare *Thlimmenos v Greece* (6 April 2000) (ECtHR) (J) (employment discrimination against Jehovah's Witness violated Art 14 combined with Art 9). See also R Wintemute, [2004] EHRLR 366–82, 484–99.

ing, and organisations of workers, employers or professionals. Ten days later, on 7 December 2000, sexual orientation was also included in the anti-discrimination provision (Article 21) of the Charter of Fundamental Rights of the European Union (Article II-81, Treaty establishing a Constitution for Europe).

The UK has implemented Directive 2000/78 for Great Britain through the Employment Equality (Sexual Orientation) Regulations 2003,[78] which entered into force on 1 December 2003, the day before the deadline for implementation. For the most part, they correctly implement the Directive and provide protection equivalent to that in the SDA or the Race Relations Act 1976 ('RRA'), but only in the areas of employment and vocational training (including all further and higher education), and without providing victims of discrimination the assistance of any enforcement agency, like the Equal Opportunities Commission (for sex discrimination), the Commission for Racial Equality, and the Disability Rights Commission.[79]

A special exception for 'employment . . . for purposes of an organised religion,'[80] included at the last minute after lobbying by the Church of England, is broader than what the Directive permits and was challenged (unsuccessfully) by Lord Lester in the legislative House of Lords. If employment tribunals are willing to consider the minister's statements regarding the intended scope of the exception,[81] under *Pepper v Hart*,[82] much of the exception's potential damage could be avoided. When several trade unions sought judicial review of the exception's validity the Administrative Court confirmed the exception's narrowness.[83]

The Regulations are not retroactive. But public and private sector LGB employees dismissed on grounds of sexual orientation between 2 October 2000 and 1 December 2003 should have a better chance of claiming unfair dismissal than in the past, because they could insist, under HRA section 3(1), that the tribunal or court interpret the concept of 'unfairness', in section 94 of the Employment Rights Act 1996, in a way that avoids sexual orientation discrimination that would violate Articles 8 and 14 of the Convention.[84]

---

[78] SI 2003, No 1661: approved by House of Lords (17 June) and House of Commons (25 June); made by Jacqui Smith, Deputy Minister for Women and Equality, Department of Trade and Industry (26 June); amended by SI 2003, No 2827 (trustees and managers of occupational pension schemes).

[79] Victims will eventually receive assistance from a planned Commission for Equality and Human Rights, which will replace the existing commissions, but not before 2007. See further in this volume chs 3 and 5. See also Equality Bill (Queen's Speech, 23 Nov 2004); <http://www.womenandequalityunit.gov.uk/equality/project>.

[80] *Ibid*, Regs 7(3), 16(3).

[81] *Hansard* (HL), 17 June 2003, cols 779–81.

[82] [1992] 3 WLR 1032 (HL).

[83] *R (Amicus) v Secretary of State for Trade and Industry* [2004] IRLR 430.

[84] But see *X v Y* [2004] IRLR 625 (CA) (no issue of direct or indirect sexual orientation discrimination where dismissed male employee had been convicted of 'gross indecency' with another adult male in a roadside public toilet while off duty).

Education, Housing and Services

The protection provided by the HRA since 2 October 2000, described above, is not limited to employment by 'public authorities', but extends to all of their acts or omissions. Thus, sexual orientation and gender identity discrimination by 'public authorities' in the provision of education, housing or other services can be challenged under HRA section 6. However, in the private sector, there is no protection with regard to (primary or secondary) education, housing or services (unlike in the case of sex, race or disability discrimination), because EC law does not require such protection for sex and sexual orientation, and the Government has refused to go beyond the requirements of EC law with respect to gender identity and sexual orientation. The Sex Discrimination (Gender Reassignment) Regulations 1999 and the Employment Equality (Sexual Orientation) Regulations 2003 are confined to employment and vocational training (which, in the case of the 2003 Regulations, has been extended to cover all education in universities and other institutions of further or higher education).[85]

This means, for example, that the former advertisements of the Sandals chain for its Caribbean resorts for 'mixed-sex couples only'[86] were perfectly legal, unless they were caught by the SDA. In the private sector, LGBT individuals and same-sex couples facing discrimination in (primary or secondary) education, housing or services (including insurance) could ask UK courts to reconsider the sex discrimination argument in light of HRA section 3(1), which was not available in the cases that rejected the argument.

Section 28 of the Local Government Act 1988

Section 28 inserted a new section 2A into the Local Government Act 1986: 'A local authority shall not (a) intentionally promote homosexuality . . .; (b) promote the teaching . . . of the acceptability of homosexuality as a pretended family relationship.' With the support of then Prime Minister Margaret Thatcher, the provision was added to slap down Labour-controlled local governments that were seen as 'promoting homosexuality', by allegedly requiring widespread classroom use of the Danish children's book *Jenny Lives With Eric and Martin*[87] (one copy was available for use by teachers in Inner London Education Authority schools), by funding services for and organisations from the LGB community (tabloid newspapers usually mocked alleged funding of bereavement or karate classes for lesbian women), and by encouraging the use of 'positive images' of lesbian women and gay men.

---

[85] See Regs 17, 20.
[86] See, 'Poster Ads for "Romantic Couples" Holidays Banned from Tube for Bias against Gays', *The Independent*, 29 September 2003.
[87] (London, Gay Men's Press, 1983).

Section 28 never applied to Northern Ireland and was repealed by the Scottish Parliament in 2000.[88] Repeal for England and Wales, blocked by the House of Lords in 2000,[89] finally succeeded in 2003.[90] Although this extraordinarily offensive statutory language must have had a chilling effect[91] on local authority funding of LGB organisations, discussion of same-sex sexual activity and partnerships in schools, and efforts by teachers to address bullying of LGB pupils, it did not give rise to a single reported judicial decision.[92]

Section 28 is survived by a provision that is facially less offensive, but succeeds in stigmatising all non-marital families. Section 403(1A) of the Education Act 1996, inserted by section 148 of the Learning and Skills Act 2000 as a replacement for Section 28, requires the Secretary of State for Education to 'issue guidance designed to secure that when sex education is given to registered pupils at maintained schools—(a) they learn the nature of marriage and its importance for family life and the bringing up of children . . .'

The resulting *Sex and Relationship Education Guidance*[93] states that '[t]here should be no direct promotion of sexual orientation'[94] (except presumably for the promotion of different-sex marriage as the ideal form of family life). The absence of a reference to 'homosexuality' appears to be an improvement on section 28. However, many people read 'sexual orientation' as meaning same-sex sexual orientation, because they do not see heterosexual individuals as having a sexual orientation. So it is possible that the harmful effects of section 28, and the hopelessly vague word 'promote', have been transferred from the statute book to the statutory guidance. The *Report of the Working Group on Sex Education in Scottish Schools* is much better, and does not refer to 'promoting sexual orientation'. Instead, it says: 'All young people should be helped to understand, at an appropriate age, that different people can have different sexual orientations.'[95]

---

[88] Ethical Standards in Public Life etc (Scotland) Act, 2000, s 34. See Peter Cumper and Mark Bell, 'Reforming Section 28: Lessons for Westminster from Holyrood' [2003] *European Human Rights Law Review* 400.

[89] *Hansard* (HL), 24 July 2000, cols 97–129.

[90] Local Government Act 2003, s 127(2) and sch 8, pt 1 (in force on 18 Nov 2003).

[91] See Wintemute, above n 4, at 507–10.

[92] Possibly the only attempt to enforce s 28 was that of Sheena Strain (backed by the Christian Institute), who sought judicial review of Glasgow City Council's funding of HIV or LGB organisations. Her complaint was settled. See <http://news.bbc.co.uk/2/hi/uk_news/scotland/746575.stm> (14 May 2000); <http://news.bbc.co.uk/2/hi/uk_news/scotland/821896.stm> (6 July 2000).

[93] See <http://www.dfes.gov.uk/sreguidance> (7 July 2000).

[94] *Ibid*, at para 1.30.

[95] See <http://www.scotland.gov.uk/library2/doc16/sexedwg.pdf> (16 June 2000), paras, 5.25–5.29.

Other Discrimination Against (De Facto or De Jure) Same-Sex Partners

Equal Access to the Rights of Unmarried Different-Sex Partners

In 1993, there was no UK legislation or case law requiring equal treatment of unmarried different-sex and same-sex partners.[96] And the ECommHR had declared inadmissible five applications from the UK challenging discrimination against same-sex partners in immigration or housing, holding that preferences for unmarried different-sex partners could be justified.[97]

In 1996, shortly after the ECJ's *P* judgment on dismissal of transsexual employees, an industrial tribunal referred *Grant v South-West Trains* to the ECJ. The case raised the question of whether an employer's providing a benefit (free rail travel) to the unmarried female partners of male employees, but not to the unmarried female partners of female employees, was direct sex discrimination violating EC Treaty Article 141. On 17 February 1998, despite a favourable opinion from Advocate General Elmer, the ECJ rejected the claim,[98] which was probably doomed to fail for several reasons unrelated to the strength of the argument: (1) a case of dismissal of an LGB employee would have been a better vehicle for extending *P*, because free rail travel might have been seen as a trivial employment benefit; (2) the absence at that time of any positive case law from the ECtHR or ECommHR on equal treatment of same-sex partners made it unlikely that the ECJ would take the lead; and (3) the insertion of Article 13 into the EC Treaty on 2 October 1997 made it easier for the ECJ to leave the issue to the EC legislature.

As mentioned above, the EC legislature exercised its new express competence under Article 13 on 27 November 2000, less than two years after the Treaty of Amsterdam came into force on 1 May 1999. Directive 2000/78 overrules the result (but not the sex discrimination reasoning) in *Grant*, by prohibiting direct sexual orientation discrimination with regard to 'pay'.[99] The UK Government accepts that the Directive requires equal treatment of unmarried different-sex and same-sex partners with regard to employment benefits,[100] and the ECJ will almost certainly agree (especially in light of the Strasbourg Court's judgment in *Karner v Austria*, to be discussed below).

---

[96] See Wintemute, above n 4, at 511–12.

[97] *Ibid*, pp 525–26; R Wintemute, 'Strasbourg to the Rescue? Same-Sex Partners and Parents Under the European Convention' in R Wintemute (ed) and Mads Andenæs (hon co-ed), *Legal Recognition of Same-Sex Partnerships: A Study of National, European and International Law* (Oxford, Hart Publishing, 2001) 713–29.

[98] Case C-249/96, [1998] ECR I-621. See also *Grant v South-West Trains* (1997), [1998] IRLR 188 (H Ct, QB Div) (unsuccessful attempt to enforce employer's equal opportunities policy as a term of the employment contract).

[99] Arts 2(1), 3(1)(c).

[100] See *Equality and Diversity: The Way Ahead* (Oct 2002), <http://www.dti.gov.uk/er/equality/wayahead.htm>, para 80.

Outside the field of employment, the first judicial breakthrough came in 1999 in the private sector housing succession case of *Fitzpatrick v Sterling Housing Association*.[101] The House of Lords held that a surviving same-sex partner could succeed to a tenancy under the Rent Act 1977 as a 'family member', but not as a 'spouse', defined as including 'a person who was living with the original tenant as his or her wife or husband.' Lord Slynn observed that: '[w]hether that result [exclusion by judicial interpretation from the category of "spouse"] is discriminatory against same-sex couples in the light of the fact that non-married different sex couples living together are to be treated as spouses . . . may have to be considered when the Human Rights Act 1998 is in force.'[102]

Reconsideration of *Fitzpatrick* took place on 5 November 2002 in *Ghaidan v Mendoza*.[103] The Court of Appeal held that, under HRA section 3(1), it is 'possible' to interpret the 'spouse' category in the Rent Act 1977 as covering a same-sex partner, to avoid sexual orientation discrimination violating Articles 14 and 8 (respect for home). On 24 July 2003, in the virtually identical case of *Karner v Austria*,[104] the ECtHR agreed that legislation interpreted as allowing unmarried different-sex but not same-sex partners to succeed to a tenancy violates these Articles. On 21 June 2004 in *Mendoza*, the House of Lords agreed with the ECtHR on the violation issue, and held that the Court of Appeal was right to use HRA section 3(1), rather than make a declaration of incompatibility under HRA section 4.[105]

Similar 'living as husband and wife' language in other Acts (such as the Fatal Accidents Act 1976, section 1(3)(b): '"dependant" means . . . any person . . . who was living . . . as the husband or wife of the deceased') will also have to be interpreted as including same-sex partners. But some provisions that expressly exclude same-sex partners (such as the Family Law Act 1996, s. 62(1)(a): '"cohabitants" are a man and a woman who . . . are living together as husband and wife') will not be repairable under HRA section 3(1) and will have to be amended.

Without waiting for the Law Lords' judgment in *Mendoza*, the UK Government began to make piecemeal amendments to legislation to ensure compliance with *Karner*. It is making both necessary amendments to 'a man and a woman' language (as in the Family Law Act 1996),[106] and amendments to sex-neutral 'living as husband and wife' language (as in the Rent Act 1977 and other housing legislation)[107] that are not necessary after *Mendoza*. In both situations, it is substituting variations on 'living with the [relevant person]—(a) as his or

---

[101] [1999] 4 All ER 705 (HL).

[102] *Ibid*, at 709.

[103] [2002] 4 All ER 1162 (CA).

[104] (24 July 2003) (ECtHR) (J).

[105] See R Wintemute, 'Same-sex partners, "living as husband and wife", and section 3 of the Human Rights Act 1998' [2003] *Public Law* 621; [2004] 3 All ER 411 (HL).

[106] See Domestic Violence, Crime and Victims Act 2004, s 3. See also *M v Secretary of State for Work and Pensions* [2004] EWCA (Civ) 1343.

[107] See Civil Partnership Act 2004, sch 8.

her wife or husband, or (b) if of the same sex, in an equivalent relationship,' or its latest creative use of language, the phrase 'living together as if they were civil partners' (as 'uncivil partners'?), which appears frequently in the Civil Partnership Act 2004, to be discussed below.

Rather than use the same expression for unmarried different-sex partners and unmarried same-sex partners (eg, 'two persons living as husband and wife'), the UK Government seems determined to create a 'separate but equal' category for unmarried same-sex partners. Allowing legislation to cover same-sex partners as persons 'living as husband and wife' would appear to be a symbolic step down the slippery slope to civil marriage for same-sex partners. This dilemma could be avoided by using the definition of 'couple' in section 144(4) of the Adoption and Children Act 2002, to be seen below, which includes: 'two people (whether of different sexes or the same sex) living as partners in an enduring family relationship.'

Equal Access to the Rights of Married Different-Sex Partners (Without Marrying)

The ECtHR having established in *Karner* that, absent a strong justification, unmarried different-sex and same-sex partners must receive equal treatment, the next question is whether same-sex partners can argue that it is direct or indirect sexual orientation discrimination to exclude them from particular rights that are granted only to married different-sex partners.[108] In the case of employment benefits, including survivor's pensions, the Employment Equality (Sexual Orientation) Regulations 2003 attempt to preclude any such arguments through an express exception: Regulation 25 provides that the Regulations do not 'render unlawful anything which prevents or restricts access to a benefit by reference to marital status.' The validity of Regulation 25, unsuccessfully challenged by several trade unions,[109] will ultimately depend on what weight the ECJ gives to non-binding Recital 22 to Directive 2000/78: 'This Directive is without prejudice to national laws on marital status and the benefits dependent thereon.'

A similar issue has already been considered by the ECJ: *KB v National Health Service Pension Agency*,[110] referred by the Court of Appeal, concerned the non-eligibility of the transsexual male partner of a non-transsexual female employee for a 'widower's pension' (limited to legal spouses of employees) if she were to pre-decease him. They were not married, and would not be eligible to marry until the Gender Recognition Act 2004 came into force. Advocate General Ruiz-Jarabo Colomer's Opinion of 10 June 2003 urged the ECJ to decide the case as

---

[108] See R Wintemute, 'From "Sex Rights" to "Love Rights": Partnership Rights as Human Rights' in N Bamforth (ed), *Sex Rights* (Oxford, Oxford University Press, forthcoming in 2005).

[109] See above, n 83.

[110] Case C-117/01, appeal of *Bavin v NHS Trust Pensions Agency*, [1999] ICR 1192 (EAT), referred by Court of Appeal to ECJ on 4 October 2000.

follows: 'The prohibition on discrimination based on sex, laid down in Article 141, precludes national rules which, by not recognising the right of transsexuals to marry in their acquired sex, den[y] them entitlement to a widow(er)'s pension.' On 7 January 2004, the ECJ agreed with the Advocate General, using similar reasoning, which it could extend in a future case, eg: 'The prohibition on discrimination based on sexual orientation, laid down in Council Directive 2000/78/EC, precludes national rules which, by not recognising the right of persons of the same sex to marry, deny them entitlement to a widow(er)'s pension.'

Exclusion of same-sex partners from benefits provided to married different-sex partners can also be challenged under the HRA 1998[111] and the European Convention. Although the Strasbourg Court has so far declined to find a violation of Articles 8 and 14 where unmarried different-sex partners (rather than their children) are treated less favourably than married different-sex partners, a key factor in its reasoning has been that the applicant unmarried different-sex partners were legally able to marry and chose not to do so, or neglected to do so.[112] The applicant same-sex partner in the pending case of *MW v UK*[113] will be able to stress that he could not qualify for bereavement benefits because he was legally unable to marry his deceased partner. Since *Thlimmenos v Greece*, the ECtHR has accepted that indirect discrimination can sometimes violate Article 14 of the Convention (combined with another Article), ie, 'when States without an objective and reasonable justification fail to treat differently persons whose situations are significantly different.'[114] And both the Constitutional Court of South Africa[115] and US state appellate courts[116] have found sexual orientation discrimination in these circumstances.

On 30 June 2003, the UK Government proposed the creation for England and Wales of a new, separate (but 100 per cent equal?) institution of 'civil partnership' open only to same-sex partners, which would allow them access to (all?) the rights and obligations of married different-sex partners.[117] The proposal

---

[111] See above, n 83.

[112] See *Saucedo Gómez v Spain* (26 Jan 1999) (no 37784/97) (ECtHR) (AD); *Shackell v UK* (27 April 2000) (no 45851/99) (ECtHR) (AD).

[113] Application no 11313/02 (communicated to UK Government). The similar case of *Mata Estevez v Spain* (no 56501/00) was declared inadmissible by the ECtHR on 10 May 2001, probably because the applicant was not represented by a lawyer, and therefore could not present the arguments for departing from the case law of the former ECommHR.

[114] (6 April 2000) (ECtHR) (J), para 44.

[115] See, at <http:www.concourt.gov.za>, *National Coalition for Gay and Lesbian Equality v Minister of Home Affairs* (2 Dec 1999), Case no CCT10/99; *Satchwell v President of Republic of South Africa* (25 July 2002, 17 March 2003), Case nos CCT45/01, CCT48/02; *Du Toit v Minister for Welfare and Population Development* (10 Sept 2002), Case no CCT40/01; *J and B v Director General, Department of Home Affairs* (28 March 2003), Case no CCT46/02.

[116] See *Tanner v Oregon Health Sciences University*, 971 P2d 435 (Ore Ct App 1998); *Levin v Yeshiva University*, 754 NE2d 1099 (NY 2001).

[117] Department of Trade and Industry, Women and Equality Unit, 'Civil Partnership: A framework for the legal recognition of same-sex couples' (30 June 2003), <http://www.womenandequalityunit.gov.uk/lgbt/partnership.htm>.

was subsequently extended to Scotland and Northern Ireland.[118] In my comments to the Department of Trade and Industry team responsible for the proposal, I argued: (1) that the proposed Bill should simply end the exclusion of same-sex couples from civil marriage (the Canadian federal government has proposed doing so by means of a two-clause Bill); or (2) (as a 'better than nothing' alternative) that a simple Scandinavian-style Bill should be drafted stating that 'civil partnership has the same legal effects as marriage, except as provided [in a list of specific exceptions].' Attempting to list all of the rights and obligations of married different-sex partners and extend them one by one to 'civil (same-sex) partners' would inevitably result in omissions that would make civil marriage and 'civil partnership' unequal.[119] On 30 March 2004, the UK Government introduced the Civil Partnership Bill in the House of Lords. It consisted of 258 pages, 196 clauses and 22 schedules. When it received Royal Assent on 18 November 2004, it had grown to 264 clauses and 30 schedules. Even eliminating provisions that do not apply to their part of the UK, few individuals will have the time or energy to determine whether the Act does in fact provide equal rights and obligations to 'civil (same-sex) partners'.

Equal Access to Civil Marriage

In a 1998 decision reached by 18 votes to 2,[120] the Court reaffirmed its interpretation of Article 12 (right to marry and found a family) as referring to 'the traditional marriage between persons of opposite biological sex.' Yet on 11 July 2002, in *Christine Goodwin v UK* and *I v UK*, the Court held by 17 votes to 0 (a dramatic reversal in only four years) that the UK violated Article 12 by refusing to permit transsexual individuals to contract different-sex civil marriages in their reassigned sex.

Several aspects of the Court's reasoning could be transferred, in an appropriate future case, to a failure to permit a same-sex civil marriage. The Court observed that 'the inability of any couple to conceive or parent a child cannot be regarded as *per se* removing their right to enjoy the [the right to marry],'[121] that '[t]here have been major social changes in the institution of marriage since the adoption of the Convention [in 1950],'[122] that 'Article 9 of the recently adopted Charter of Fundamental Rights of the European Union departs, no doubt deliberately, from the wording of Article 12 of the Convention in removing the reference to men and women,'[123] and that 'it is artificial to assert that

---

[118] Scottish Executive, 'Civil Partnership Registration: A legal status for committed same-sex couples in Scotland' (10 Sept 2003), <http://www.scotland.gov.uk/consultations/justice/cprs.pdf>; Office of Law Reform, 'Civil Partnership: A legal status for committed same-sex couples in Northern Ireland' (18 Dec 2003).

[119] See <http://www.lagla.org.uk/files/lagla_civil_partnership_response.pdf>

[120] *Sheffield and Horsham v UK* (30 July 1998) (ECtHR) (J).

[121] *Christine Goodwin v UK* (11 July 2002) (ECtHR) (J), para 98.

[122] *Ibid*, para 100.

[123] *Ibid*.

post-operative transsexuals [LGB individuals] have not been deprived of the right to marry as, according to law, they remain able to marry a person of their former [their current] opposite sex.'[124]

On 10 April 2003, in *Bellinger v Bellinger*,[125] the Law Lords could have given effect to *Christine Goodwin* and *I* immediately by allowing post-operative transsexual women and men to contract different-sex civil marriages in their reassigned sexes. They could have done so by using HRA section 3(1) to interpret the words 'female' and 'male' in section 11(c) of the Matrimonial Causes Act 1973 as including (at least) transsexual women and men who have undergone gender reassignment surgery. However, they chose instead to make a declaration of incompatibility under HRA section 4 and leave compliance with *Christine Goodwin* and *I* to the UK Government and the UK Parliament.

The Gender Recognition Act 2004 allows unmarried transsexual individuals to contract factually and legally different-sex civil marriages after a 'full gender recognition certificate' has been issued.[126] (To contract legally different-sex but factually same-sex civil marriages, they must elect not to have their gender reassignments recognised). Married transsexual individuals may only be granted an 'interim gender recognition certificate' until the marriage is annulled or dissolved, or the other spouse dies (to ensure that the marriage will not become legally a same-sex marriage), after which a 'full gender recognition certificate' may be issued.[127] Clergy of the Church of England and the Church of Wales are exempted from solemnising the different-sex civil marriage of a transsexual individual in their reassigned sex.[128]

Neither the UK Government nor the Scottish and Northern Ireland Executives have any plans to open up civil marriage to same-sex partners, unlike the governments of the Netherlands, Belgium and Spain.[129] Would UK courts be willing to do so, as in Ontario, British Columbia and Massachusetts?[130] Unfortunately, they could only make a declaration of incompatibility under HRA section 4 in relation to section 11(c) of the Matrimonial Causes Act 1973, which expressly renders a marriage void 'if the parties are not respectively male and female.' If a

---

[124] *Ibid*, para 101.
[125] [2003] 2 All ER 593.
[126] Section 11, sch 4.
[127] Sections 4–5, sch 2.
[128] Sch 4, para 3.
[129] See Netherlands, Act of 21 December 2000 amending Book 1 of the Civil Code, concerning the opening up of marriage for persons of the same sex (in force 1 April 2001); Belgium, Law of 13 February 2003 opening up marriage to persons of the same sex and modifying certain provisions of the Civil Code (in force 1 June 2003); Spain, *Anteproyecto de ley* (draft Bill), 1 Oct 2004.
[130] See *Halpern v Canada (Attorney General)* (10 June 2003, date of first marriages), <http://www.ontariocourts.on.ca/decisions/2003/june/halpernC39172.htm> (Ont CA); *EGALE Canada Inc v Canada (Attorney General)* (indexed as *Barbeau v British Columbia (Attorney General)*) (1 May 2003), <http://www.courts.gov.bc.ca/../../../../jdb-txt/ca/03/02/2003BCCA0251.htm> (8 July 2003, date of first marriages) <http://www.courts.gov.bc.ca/Jdb-txt/CA/03/04/2003BCCA0406.htm> (BCCA); *Goodridge v Department of Public Health* (18 Nov 2003), <http://www.glad.org> (Mass Sup Jud Ct) (first marriages celebrated on 17 May 2004).

UK court did so, the UK Government, the Scottish Executive, and the Northern Ireland Executive could ignore the declaration and refuse to change the law. As for the ECtHR, given that civil marriage has so far been opened up to same-sex partners in only two or three of 46 Council of Europe Member States, it seems unlikely that the Court would yet be willing to find a violation of Article 12 or Articles 12 and 14.

Other Discrimination Against LGBT Parents

In 1999, in *Salgueiro da Silva Mouta v Portugal*,[131] the ECtHR held that if, when deciding on the custody of children from dissolved different-sex marriages, a court treats as a negative factor the sexual orientation of an LGB parent (and probably also the gender identity of a transsexual parent), it violates Article 14 together with Article 8 (respect for family life). In 2002, in *Fretté v France*,[132] the Court's Austrian, Belgian and UK judges were willing to extend the principle of *Mouta* to the opportunity for unmarried individuals to adopt children as individuals (ie, where any partner they may have acquires no parental rights). However, their votes were cancelled out by those of the French, Czech and Albanian judges, who thought that Article 14 could not be invoked because the difference in treatment had not sufficiently affected the Article 8 rights of the applicant (a gay man found ineligible to adopt a child because of his sexual orientation). This meant that the Lithuanian judge decided the case and determined the reasoning of the majority: Article 14 is applicable, but the difference in treatment is justifiable and therefore not discriminatory.

The *Fretté* judgment reflects the fact that, in many Continental European countries, adoption of children by LGB individuals or same-sex couples is a more sensitive issue than access to civil marriage for same-sex couples. Courts in Great Britain and the UK Government have taken the opposite view, and have gone beyond the minimum standards of the ECtHR. With regard to individual adoption, English and Scottish courts have interpreted the relevant legislation as permitting LGB individuals to adopt.[133] And the new Adoption and Children Act 2002 (once it comes into force, probably in September 2005) will expressly permit same-sex couples to adopt each other's children (second-parent adoption), and to adopt an unrelated child jointly (joint adoption).[134] In the case of intercountry adoptions, most if not all countries sending children to the UK for adoption would veto a proposed adoption by same-sex partners. Instead, one

---

[131] (21 Dec 1999) (ECtHR) (J).

[132] (26 Feb 2002) (ECtHR) (J).

[133] See *T, Petitioner*, [1997] Scots Law Times 724 (Ct Session, Inner House); *Re W (a minor) (adoption: homosexual adopter)*, [1997] 3 All ER 620 (H Ct, Fam Div); *Re E (Adoption: Freeing Order)*, [1995] 1 Fam LR 382 (CA).

[134] See ss 50(2) and 51(2) on second-parent adoption, and s 50(1) on joint adoption by a couple, defined in s 144(4) as '(a) a married couple, or (b) two people (whether of different sexes or the same sex) living as partners in an enduring family relationship'.

same-sex partner would have to adopt as an individual (and might have to hide their sexual orientation from officials in the child's country), and the other partner would have to adopt as a second parent once the child arrived in the UK.

Where a child is born to a heterosexual, non-transsexual woman after donor insemination, section 28(2)–(3) of the Human Fertilisation and Embryology Act 1990 provides that her husband or male partner is automatically the legal father of the child and is therefore not required to adopt it. *Christine Goodwin* and *I* implicitly require the same treatment for a transsexual husband or male partner, and implicitly reverse the outcome in *X, Y & Z v UK*.[135] The 2004 Gender Recognition Act's general principle of legal recognition of the acquired gender 'for all purposes' means that the 1990 Act's automatic fatherhood provision will apply to a transsexual husband or male partner, but not retroactively.[136] However, if a child is born to a lesbian, non-transsexual woman after donor insemination, her non-transsexual female partner will not be recognised as a legal parent until she adopts the child. This could cause problems for the child if the partner were to die suddenly before the new parents found the time, energy and money to organise a second-parent adoption. Because of its wording, section 28 of the 1990 Act cannot be repaired under HRA section 3(1) and *Mendoza*, and must be amended. The Civil Partnership Act 2004 did not make such an amendment for female–female couples, whether they are 'civil (same-sex) partners' or cohabiting.[137]

Where a child is born to a surrogate mother commissioned by a married different-sex couple who supplied the sperm, egg or both, section 30(1) of the 1990 Act permits the couple to apply for a court order treating them as the legal parents of the child. The same would be true of a transsexual individual who was able to contract a different-sex civil marriage in their reassigned sex. However, where a male–male or female–female couple commission a surrogate mother and one partner supplies the sperm or the egg, the other partner can only apply to adopt the child, which could cause the problems mentioned above. The Civil Partnership Act 2004 did not make such an amendment for same-sex couples who are 'civil (same-sex) partners'.

HOW HAVE HUMAN RIGHTS MADE A DIFFERENCE?

Reviewing the reforms that have taken place since 1993, it is clear that many of them have been adopted *involuntarily* to comply with judgments and reports of

---

[135] (22 April 1997) (ECtHR) (J) (Convention did not require recognition of mother's transsexual male partner as the legal father of her children by donor insemination) .

[136] Section 9(2). Cl 8(2) of the 11 July 2003 draft of the Bill (see <http://www.pfc.org.uk/gr-bill/grb-dr.htm>) would have made this reform retroactive, so that it would have covered the family in *X, Y and Z v UK*, but this provision was deleted from s 12 of the Act.

[137] In several jurisdictions, the female partner is now automatically the second legal parent of the child, and does not have to adopt it. See 15 Vermont Statutes Annotated s 1204(f) (2000); Western Australia, Artificial Conception Act, s 6A (2002); Québec, Civil Code, Arts 538.3, 539.1 (2002); CCT46/02, *J and B v Director General, Department of Home Affairs* (Constitutional Court of South Africa, 28 March 2003), http://www.concourt.gov.za

the ECtHR and ECommHR. No matter how well-intentioned a UK government, it will often refrain from enacting reforms sought by the LGBT minority,
who have relatively few votes to deliver and may be seen by a Labour government as a 'captive minority' who could only expect worse treatment if they
voted Conservative. Reforms providing equal rights to LGBT individuals and
same-sex couples could alienate more Middle England voters than they would
attract, and in any case would be likely to encounter vehement opposition from
Conservative MPs, lords and newspapers. Thus, as part of the process of making itself electable, the Labour Party dropped its 1992 manifesto commitment to
'introduce a new law dealing with discrimination on grounds of sexuality,
repeal the unjust Clause 28 and allow a free vote in the House of Commons on
the age of consent.'[138] Instead, its 1997 manifesto said cryptically: 'We will
uphold family life . . . [O]ur attitudes to race, sex and sexuality have changed
fundamentally. Our task is to combine change and social stability.'[139]

At least five major involuntary reforms might not yet have been adopted or
proposed, but for test cases brought by LGBT individuals under the European
Convention, with the support of non-governmental organisations such as
Stonewall, Press for Change, Liberty and ILGA-Europe (the European Region
of the International Lesbian and Gay Association): (1) equalisation of the age of
consent; (2) elimination of other direct sexual orientation discrimination by the
Sexual Offences Act 2003; (3) the provisions of the Gender Recognition Act 2004
on amended birth certificates and marriage for transsexual individuals;
(4) the lifting of the ban on LGB members of the armed forces; and (5) the comprehensive equalisation of the rights and obligations of unmarried different-sex
and same-sex partners (which is likely to follow the judgments of the ECtHR
in *Karner* and the House of Lords in *Mendoza*). A sixth involuntary reform
might not yet have been adopted, but for a test case under European
Community anti-discrimination law (which is influenced by the European
Convention): (6) the Sex Discrimination (Gender Reassignment) Regulations
1999.

It would be unfair to claim that the UK Government never takes voluntary
action against sexual orientation or gender identity discrimination. It has done
so in at least seven cases where there was not yet any European Convention or
European Community case law requiring the reform, but it was persuaded by the
human rights arguments of LGBT organisations lobbying for change. Still, in
three of these cases, the reform might not yet have been adopted if it had required
an Act of the UK Parliament: (1) the provisions of the Immigration Rules allowing UK residents to sponsor unmarried partners for immigration;[140] (2) the provision of the Criminal Injuries Compensation Scheme 2001 allowing same-sex
partners to claim;[141] and (3) the Employment Equality (Sexual Orientation)

---

[138] 1992 Manifesto, at 24.
[139] 1997 Manifesto, at 25.
[140] See paras 295AA–295O (first introduced in October 1997).
[141] See para 38(a)(i).

Regulations 2003, implementing the sexual orientation provisions of Council Directive 2000/78/EC. The UK Government had the power to veto the Directive, but was able to support it quietly in the Council of the European Union knowing that there would be little publicity in the UK.

The four other cases of voluntary action are: (4) the unmarried couple provisions of the Adoption and Children Act 2002, which the UK Government presented as entirely about the best interests of children needing adoptive parents, emphatically denying that they had anything to do with extending equal rights to LGB prospective parents; (5) the repeal of Section 28, which was facilitated by the outrageousness of the discrimination, and qualified by the 2000 statutory guidance banning 'direct promotion of sexual orientation'; (6) the partial 'hate crimes' legislation, introduced discreetly in the UK Parliament without a Home Office press release; and (7) the Civil Partnership Act 2004. The latter is the first major reform that is voluntary (because it is not yet required by case law of the ECtHR, the ECJ or a UK court), requires an Act of the UK Parliament, cannot be disguised as having a purpose other than equality for LGBT individuals, and introduces new, positive, statutory rights.

CONCLUSION

LGBT individuals in England and Wales have made rapid progress towards full legal and social equality since 1993. Indeed, most reforms have occurred since 1997, when LGBT applicants from the UK began to achieve success before the ECommHR and ECtHR, and the newly elected Labour Government showed its willingness to make voluntary changes in limited areas. What remains to be done?

On the legislative side, the UK Government should introduce Bills in the UK Parliament: (1) providing the same protection for victims of offences 'aggravated by reference to sexual orientation or gender identity' as for 'racially or religiously aggravated' offences; (2) prohibiting the stirring up of 'sexual orientation or gender identity hatred'; (3) prohibiting (by means of an Equality Act consolidating all anti-discrimination legislation for Great Britain) sexual orientation and gender identity discrimination, not only in employment and vocational training but also in (primary and secondary) education, housing and the provision of services, and imposing on public authorities the same positive duties to promote equality as exist for race in Great Britain and sexual orientation in Northern Ireland;[142] (4) opening up civil marriage to legally and factually same-sex partners (and either abolishing the institution of 'civil partnership' or extending it to unmarried different-sex partners); and (5) ensuring equal treatment of LGBT individuals and same-sex couples in relation to donor insemination, surrogacy and other aspects of assisted procreation.[143]

[142] See Race Relations Act 1976, s 71 (amended in 2000); Northern Ireland Act 1998, s 75.
[143] Including repeal of the reference to 'the need of that child for a father' in the Human Fertilisation and Embryology Act 1990, s 13(5).

On the judicial side, UK courts should: (6) be open to arguments that the legislative drafting, executive enforcement, or judicial interpretation of neutral laws involves direct or indirect sexual orientation or gender identity discrimination (eg, the new criminal offence of 'sexual activity in a public lavatory'). Finally, it would be absolutely certain that UK courts could review all sexual orientation and gender identity discrimination by public authorities, and no cases could ever fall through the cracks of the Article 14 'within the ambit' test, if the UK: (7) signed and ratified Protocol No 12 to the European Convention, establishing a general right to non-discrimination.[144] This list of seven items is a long one. But given the rapid progress since 1993, I am optimistic that, by 2015, every item will have been ticked off, and (at least formal) legal equality for LGBT individuals and same-sex couples will have been achieved.

---

[144] See <http://conventions.coe.int>, ETS No 177.

11

Religious Discrimination

———◆◆◆———

MOHAMMED AZIZ

INTRODUCTION

THE RIGHT TO freedom of religion is said to part-constitute a foundational pillar in Western civilisation and society, and the human rights ideology that provides its underpinning for state-individual relations as well as relations between individuals. The right certainly takes a prominent place in the leading international and European human rights instruments. Alongside this right to freedom of religion, the same instruments, with equal force, provide a right not to be discriminated against in the enjoyment of that basic right.

The objective of this chapter is to consider how the right to freedom of religion and the right not to be discriminated against on the ground of religion (freedom from religious discrimination) operate in practice in the UK; and how they are accessed and enforced by religious communities. In order to make the task manageable, this will be done through a case study of one particular religious group, the Muslim community in the UK. The chapter will also address the issue of whether there is yet a 'human rights culture' in accessing and enforcing these rights and consider strategies available for making real such a culture.

THE MUSLIM COMMUNITY IN THE UK

According to the 2001 Census, British Muslims constitute approximately 1.6m (just under 3 per cent) of the UK population. Not only is Islam the UK's second largest religion, but it is also the largest minority religion. The total number of UK Muslims also exceeds the total number of members of all other minority faith communities. The experience of British Muslims is therefore a good barometer for assessing the presence and extent of religious discrimination in the UK.

THE RIGHTS IN UK LAW AND PRACTICE

The ideal place to start an assessment of the rights in practice in the UK is perhaps their place in domestic law. The right to freedom of religion was for the first time positively and clearly enshrined in statutory form in the Human Rights Act 1998 (HRA). Article 9 of the European Convention on Human Rights (ECHR) states:

1 Everyone has the right to freedom of thought, conscience and religion; this right includes freedom to change his religion or belief and freedom, either alone or in community with others and in public or private, to manifest his religion or belief, in worship, teaching, practice and observance.

2 Freedom to manifest one's religion or beliefs shall be subject only to such limitations as are prescribed by law and are necessary in a democratic society in the interests of public safety, for the protection of public order, health or morals, or for the protection of the rights and freedoms of others.

The right enshrined in Article 9 has, for our purposes, three important features or elements. First, it provides the absolute right to belief in a religion of one's choice. The provision is uncompromising on the issue of forced religion or belief, no matter what the reason may be for applying the force. Secondly, it provides the qualified right to manifest that religion in private or public. Article 9(2) provides the grounds on which this aspect of the right may be limited: it may only be done through law and only where it is necessary in a democratic society in the interests of (a) public safety, (b) the protection of public order, health or morals, and (c) the protection of the rights and freedoms of others. Thirdly, it provides the right to manifest that religion in community with others—that is, a right to organisation and collective action on the basis of religion. This is a much overlooked element of the Article 9 right; however, it includes not only the right to organised worship but also, for instance, the right to organised education and services, for example, schools and housing associations based on a religious ethos. This element of the right is again limited by Article 9(2).

Article 9, however, does not provide protection against religious discrimination. That protection is provided in Article 14, which states:

The enjoyment of the rights and freedoms set forth in this Convention shall be secured without discrimination on any ground such as sex, race, colour, language, religion, political or other opinion, national or social origin, association with a national minority, property, birth or other status.

For our purposes, there are three important features or elements attaching to this provision. First, it requires that the enjoyment of the right will be secured by the state without discrimination between different faith communities. Secondly, it requires that the other rights and freedoms must be secured without any discrimination on the basis of religion. And thirdly, the provision only applies to the rights and freedoms enshrined in the European Convention and not beyond. This is a significant limitation, and, together with the fact that the HRA applies only to public authorities, carries significant implications for religious discrimination. We consider below how each of these elements operates in practice with regards to the Muslim community in the UK.

SECURING THE RIGHT TO FREEDOM OF RELIGION

As noted above, under Article 14, the state is required to secure the enjoyment of the right to freedom of religion without discrimination. The enjoyment of the right to freedom of religion may be undermined, even breached, in various ways: (a) stereotypes, prejudice and vilification directed at followers leading to hatred and incitement of hatred, harassment and violence; (b) irreverence, defilement and damage of religious spaces (for example, places of worship or burial), ceremonies and sacred objects; (c) scurrilous attacks on religious beliefs and practices; and (d) various forms of religious discrimination. In UK law these breaches are broadly identified and addressed through two categories of offences: criminal (which would include a, b and c) and civil (which would include d). We assess here, however, whether these provisions are adequate to secure the enjoyment of the right and whether the provisions that are available operate without discrimination on the ground of religion.

Religious Offences in Criminal Law

Most helpfully, a select committee of the House of Lords (HL Select Committee on Religious Offences) recently addressed and produced a report on the religious offences that fall into the criminal category. The findings of the committee are particularly pertinent for our purposes.

Attacks on Followers of Religions

Unlawful harassment and assault of individuals is, of course, addressed by the normal course of the law. But if the harassment or assault, or indeed incitement to hatred leading to such harassment or assault, is based on religious affiliation, this could be a significant means of undermining the enjoyment of the right, not just by the individual but by whole communities of believers. The select committee noted that under present race relations laws, the UK provides protection against incitement and attacks on members of faith communities under two main headings. First, incitement legislation, which ensures that the right to freedom of religion is not undermined by hate campaigns against religious groups. And secondly, aggravated offences legislation, which ensures that the religious hate motive behind attacks is punished over and above the act of the attack. This is in order to send out a strong message that such motive and action is not tolerated, thus creating meaningful space for access to the right to freedom of religion without fear. Such protection, as developed by case law, however, extends at present only to mono-ethnic religions (eg, the Sikh and Jewish communities) and not to multi-ethnic religions (eg, Christians and Muslims). In order to remedy this anomaly and resulting discrimination in the law, the Government sought to extend the relevant provisions (in the Public Order Act 1986 (POA) on incitement to hatred and the Crime and Disorder Act 1998 (CDA) on aggravated offences) to cover all religions in the Anti-terrorism, Crime and Security Bill 2001. However, while the final Act remedied the shortfall in the Crime and Disorder Act, it failed to achieve this for the Public Order Act due to opposition in the House of Lords. Thus, while all religious communities in the UK are now protected from aggravated offences, many, including the Muslim community, are still not protected from incitement to religious hatred.

The select committee observed that while the Government and all law enforcement agencies remain in favour of legislation against incitement to religious hatred, particularly in view of the strong call for such legislation from national and international human rights organs, there is yet some concern about such legislation from various quarters. These concerns have been stated as follows: whether there is indeed a gap in the law requiring new legislation and whether the legislation proposed would effectively deal with the mischief it is intended to address; whether the proposed legislation would unnecessarily and unacceptably infringe the right to freedom of expression; whether it is possible to frame and implement such legislation; and whether such legislation is necessarily open to abuse. The select committee's response to these concerns was as follows:

> If Sikhs and Jews are to be protected from incitement to religious hatred and if this is considered to be a legitimate restriction of free speech, the same standard should be applied to Muslims, Christians and other faith communities, otherwise there is clearly a breach of Article 9 combined with Article 14 of the European Convention on Human Rights.[1]

The former Home Secretary, in July 2004, stated that the Government intended to introduce an offence of incitement to religious hatred 'as soon as possible'.[2] The new provisions were included in the Serious Organised Crime and Police Bill.

In practice, the inadequacies of the present incitement provisions are particularly acutely felt in the Muslim community. This is because 'Far Right' organisations have adopted a deliberate strategy to benefit from the loophole in the law to mobilise their campaigns specifically along Islamophobic lines. There are now many local councillors who have been elected on the basis of that particu-

---

[1] House of Lords Select Committee on Religious Offences in England and Wales (2002–2003) Vol I HL 95-I para 15. See also 'The Government Reply to the Report from the Religious Offences Committee' (2003).

[2] See David Blunkett, 'New Challenges for Race Equality and Community Cohesion in the 21st Century' speech delivered to the IPPR, 7 July 2004. See also Home Office, *Strength in Diversity: Towards a Community Cohesion and Race Equality Strategy* (2004).

lar agenda, seeking to curtail the rights of Muslims. The result is not only that Muslim communities feel more the absence of such legislation, there is also a strong feeling of hierarchy of protection and resentment, an awareness that the weight of right-wing activities has shifted and religion is a surrogate for racist activity. Incitement of hatred, legal under the law, leaves the impression that some religions are less welcome than others—undermining the right to freedom of religion of some believers. The discriminatory provisions in the law, therefore, have a direct impact on accessing the right.

Attacks on Sacred Spaces

The select committee found that section 2 of the Ecclesiastical Courts Jurisdiction Act 1860 (ECJA) dealt with certain offences against sacred places and space (eg, places of worship and burial) that would otherwise not be addressed by UK law. It provides the protection required to safeguard the sanctity of religious places of worship/burial, ceremonies and objects to be found in those places or used in those ceremonies. Thus, for example, if a pig's head was left in a mosque or synagogue, or a cow's head was left in a Hindu temple, or if the same was done at the respective cemeteries of these faith communities, at a time when worshippers and custodians were absent, then the only law under which such sacrilegious action could be prosecuted would be an offence which sought specifically to protect the 'sanctity' (as opposed to security) of places of worship/burial, such as the 1860 Act. Such protection is unlikely to fulfil the high threshold requirements of either a blasphemy offence or other public order offence, although in itself capable of causing much affront and undermining the enjoyment of the right to freedom of religion—that is, affront and detriment far beyond that which should be tolerated by any ordinary citizen. The strength of the ECJA provision is that it is thought to provide protection across the religions. It is stressed, however, that if section 2 of the ECJA is to be retained it needs to be reformulated in a more modern form and language, with perhaps a set minimum penalty to reflect the seriousness of the offence. The argument is that if the set minimum penalty is too low, the protection is undermined, which in turn would undermine the enjoyment of the right to freedom of religion.

Attacks on Religious Beliefs and Practices

In UK law protection against attacks on religious beliefs and practices is provided by the common law offence of blasphemy. Developed through case law, the content and scope of this offence is very obscure. However, when the Select Committee on Religious Offences in England and Wales asked David Feldman, formerly the legal adviser to the Parliamentary Joint Committee on Human Rights, to construct as best he could a modern definition of the elements of the common law offence, he suggested that from the decided cases it would seem that blasphemy is committed by anyone who makes public words, pictures or conduct whereby the doctrines, beliefs, institutions, or sacred objects and rituals of the Church of England by law established are denied or scurrilously vilified or there is objectively contumelious, violent or ribald conduct or abuse directed towards the sacred subject in question, likely to shock and outrage the feelings of the general body of Church of England believers in the community.

The law on blasphemy as it stands today has been criticised on a number of grounds: it is uncertain, and therefore, possibly retrospective—thus, possibly in breach of Article 7; it is an offence of strict liability; it is an unacceptable infringement of the right to freedom of expression; it protects only the Church of England and not other faith communities, and is therefore in breach of Article 9 read with Article 14. The observation of the select committee was as follows:

> No blasphemy case has been prosecuted in England and Wales since the passage of the Human Rights Act 1998 (incorporating elements of the European Convention on Human Rights), but it is a reasonable speculation that as a consequence of that legislation any prosecution for blasphemy today—even one which met all the known criteria—would be likely to fail or, if a conviction were secured, would probably be overturned on appeal (if not by the House of Lords then by the European Court of Human Rights) on grounds either of discrimination, or denial of the right to freedom of expression, or of the absence of certainty. Such an outcome would, in effect, constitute the demise of the law of blasphemy.[3]

Criticisms of, and the select committee's verdict on, the current law of blasphemy does not mean, however, that legal protection against attacks on religions is not possible. That possibility was eloquently articulated in the *Otto-Preminger* case[4] in the European Court of Human Rights:

> Those who choose to exercise the freedom to manifest their religion, irrespective of whether they do so as members of a religious majority or minority, cannot reasonably expect to be exempt from all criticism. They must tolerate and accept the denial by others of their religious beliefs and even the propagation by others of doctrines hostile to their faith. However, the manner in which religious beliefs and doctrines are opposed or denied is a matter which may engage the responsibility of the state, notably in its responsibility to ensure the peaceful enjoyment of the right guaranteed under Article 9 to the holders of those beliefs and doctrines. Indeed, in extreme cases the effect of particular methods of opposing or denying religious beliefs can be such as to inhibit those who hold such beliefs from exercising their freedom to hold and express them. In the *Kokkinakis* judgment the Court held, in the context of Article 9, that a state may legitimately consider it necessary to take measures aimed at repressing certain forms of conduct, including the imparting of information and ideas, judged incompatible with the respect for the freedom of thought, conscience and religion of others . . . The respect for the religious feelings of believers as guaranteed by Article 9 can legitimately be thought to have been violated by the provocative portrayal of

---

[3] Vol 1, para 20 in the main report; see also end of para 43 in the main report and para 10 under app 3.

[4] *Otto-Preminger Institut v Austria* (1995) 19 EHRR 34.

objects of religious veneration; and such portrayals can be regarded as malicious violation of the spirit of tolerance, which must also be a feature of democratic society. The Convention is to be read as a whole and therefore the interpretation and application of Article 10 in the present case must be in harmony with the logic of the Convention.[5]

In practice, then, it is arguable that the protection that currently exists against attacks on religion is meaningless, and that even if it is of legal value it is discriminatory. It simply does not extend protection to the Muslim community[6] or any other faith community except the Church of England. It is possible to argue that the UK is in breach of Article 14 on two counts: first, on the ground of apparently discriminatory provisions (albeit that the provisions may be meaningless), and secondly, on the ground of failing to 'secure' the right to freedom of religion as it could be secured.

Religious Offences in Civil Offences

The case law by which protection under the POA and CDA is extended to mono-ethnic religious communities itself developed from a statutory provision firmly rooted in civil law, the Race Relations Act 1976 (RRA). Having outlawed direct and indirect discrimination on 'racial grounds' and against 'racial groups', the Act goes on to state:

3 (1) In this Act, unless the context otherwise requires:

— 'racial grounds' means any of the following grounds, namely colour, race, nationality or ethnic or national origins;
— 'racial group' means a group of persons defined by reference to colour, race, nationality or ethnic or national origins, and references to a person's racial group refer to any racial group into which he falls.

(2) The fact that a racial group comprises two or more distinct racial groups does not prevent it from constituting a particular racial group for the purposes of this Act.

In two subsequent test cases,[7] 'ethnic group' was defined to include the Jewish and Sikh communities. In *Mandla*, the House of Lords identified seven characteristics relevant to identifying an ethnic group. The essential characteristics are:

— a long shared history, of which the group is conscious as distinguishing it from other groups; and the memory of which it keeps alive; and
— a cultural tradition of its own, including family and social customs and manners, often but not necessarily associated with religious observance.

---

[5] This approach is evident in the select committee's report (para 36) and the contribution made by Lord Parekh in the House of Lords on 10 December 2001 (*Hansard*: col 1186).

[6] See the case of *R v Chief Metropolitan Stipendiary Magistrate, ex parte Choudhury* [1991] 1 QB 429.

[7] *Seide v Gillette Industries Ltd* [1980] IRLR 427; *Mandla v Dowell Lee* [1983] 2 AC 548.

The other five relevant but not essential characteristics are:

— Either a common geographical origin, or descent from small number of common ancestors.
— A common literature, peculiar to that group.
— A common language, not necessarily peculiar to the group.
— A common religion, different from that of neighbouring groups or from the general community surrounding it.
— Being a minority or being an oppressed or a dominant group within a larger community.

Applying these same characteristics, however, in a number of test cases the courts have ruled that Muslims do not fall within the ambit of the Act. It is difficult to make sense of these decisions; difficult to see, for example, how the Jewish community fits the above criteria any more than the Muslim community, except perhaps on common ancestors, which in any case is not essential. The shorthand explanation often given is that the Act accommodates mono-ethnic religions but not multi-ethnic religions. There is no justification for such a distinction, and in view of section 3(2) of the Act—that for the purposes of the Act, a particular group need not comprise one distinct racial group but may comprise two or more distinct racial groups—and the fact that 99 per cent of British Muslims come from one or other racial or ethnic minority group, the judicial decisions and resultant shorthand distinction and explanation seem patently wrong.

The practical consequences of the courts' decisions were very significant. First, they legalised and legitimised very crude forms of religious discrimination against Muslims. Muslims could be discriminated against with impunity in employment, provision of goods, facilities and services, membership of organisations and disposal or management of premises, and law enforcement, regulatory and control functions, simply on the grounds of being Muslim. If the victim was from an ethnic community in which Muslims are a majority, for example, the Bangladeshi or Pakistani community, then they could challenge the discrimination under *indirect* racial discrimination. But if, for example, they were a Chinese, English or Caribbean Muslim, they would not be covered under indirect discrimination. In any case, even where they were covered under indirect racial discrimination, the offender would still not have to pay any compensation if there was no 'actual' *racial* motivation.

Secondly, they opened an enormous loophole in the laws against racial discrimination as provided in the Race Relations Act. Arabs, Bangladeshis, Pakistanis, Somalis, Turks, etc could now be legitimately targeted for discrimination, so long as the discrimination was based on religion and not race. The smart racists, of course, soon saw the possibility of using religion as a surrogate for continuing their racist policies and practices. As well as discrimination against Muslims purely on the basis of religion, there is now considerable evidence of how this surrogacy approach and mechanism operates. Campaigns by the BNP—for example, the campaign on 'Say NO to Muslim Businesses', demonstrate an overt exploitation of this surrogacy loophole. But the surrogacy loophole is also exploited in far more subtle forms which are not easily detectable except through long term monitoring of trends. Large-scale exploitation of this loophole, as is sometimes the case, of course, also makes a mockery of the original intentions behind the race relations legislation.

Thirdly, with a legitimate target being provided by the state while protecting other racial and religious minority groups, the focus of racial and religious discrimination by bigots, particularly those persistently seeking scapegoats, intensified disproportionately against Muslims. At a more subtle and possibly subconscious level, this was augmented by society generally through stereotypes and prejudices arising out of the rise of Islam internationally as the new enemy of the West; replacing Communism after the end of the Cold War. It is not surprising, therefore, that a Runnymede Trust report in 1997 on Islamophobia concluded:

> Such dread and dislike has existed in western countries and cultures for several centuries. In the last twenty years, however, the dislike has become more explicit, more extreme and more dangerous. It is an ingredient of all sections of our media, and prevalent in all sections of our society. Within Britain it means that Muslims are frequently excluded from the economic, social and public life of the nation . . . and are frequently victims of discrimination and harassment.

Nor is it surprising that a report commissioned by the Home Office from the University of Derby found that Muslims are most likely to feel religious discrimination.

Fourthly, it drove a wedge between those communities protected by race relations legislation and initiatives, the agencies enforcing these provisions, and the Muslim community. Muslims feel strongly that they are unjustly denied access to legislation and resources for protection against discrimination, that was initially intended for all ethnic communities. They perceive that the interpretation of the legislation by the courts has produced a hierarchy of protected race and faith groups, in which Muslims are at the bottom. They perceive British society as constituting different levels of citizenship and Muslims as third-class citizens. This perception of the law is fuelled by socio-economic disadvantage and underrepresentation in the major public and private sector institutions as discussed below. The result is alienation from state and society, sometimes leading to the disturbances such as those witnessed in northern cities in 2001. This then leads to further punishment of the community as a whole.

These inconsistencies, inequities and the hierarchy of protection creates the perception that some are more equal than others, some have greater rights to protection than others, some have a higher status of citizenship than others. This has been further ingrained and reinforced by the Race Relations Amendment Act 2000, which has upgraded the protection of some faith communities but not the protection of the Muslim community. Thus, for example, with regard to the Jewish and Sikh communities, all public sector agencies have a positive duty to proactively seek to eliminate discrimination and promote equality of opportunity, but not with regard to the Muslim community.

Such legalisation and legitimisation of discrimination undermines the very essence of the right to freedom of religion for Muslims. The recent regulations against discrimination on the grounds of religion or belief in employment are therefore a welcome change in direction. However, Muslims are still not to be protected against discrimination in delivery of goods and services, and law enforcement, regulatory and control functions. They are also still not to be supported by an equality commission until the creation of the new Commission for Equality and Human Rights, which will be restricted in the case of Muslims, but not some others, in the assistance that it may provide. It is clear from the above that the UK Government has failed in practice to fulfil its duty under Article 14, first, to secure adequately the Article 9 right, and secondly, where it has made certain provisions towards fulfilling this duty, it has failed to do so without discrimination between different faith communities. There are signs that these concerns are being recognised.

SECURING THE OTHER CIVIL AND POLITICAL RIGHTS IN THE HUMAN RIGHTS ACT

It is neither the intention, nor would it be possible within the space of this chapter, to address individually each of the other rights contained in the Human Rights Act in terms of how they are provided by the state across faith communities or accessed by the British Muslim community. However, we may nevertheless test with a few thematic case studies where in practice the UK stands with regards to Article 14 in terms of providing the other civil and political rights. We will do this with four thematic case studies on: (1) national security and anti-terrorism initiatives; (2) immigration and asylum; (3) crime, policing of crime and treatment by the criminal justice system; and (4) participation and representation in mainstream public life.

National Security and Anti-Terrorism Initiatives

The Terrorism Act 2000 provides a very wide definition of terrorism and gives the Home Secretary the power to proscribe organisations as terrorist without having to prove a case in court. The right of appeal against proscription is only to a special communion and not the courts. As a result of the very wide definition, the most tenuous association with any proscribed organisation may result in prosecution. The Act also gives the police 'a special arrest power' to enable them to arrest without warrant or evidence of any offence someone they suspect of 'involvement with terrorism'; general powers to stop and search people and vehicles 'for the prevention of terrorism'; and power to detain suspects for 48 hours without access to a lawyer if they believe that this access would lead, for example, to interference with evidence or alerting another suspect. Furthermore, the Act creates offences where the burden of proof may be placed on the accused to prove his innocence.

The Anti-terrorism, Crime and Security Act 2001 gives the police further powers to search and take photographs of anyone detained at a police station to determine their identity, using force if necessary, and require any person to remove face coverings or other items that conceal their identity. The Government has also derogated from the European Convention on Human Rights (ECHR), to enable the detention of foreign citizens suspected of terrorism. In December 2004 the House of Lords held that the practice violates the European Convention.

The provisions of the two terrorism Acts have raised concerns in many quarters. For example, in December 2001, the UNHRC criticised the powers of detention and questioned their compatibility with the UN Covenant on Civil and Political Rights, particularly Article 9 on arrests and Article 14 on fair criminal process. The committee warned also that they may have potential far reaching effects on other rights guaranteed in the Covenant. The committee suggested that there are other far less intrusive ways of achieving the same ends. The Joint Committee on Human Rights has questioned whether some of these powers are proportionate to the problems they seek to address, pointing out potential interference with rights guaranteed to ordinary citizens under the European Convention, such as the right to privacy.[8] MPs on the Home Affairs Select Committee have also voiced concerns,[9] as have many prominent and respectable NGOs, for example, Liberty, Justice and Amnesty International. The judgment of the Law Lords confirms many of these criticisms. The reality is that the anti-terrorism provisions have the potential to undermine the commitment to a culture of respect for human rights, eroding, for example: right to life; freedom from inhuman or degrading treatment; right to liberty and security of person; right to a fair trial; right to family life and privacy; right to freedom of religion; right to freedom of expression and information; right to assembly and association; right to peaceful enjoyment of possessions; right to education; right to free elections; and freedom from discrimination. Few disagree that, with the present levels of terrorist threats to the UK, the fight against terrorism must be robust. The concern, however, is that the present provisions are disproportionate and excessive, and therefore unacceptably infringe the civil rights of innocent people. There is yet a dearth of research to establish how the new provisions impact on people across different race and religious groups. However, the initial indications are that they have disproportionately targeted the British Muslim community. Thus, it would not be inappropriate to conclude that while

---

[8] Paras 61–64, 2001.
[9] HC 352, 15 November 2001.

the anti-terrorism provisions appear to be neutral, in practice they have impacted on the Muslim community disproportionately, and have therefore infringed the civil rights of that community disproportionately as compared to other faith communities. The provisions, therefore, discriminate in practice against the British Muslim community on their access to the other civil and political rights in the Human Rights Act.

Immigration and Asylum

The Race Relations Acts provide few exceptions to the general law applicable on racial discrimination. One notorious exception retained by the Race Relations (Amendment) Act 2000, however, is in the area of immigration and asylum. Thus, while racial discrimination is generally unacceptable, even by immigration officials, there is an exemption for nationality, immigration and asylum law, which allows the Home Secretary to discriminate on grounds of nationality or national or ethnic origin, or to authorise his officials to do so by way of guidance or instructions. Therefore, this specifically permits institutionalised racial discrimination without the need to justify differential treatment. The exemption permits instructions to be issued to officials to examine the claims of people from certain backgrounds more closely or sceptically, or to target them for detention or enforcement and action. In the context of the 'war on terrorism' (targeting particularly Islam and Muslims), the exemption allows the immigration service to be instructed to be discriminatory towards claimants from predominantly Muslim countries. Whether or not such instructions have actually been made, there is evidence that the discriminatory approach is being exercised in practice. In an article in *The Guardian*, suitably entitled 'Muslims need not apply', based on an analysis of statistics from British embassies, Raekha Prasad reports that 'applications to visit relatives in Britain from countries with large Muslim populations are twice as likely to be turned down than they were just over a year ago.'[10] She notes also that the 'biggest rises in refusals were for applications from the Middle East and the Indian sub-continent,' precisely where the vast majority of British Muslim families originate. The recent deliberate and specific targeting of Muslims is, of course, over and above the general impact of our draconian provisions against immigrants, asylum seekers and refugees. The experience of the recent deliberate and specific targeting is therefore additional to an already existing layer of historic and structural racial discrimination, particularly affecting Muslims. Thus, whilst our immigration and asylum provisions raise human rights concerns in general, they have a particularly detrimental impact on British Muslims.

---

[10] 16 April 2003.

Crime, Policing of Crime and Treatment by the Criminal Justice System

Analysis of the British Crime Survey in 2000 revealed that while minority populations are concentrated in large cities, in particular in conurbations where crime risks are high for everyone, ethnic minorities generally, and Muslims (Bangladeshis and Pakistanis) in particular, are at greater risk of victimisation. People from ethnic minorities, and Muslims in particular, worry more about crime than their white counterparts. This finding holds even when account is taken of the type of area in which respondents live, and their experience of crime. In terms of actual experience of crime, Muslims have a significantly higher risk of being victims of crime. Muslims are also least satisfied with the police response to sought contact and police efforts to keep them informed following their enquiry.[11]

The British Muslim experience of law enforcement agencies and the criminal justice system generally is negative, whether this is as victims, defendants or inmates.[12] The statutory sector's handling of the disturbances in the Northern cities highlighted many of the concerns regarding law enforcement and the criminal justice system long felt by the Muslim community. First, the issue of heavy-handed policing or unfair policing compared with others (eg, Muslims are more likely to be dealt with through arrests rather than summons). Secondly, disproportionately higher levels of charging by the police and the Crown Prosecution Service (eg, Muslims are more likely to be prosecuted than cautioned and charged with more serious offences than others). Thirdly, disproportionately harsher treatment by the courts (eg, Muslims are more likely to be remanded in custody and given higher levels of sentences). The net result of this sequence of discriminatory treatment by the law enforcement agencies is that it contributes to a disproportionately higher presence of Muslims in prisons. According to prison statistics for England and Wales, on 30 June 2000, there were 4,445 Muslims, as compared with 418 Sikhs and 254 Hindus, in prison.[13] The fourth major concern highlighted was the treatment of Muslim inmates, reinforced by the events leading up to and following the death in custody of Zahid Mubarak. What is of particular concern is not only the discriminatory provisions in legislation, but the sharp end of Islamophobia among prisoners and officers commonplace in day-to-day life in many prisons.

---

[11] A Clancy et al, *Crime, Policing and Justice: The Experience of Ethnic Minorities—Findings from the 2000 British Crime Survey* (BCS) (London, Home Office, 2001).

[12] See, eg, *Muslim Profiling* (London, Islamic Human Rights Commission, September 2002); S Tafadar, *The Hidden Victims of September 11: Prisoners of UK Law* (London, Islamic Human Rights Commission, September 2002); N Garcia, *A Report to the IHRC on Detentions under the Anti-terrorism, Crime and Security Act 2001* (London, Islamic Human Rights Commission, September 2002).

[13] It would be wrong to attribute the whole of this high presence of Muslims in prison to discrimination in the criminal justice system. Other contributing factors include, for example, the socio-economic and age profiles of the Muslim community. However, the presence of religious discrimination in the criminal justice system certainly contributes to the high presence of Muslims in prison.

Discriminatory treatment against Muslims by the law enforcement agencies in the manner described above, of course, carries practical implications for the level of access British Muslims have to the civil and political rights enshrined in the ECHR. These rights are disproportionately infringed as compared with others, and thus not equally secured as compared with people of other faiths.

Participation and Representation

There are three clearly identifiable areas that require attention: representation in politics and policy-making; media and popular culture; and mainstream public institutions. Representation here includes both visibility of Muslims in these sectors of British society and fair portrayal by these sectors. In politics and policy making, the Muslim complaint is primarily one of under-representation. If it is true that black and ethnic minorities are under-represented in mainstream politics,[14] then this is more so with representation of Muslims in mainstream British politics. Muslims make up 3 per cent of the British population but only 0.05 per cent of MPs. The absence of Muslims in the senior Civil Service and similar policy impacting positions is marked. The result is that Muslim concerns and viewpoints scarcely feature in mainstream politics and policy circles, and when they do so, they usually receive very negative and unsympathetic treatment; for example, the treatment in recent years of issues such as extremism and terrorism, immigration and asylum, law and disorder, and family-related matters. Each of them alienating the Muslim community that much further, presenting additional barriers to inclusion and mainstream participation, and affecting many civil and political freedoms and rights.

With regard to Muslim visibility in senior positions in public authorities, the under-representation of Muslims is again strongly felt, and the result is that the lack of sensibility and sensitivity to Muslims is not only felt at the political and policy level, but at the service delivery level. The combination of this with poor socio-economic conditions can then contribute both to alienation and social exclusion, and eventually to disenchantment and disturbance.[15]

In media and popular culture (the arts and sports), the complaint is again one of under-representation. But in addition to this, the most serious Muslim complaint is about how the media portrays Islam and ordinary Muslims. The perception here is not only that the media is Islamophobic, but that at least some sections of it are rabidly Islamophobic and that this is acceptable to a large

---

[14] See *A Progressive Future: IPPR's Agenda for a Better Society*, downloadable at: www.ippr.org.uk/about/pdf/agenda.pdf

[15] Many reports from the Muslim community have cited this combination as one of the primary reasons for the disturbances in the northern cities. See, for example, N Ahmed et al, *The Oldham Riots: Discrimination, Deprivation and Communal Tensions in the United Kingdom* (London, Islamic Human Rights Commission, 2001) and R Tarafder, *The Oldham Riots: Shattering the Myths* (London, Black Racial Attacks Independent Network, 2001).

section of the British public. This to some Muslims is very alienating and an immense barrier to feeling at ease with being British.[16]

The additional challenge with regard to representation is the ability to represent different parts of the British Muslim community. The challenge is to ensure that representation is not restricted to middle class, middle-aged Asian Muslim men. To overcome the representational barrier to citizenship, and provide equal access to civil and political freedoms and rights, means extending institutional engagement with Muslims to Muslim women, working class youth[17] and Muslims of different ethnic backgrounds.[18] As mentioned earlier, the rights in the HRA apply only in respect of the public sector. However, it is conceivable that such rights may be abused by the private and voluntary sector against Muslims, as against people of other religions. There is limited protection against such religious discrimination.

SECURING SOCIAL, ECONOMIC AND CULTURAL RIGHTS BEYOND THE HUMAN RIGHTS ACT

The HRA does not extend to social, economic and cultural rights, and as mentioned above, does not contain a free-standing non-discrimination clause that provides protection against religious discrimination in these additional fields of human rights. For protection against religious discrimination in these fields, faith communities must, on the whole, still rely on international and regional human rights instruments, institutions and mechanisms.

The socio-economic condition of the British Muslim community, as highlighted through the indicators of education, employment and wages, housing and health, in recent research,[19] is arguably the main reason for exclusion and a barrier to full citizenship. Economic and social exclusion is, in our view, involuntary. However, extreme economic and social exclusion can be a major contributory factor to the voluntary isolation of certain sections of the Muslim community, who then prefer to separate from mainstream economic, social and political activity. This may be the case particularly where it is perceived that the law provides little protection and reassurance against such economic and social exclusion. Socio-economic exclusion, leading to social isolation, was perhaps at

[16] See, eg, T Choudhury, *Monitoring Minority Protection in the EU: The Situation of Muslims in the UK* (London, Open Society Institute, October 2002).

[17] A frequent complaint by the youth in the northern cities during the disturbances, for example, was that they did not feel represented by the local Muslim political leaders (eg Councillors, etc) or the Muslim religious leaders.

[18] A stark example of 'under-representation amongst the under-represented' is the fact that although there are approximately 300,000 Arab Muslims in Britain, there are no Arab Muslim members of the House of Lords, MPs, MEPs and very few councillors, if any.

[19] T Modood, R Berthoud, *et al*, *Ethnic Minorities in Britain: Diversity and Disadvantage* (London, Policy Studies Institute, 1997); *Improving Labour Market Achievements for Ethnic Minorities in British Society—Interim Analytical Report* (Performance & Innovation Unit, February 2002).

the root of the breakdown in community cohesion in some northern cities in the summer of 2001. The socio-economic reintegration of the Muslim community, as a step towards better political engagement with the state and its institutions and fuller participatory citizenship, is therefore a key area for policy work and concrete strategic initiatives.

DEVELOPING A HUMAN RIGHTS CULTURE IN THE UK

We have so far highlighted where and how UK Muslims suffer religious discrimination. The remaining part of this chapter will consider how British Muslims, and faith communities generally, along with wider society may assist in developing 'a human rights culture'. The focus is on examining the potential for using 'human rights' as a strategy for addressing issues of concern to faith communities and the space human rights focused mechanisms can create for influencing policy to meet such concerns.

First, however, it is important to stress the importance of human rights as a language for public discussion and debate. Human rights are not just about law. Human rights provide a language and framework for discussion of public issues in a multi-faith and multi-cultural society. The title of Francesca Klug's book on the development of human rights legislation and policy in the UK, *Values in a Godless Age,* reflects her argument that, in a secular and multi-faith society, human rights provide the accepted language through which public debate and discussion can take place. It provides a way to articulate claims and a framework through which arguments about the priority between competing or conflicting interests can be weighed.

The idea behind the HRA was to generate cultural change in our institutions and public bodies and to provide a framework for officials (everyone from hospital administrators and probation officers to teachers and those running the local community leisure centre) to think about how they act and the services they provide. The Act has the potential, if the idea of using it for achieving cultural change is taken seriously, to impact on the way public services are delivered to faith communities. It provides an avenue through which faith communities can articulate their concern. This seems to have been lost, as the Act has shrunk to purely a legal instrument. An example of how human rights can be used to address issues of concern for faith communities can be seen in the case of *R v Newham LBC*.[20] In that case the education authority sent pamphlets to parents of prospective pupils setting out its policy on the allocation of places in secondary schools. The preference of parents for single sex schools was one criterion for selection. The applicant, K, had put down single sex schools for his first, second and third preference. The authority offered Z (K's child) a place in a co-educational (mixed sex) school. In his appeal to the High Court the

---

[20] [2002] EWHC 405 (Admin).

applicant argued that under the HRA the education authority was required by Article 2 of the First Protocol to the Convention to respect the right of parents to education and teaching in conformity with their religious convictions. The court accepted that in order to secure this right there were some positive duties on the state authorities. In particular, the education authority had to ascertain a parent's religious conviction and take this on board in formulating the education policy. In practical terms, this meant that the application form for places in secondary schools should include space in which parents could give reasons for their preferred option. As the education authority in this case had not done so, its decision was quashed and remitted for reconsideration. This example illustrates how issues that concern faith communities can be raised using the Act. It also shows the limitations that are contained in the Convention; the state is required to 'respect' the right of parents to education in conformity with religious convictions. The content of what is required to meet the duty of 'respect' is contested. In this instance the court held that respect requires the education authorities to take some actions, but it does not go so far as to require them to guarantee a place in a single sex school. The fact that this resulted in court action is to some extent a sign of ongoing failure to achieve a human rights culture within public authorities. A more active human rights culture would have picked this up at an earlier stage in the development of policy.

The next section explores the possible avenues through which the concerns of faith communities can be addressed.

ADDRESSING THE CONCERNS OF FAITH COMMUNITIES THROUGH A HUMAN RIGHTS CULTURE

One approach for faith communities would be to consider what are the pressing issues and concerns for them, as we have done for the Muslim communities above, and then to ask what role human rights can play in addressing those concerns. Once the issues have been identified, the next step is to identify the strategies human rights offer for addressing them. In relation to each issue there may be a variety of ways in which human rights provide an avenue for ensuring that the concerns of faith communities are considered in public policy. There are then a variety of mechanisms through which those concerns can be raised. In this final part of the chapter, we explore some possibilities.

Awareness Raising, Training and Guidelines

This includes awareness raising within the faith communities of the possibilities under the current provisions. The introduction of the Human Rights Act was accompanied by large-scale training and additional guidance to those working in public authorities, but that level of awareness raising and training needs to stretch far wider. The guidance and the training provide ways in which the concerns of faith communities can be raised. Where the policies or activities of public authorities raise concerns, an audit of the guidance and content of human rights training may be useful in addressing these.

Strategic Litigation

Strategic litigation provides an additional avenue. It involves taking up cases that have an importance beyond the immediate individual case. There are several options for faith communities seeking to raise issues through strategic litigation. The first would be to set up organisations with the capacity to undertake such litigation. This would require significant resources and require qualified lawyers and researchers. An alternative would be greater engagement and dialogue with human rights NGOs that already undertake such litigation. Research and policy papers would play an important part in highlighting the issues that concern faith communities that could then be advanced by such groups. Grassroots organisations will have access to local communities and be able to provide evidence of the experiences of those who have suffered human rights violations. Strategic litigation would also be an important way of testing out new laws, such as powers under anti-terrorism legislation, or the new employment directive on religious discrimination.

Casework

Casework would allow individuals to seek redress through the judicial process. Unlike strategic litigation, casework would seek redress in individual cases even where there is no wider public interest. The ability to undertake casework is closely linked to public funding for cases. Are there significant gaps in the funding of cases that are of significance to faith communities? One gap that may arise is in respect of funding for religious discrimination cases once the employment directive comes into effect. Is there a need for specific casework organisations, such as, for example, the Noor legal clinics for Muslim women? What, if any, support and assistance is needed for existing casework organisations such as law centres and CABs to ensure that they provide appropriate services to faith communities? Casework requires awareness on the part of members of faith communities of their rights and of the avenues for redress, so it would require development of effective strategies for reaching those who are often the most marginalised within the faith communities.

Engaging with Regional and International Human Rights Mechanisms

In the UK the ability to address effectively issues in terms of human rights is limited by the focus on the European Convention and its restriction to civil and political rights. Several European and international treaties provide further avenues, through their various reporting mechanisms, to raise concerns about violations of such civil and political rights. Some of the treaties, such as the International Covenant on Economic, Social and Cultural Rights and the European Social Charter, provide an international setting in which to focus attention on the issues of economic and social disadvantage experienced by faith communities. Additionally, the Council of Europe's Framework Convention for National Minorities provides an example of how an international process could provide a further level within which the views of minority faith communities can be raised. Faith communities, in recent years, have campaigned for statistics to be collected on the basis not only of ethnic identity, but of minority faith identities. The committee of experts that examined the UK's latest report under the Framework Convention also requested that in future information about faith communities be included in the report.

Policy-making Processes

Where there are government policies that adversely affect faith communities then, as well as the general policy consultation process, there are human rights focused review processes to follow. For example, concerns can be raised before the Joint Committee on Human Rights, the Human Rights Unit at the Department for Constitutional Affairs, and, in Northern Ireland, the Human Rights Commission.

CONCLUSION

Faith communities in the UK suffer infringements of human rights and religious discrimination. The degree to which they suffer depends on the religion in question. The case of UK Muslim communities serves to illustrate the nature and extent of the problem. Much can and needs to be done to redress this discrimination. This will be a key challenge for any new mechanisms established to protect and promote equality and human rights in Britain.

12

Children's Human Rights as a Force For Change

CAROLYNE WILLOW

INTRODUCTION

A T THE BEGINNING of the new millennium, a young person from the Article 12 self-advocacy organisation wrote for a Carnegie Young People Initiative pamphlet:

> To be a young person now is simply to see life from the outside. Not being able to interfere or effect any action that goes on around you. We see things—natural disasters, wars, politics—and we are neither asked about them, [nor] given the chance to change anything . . . To be a young person in the future is hopefully to see life from the inside.[1]

The year before, in January 1999, Paul Boateng, then Home Office minister, promised that the Human Rights Act 1998 would '. . . make a real difference to children's lives—and to the working practices of all public authorities who deal with children.'[2]

The Human Rights Act 1998 (HRA) has now been in force since October 2000. With the Act came high hopes—the three Cs. First, that human rights *casework* would increase, now that citizens of all ages could use domestic courts to seek a remedy for human rights violations. Secondly, that government would actively seek to ensure the *compatibility* of new legislation with the European Convention on Human Rights (ECHR). Thirdly, that over time this would lead to a transformation in the *culture* of our society. To what extent have human rights been a force for change in children's lives?

---

[1] The pamphlet explores young people's changing status and experiences at the turn of the new century—R Frost (ed), *Voices Unheard. Young People at the beginning of the 21st Century* (London, Carnegie Young People Initiative and The National Youth Agency, 2000).

[2] Extract from speech given at joint Children's Rights Alliance for England/Institute of Public Policy Research conference on *Children and the Human Rights Act 1998*, 26 January 1999.

THE STATE OF CHILDREN'S RIGHTS IN ENGLAND

A brief examination shows that all is not well with the state of children's rights in England.[3] The potential breaches of children's ECHR rights are plain to see. That there has been no legal challenge to most of these illuminates children's unique powerlessness; it also emphasises the failure to date of children's and human rights NGOs to use the HRA to protect children and their rights.

Civil and Political Rights

Children are the single biggest minority group in our country: 23 per cent of the population is aged 17 and under.[4] That is nearly 1 in 5 that has no vote. Simply being a child is seen as a legitimate reason for exclusion from the democratic process. Adults serving prison sentences are the main other class of people deemed unfit to mark their cross at election time.[5]

Babies and children are the only people whom it is legal to hit in the UK. The family home has been slowly opened to state intervention to give women better protection from violent partners, yet it remains firmly closed when it comes to the common assault of babies and children. The 'reasonable chastisement' defence was given statutory confirmation in the 1933 Children and Young Persons Act and has its roots in the 1860 case (*R v Hopley*) where a teacher beat to death a 13-year-old pupil. Section 58 of the Children Act 2004 leaves the defence of 'reasonable chastisement' intact in relation to the offence of common assault, removing it only in relation to more severe charges such as actual and grevious bodily harm and wounding. This means that parents appearing in court on a charge of common assault of a baby or child can still use the archaic defence—the prosecution not only has to prove that the parent assaulted the child, but that the assault was 'unreasonable'. In 2000, the Government issued a consultation document that asked whether the law should state that physical punishment which causes, or is likely to cause, injuries to a child's brain, eyes or ears can never be defended as reasonable.[6] At the end of 2002, the Secretary of State for Education and Employment was quoted in a Court of Appeal judgment as accepting that the ban on corporal punishment in schools did not interfere with parents' right to freedom of thought, conscience and religion because the

---

[3] For a fuller examination, see Children's Rights Alliance for England, *State of Children's Rights in England* (London, CRAE, 2004).

[4] Office for National Statistics, *Census 2001: Key Statistics for Local Authorities in England and Wales* (London, The Stationery Office, 2003).

[5] In 2003 the Electoral Commission carried out a public consultation, including with young people, on whether the voting age and candidacy should be reduced to 16 years.

[6] Department of Health, *Protecting Children, Supporting Parents. A Consultation Document on the Physical Punishment of Children* (London, DoH, November 1997)

law did not prevent a parent from administering corporal punishment *on behalf of a child's school.*[7]

Local authorities and the police have the power to 'curfew' children en masse; and police 'truancy sweeps' are an official mechanism for getting them back into school (imagine the outcry if the police were given the power to return alienated workers to their places of work). As direct advertising to 'tweenagers' booms, and 'pester power' enters our common language, it is becoming the norm for local shops to have a note on their door pronouncing 'no child without an adult' or 'only two children allowed in the shop at the same time.'

Education Rights

In education, crucial decisions about individual children are made in their absence. Parents not children have the legal right to appeal school exclusions, to be present at an appeal hearing, and to be notified of the decision. There is no requirement on schools to consult children about school uniforms. Children can be excluded for persistent and 'openly defiant' breaches of rules on uniform and appearance; aspects of the child's identity affected by such rules include hair colour and style, choice of footwear and coat, and the wearing of jewellery.

Children's behaviour outside school while on 'school business' is subject to the same behaviour policy. Even a child's behaviour while not on school business can be used as grounds for exclusion—if it takes place 'in the immediate vicinity of the school or on a journey to or from school.'[8]

Another issue relating to the right to freedom of expression is children being punished at school for expressing political opinions. Sixteen-year-old Sachin Sharma was temporarily excluded from school in March 2003 for urging fellow pupils to demonstrate against the invasion of Iraq.[9]

More than 100,000 disabled children continue to be educated in special schools, set apart from their neighbourhoods and their non-disabled peers. Segregated education infringes many of the human rights of disabled children.[10] It also impacts on their future quality of life, in adolescence and beyond and diminishes all children's experiences.[11] Children can still be withdrawn from sex education classes at the direction of their parents.[12]

Section 176 of the Education Act 2002, which provides for the Secretary of State to issue guidance on pupil participation, specifically excludes children in

[7] *R (Williamson and others) v Secretary of State for Education and Employment* [2002] EWCA Civ 1926.

[8] Department for Education and Skills, *Improving Behaviour and Attendance: Guidance on Exclusion from Schools and Pupil Referral Units* (London, DfES, January 2003).

[9] D Birkett, 'It's Their War Too', *The Guardian*, 25 March 2003.

[10] S Rustemier, *Social and Educational Justice. The Human Rights Framework for Inclusion* (Bristol, Centre for Studies on Inclusive Education, 2002).

[11] P Murray, *Hello! Are You Listening? Disabled Teenagers' Experience of Access to Inclusive Leisure* (York, Joseph Rowntree Foundation, 2002).

[12] S 405 Education Act 1996.

nursery education thus feeding the notion that babies' and young children's thoughts and feelings are not as important as older people's. Non-statutory guidance on complaints procedures in schools was finally issued in May 2003, but again it does not refer to children themselves making a complaint.[13]

Economic Rights

Childhood, like adulthood, can be blighted by poverty. From the age of 13, children can work part-time, and compulsory education ends at 16. The minimum wage was in October 2004 extended to 16 and 17-year-olds who have left full-time education, though the Government has introduced a third tier for this age group (in 2002, the UN Committee on Economic and Social and Cultural Rights criticised the UK for having a two-tier system, at that time applying to 18 to 20-year-olds and workers aged 22 and above). Asylum-seeking families continue to receive significantly less financial support from the state than other destitute families, with benefit rates for parents 24 per cent lower than non asylum-seeking parents.

Over one million children have been lifted out of poverty since 1997. The Treasury has introduced tax credits for low income parents and Child Trust Funds will give children born since September 2002 a small sum of money that can be added to throughout their childhood years. 'Sure Start' initiatives across the country are working with parents to improve the lives and future prospects of young children. Primary schools now give a piece of fruit daily to children; and various schemes have brought books to babies and young children in deprived areas. Educational maintenance allowances have been extended across the country, tackling the 'employment pull' faced by many 16 and 17-year-olds in poor families. None of this makes up for the outrage of the UK having the fourth richest economy in the world, while one in three of our children live in poverty.[14]

Lack of money has a particularly pernicious effect on the young: it takes its toll on children's developing bodies as well as on their growing minds. A national consultation with over one hundred 5 to 16-year-olds living in poor neighbourhoods in England found that childhood dreams can be wiped away by the daily grind of poverty. One teenage boy said that children's hopes and dreams could disappear at the age of 7 or 8 'when they notice they haven't got money or work.' A 12-year-old reported that dreams are wiped out 'not by you, but by your life'.[15]

---

[13] Department for Education and Skills, *School Complaints Procedure* (London, DfES, May 2003).

[14] Department for Work and Pensions, *Households below average income 2001/02* (London, DWP, 2003). This figure represents the number of children below 60 per cent contemporary median income.

[15] C Willow, *Bread is Free. Children and Young People Talk about Poverty* (London, Children's Rights Alliance for England and Save the Children, 2001).

Juvenile Justice

From the age of 10, children in England and Wales can be held criminally responsible for their actions. Few children's rights advocates would dispute the Government's view that children from this age usually understand their actions. The point of having a high age of criminal responsibility is not to infantilise children, or to give them special licence to hurt others. It is to keep children away from a system that is not geared to responding constructively to them as young people. In recent times, this was most graphically displayed when two 11-year-old boys were tried in 1993 for killing two-year-old James Bulger. A carpenter was brought in before the trial to raise the witness stand at Preston Crown Court; the boys would otherwise not have been able to see the courtroom. Mr Justice Morland, the presiding judge, decided the court would sit in school hours, in view of the young defendants' ages. There were few other concessions.[16]

Capital punishment in this country was abolished for children in 1908 and for adults in 1965.[17] The most serious penalty for criminal behaviour is, therefore, imprisonment. The UK has one of the worst records in Europe for locking up children. At any one time there are about 3,000 children behind bars in England alone. Just like poverty, incarceration has a profound impact on children's developing bodies and maturing minds. Hunger, lack of exercise and being kept away from fresh air and the sun all harm growing adolescents. So do broken ties with family, friends and formal education. At this stage in life, time counts for everything—adolescence is, after infancy, the most intense and life-changing period of human development.

In 1997 the then Chief Inspector of Prisons, Sir David Ramsbotham, called on the Government to remove responsibility for young offender institutions from the Prison Service.[18] The parliamentary Joint Committee on Human Rights (JCHR) repeated this recommendation in 2003.[19] The Government rejects the proposal, arguing that the Prison Service is capable of meeting the needs of children in custody. At the same time, it resists growing pressure to require the Prison Service to uphold the Children Act 1989, to safeguard and promote children's welfare.

Twenty-seven boys have died in custody since 1990: two were aged 14, four were aged 15, eight were 16-years-old, and 14 were 17-years-old. Seven were on

---

[16] B Morrison, *As If* (London, Granta, 1997).

[17] S 103 Children Act 1908 abolished capital punishment and life imprisonment for under-18s. On December 10 1999, the UK ratified the second Optional Protocol to the International Covenant on Civil and Political Rights, thus fully abolishing capital punishment (it was until that date still theoretically available for adults committing the offences of high treason and piracy).

[18] *Young Prisoners: A Thematic Review by HM Chief Inspector of Prisons for England and Wales* (London, HM Prisons Inspectorate, October 1997).

[19] Joint Committee on Human Rights, *The UN Convention on the Rights of the Child* (London, The Stationery Office, June 2003).

remand and had not been convicted.[20] Joseph Scholes hanged himself from the bars of his cell a month after his 16th birthday, just nine days after being given a two-year sentence for street robbery. His one previous offence was for affray, when he got into an altercation with ambulance staff after trying to kill himself. INQUEST and Nacro have joined forces with Joseph's mother in calling for a public inquiry. They report:

> Joseph was a deeply disturbed boy who had been repeatedly sexually abused from an early age . . . two weeks before his court appearance he disappeared into his room at the children's home and, taking a knife, slashed his face more than 30 times.[21]

In its response to the JCHR's critical report on the implementation of children's human rights, especially in the juvenile justice system, the Government retorts that we must remember that children who commit crimes *are not just children*.[22]

A flashback perhaps to the early 1990s, when Robert Thompson and Jon Venables, the two children who murdered the toddler James Bulger, were described by the presiding judge as acting with 'unparalleled evil and barbarity.'[23] The recent 'Shop a Yob' campaign run by *The Sun* newspaper to expose 'the animals that make your life a misery' is reminiscent of its campaign 10 years ago to have the two boys Thompson and Venables 'rot in jail'. Two days after *The Sun's* 'Shop a Yob' campaign began, the newspaper reported with satisfaction that a 16-year-old was 'caged' for three months for breaching an Antisocial Behaviour Order that prohibited him from drinking alcohol in public.[24] The 'Shop a Yob' campaign is not exclusively directed at children, though the ultimate solution to antisocial behaviour is seen to be located with them:

> . . . For years, teachers haven't been able to cane unruly pupils. The police can't deliver the old-fashioned short, sharp shock of a clip round the ear. There are even moves to ban parents from smacking children. Too many people in authority have been brainwashed that children lose self-esteem if they are punished.[25]

Children's falling independent mobility and decreasing use of public space was well documented over a decade ago,[26] before the proliferation of home computer games and the growth in parental fear of child abductors and paedophiles. Their diminishing freedom in public places has huge implications for children's quality of life, and for the status of childhood itself. The increasingly

---

[20] INQUEST and Nacro Campaign Briefing, *A Child's Death in Custody. Call for a Public Inquiry* (London, November 2003).

[21] INQUEST and Nacro Campaign Briefing, *A Child's Death in Custody. Call for a Public Inquiry* (London, November 2003).

[22] Joint Committee on Human Rights, *The Government's Response to the Committee's Tenth Report of Session 2002–03 on the UN Convention on the Rights of the Child* (London, The Stationery Office, 25 November 2003).

[23] E Pilkington, 'Boys Guilty of Bulger Murder' *The Guardian*, 25 November 1993.

[24] *The Sun*, 17 October 2003.

[25] *The Sun*, 15 October 2003.

[26] M Hillman, *One False Move . . . A Study of Children's Independent Mobility* (London, Policy Studies Institute, 1991).

cosseted lives of children arose from adult fears for them. Ironically, the more they have (been) moved indoors, the greater has become adults' fear of them. Cars certainly appear more welcome in our streets than groups of children. Cars emit noxious fumes, they take up a lot of space and they are noisy. Every day, two pedestrians in the UK die from being hit by a car. Still, there is no concerted campaign by government to rid our roads of nuisance cars, as there is with children. A recent DEMOS pamphlet argues that:

> Geography is a powerful metaphor for a wider issue—the space within which a child can be is physical, emotional, conceptual, virtual, social and political. Our tendency has been to enclose childhood, corralling it into dedicated spaces and institutions when, in fact, we need to learn how to integrate it into the whole of society . . .[27]

The Children's Society puts it more bluntly—in sharing the results of its poll of 2,600 7 to 16-year-olds about playing outside, the charity comments:

> Playing outdoors is a fundamental part of everyone's childhood, but that is being threatened by a culture of intolerance towards children's play in public. We are in danger of letting grumpy grown ups tidy our children away.[28]

New Attacks on Civil Rights

An Act has been passed through Parliament that criminalises any consensual sexual activity between children under the age of 16 (including kissing).[29] The Antisocial Behaviour Act 2003 gives the police powers to take home a person under the age of 16 who is out after 9 pm unsupervised by an adult;[30] and it grants the police, local education authorities and head teachers the power to issue fixed penalty notices to the parents of children who truant.[31] The Children Act 2004 provides for an electronic database to hold basic information on every child in the country. No evidence has been put forward from the Government that the electronic recording of the entire child population will enhance child protection.

WHAT HAVE HUMAN RIGHTS DONE FOR CHILDREN?

The European Convention on Human Rights

The European Convention on Human Rights (ECHR) was not designed with children in mind. Coming after the atrocities of Hitler (which deeply affected

---

[27] G Thomas and G Hocking, *Other People's Children. Why their Quality of Life is our Concern* (London, DEMOS, 2003).

[28] The Children's Society Press Release, *Grumpy Grown-ups Stop Play, Reveals Playday Research*. 6 August 2003.

[29] Ss 9–13, Sexual Offences Act 2003.

[30] S 30, Antisocial Behaviour Act 2003.

[31] *Ibid*, s 23.

[32] Up to one and a half million Jewish children, Gypsy children and disabled children were killed by the Nazis in Germany and Occupied Europe.

babies and children too),[32] the focus was on protecting the civil and political rights of adults. Despite its shortcomings as a treaty for children, it has brought some significant advances in UK law: the most notable being the abolition of corporal punishment in schools. The European Court of Human Rights in the 1982 *Campbell and Cosans* case[33] declared that objection to corporal punishment was a legitimate 'philosophical conviction' under the second sentence of Article 2, the state's obligation to respect the right of parents to ensure that children's education complies with their religious and philosophical convictions. The Court examined the ECHR as a whole and stated that philosophical convictions included those convictions 'as are worthy of respect in a "democratic society" . . . and are not incompatible with human dignity.' Further, the Court found that Jeffrey Cosans, who was suspended from school at the age of 15 for refusing to accept corporal punishment, had suffered a breach of his right to education. Jeffrey never returned to school after the incident, his parents' active objection to corporal punishment was seen as contravening school rules, and his suspension continued. The Court ordered the state to pay him £3,000 'moral damages'.

This case brought considerable weight to the 20-year campaign to outlaw corporal punishment in schools: Peter Newell reports, 'undoubtedly the crucial event of the campaign was the decision of the European Court of Human Rights . . . This forced the government's hand and ultimately led to abolition.'[34] Abolition in state schools across the UK came in 1987 and in private schools in England and Wales in 1998 and in Scotland in 2000. (In 2003 full abolition across the UK was finally achieved when corporal punishment was prohibited in private schools in Northern Ireland.)

Two European Court judgments in 2001 concern the responsibility of the state to protect children from abuse and neglect. The case of *TP and KM v UK*[35] concerned a four-year-old child (KM) who was taken into the care of a local authority after a disclosure of sexual abuse. The child's mother (TP) was deemed unfit to protect the child because her partner was the alleged perpetrator. Crucial to the case was a video recording of the child's disclosure: the mother was prohibited from seeing the video because of her relationship with the alleged perpetrator. A year after the forced separation between child and parent, the local authority acknowledged that there was 'doubt' about the identity of the alleged perpetrator. The Court held that there had been a breach of Article 8 in the failure of the local authority to seek a court decision about granting the mother access to the crucial video recording. There was also a breach of Article 13, in that neither applicant had an effective remedy. The Court awarded each applicant £10,000 compensation.

Z and others v UK ('the Bedfordshire case')[36] concerned the chronic neglect and abuse of four siblings, who were aged between 13 and 19 years by the time

---

[33] *Campbell and Cosans v UK* (1982) 4 EHRR 293.

[34] P Newell, *Children are People Too. The Case against Physical Punishment* (London, Bedford Square Press, 1989) 114.

[35] *TP and KM v UK* (10 May 2001) ECtHR Application no 28945/95.

[36] *Z and others v UK* (10 May 2001) ECtHR Application no 29392/95.

their case was heard by the European Court. Social services had known about the family since 1987, a year before the youngest applicant was born; the other three children were then aged five, three and one. It was not until 1992 that the children were taken into emergency care, at the mother's request. During the previous five years, the children had been subjected to 'horrific experiences' according to the consultant child psychiatrist. The Government did not dispute that the children's Article 3 right to protection from inhuman and degrading treatment had been violated. The Court reported, '[There is] no doubt as to the failure of the system to protect these child applicants from serious, long-term neglect and abuse.'

Significantly, in 1995, the House of Lords had rejected an appeal for a damages claim against the local authority, brought by the Official Solicitor. Lord Browne-Wilkinson judged that there had been no breach of statutory duty on the part of social workers or the local authority, noting:

> . . . it would require exceptionally clear statutory language to show a parliamentary intention that those responsible for carrying out these difficult functions should be liable . . . This is fertile ground in which to breed ill-feeling and resources will be diverted from the performance of the social service for which they were provided . . .

Lord Browne-Wilkinson declared that the statutory complaints procedure (under the Child Care Act 1980, now Children Act 1989) and the local authority ombudsman provided an effective remedy for maladministration in the child protection system. The European Court did not agree, declaring a breach of Article 13:

> . . . the outcome of the domestic proceedings [the children] brought is that they, and any children with complaints such as theirs, cannot sue the local authority in negligence for compensation, however foreseeable—and severe—the harm suffered and however unreasonable the conduct of the local authority in failing to take steps to prevent that harm. The applicants are correct in their assertion that the gap they have identified in domestic law is one that gives rise to an issue under the Convention . . . under Article 13 . . .

The compensation awarded to each of the applicants by the European Court ranged from £14,500 to £200,000, which took into account the need for ongoing psychiatric treatment for all four applicants. The Government observed that in future the HRA would enable victims of such negligence to seek redress, including compensation, in a domestic court.

In 2002, the European Court heard another case concerning child protection—*E and others v UK*.[37] Four siblings brought a claim to the European Commission in 1996. They contended that their local authority, Dumfries and Galloway Regional Council, had failed to protect them from abuse by their stepfather and that they had no effective remedy given the Bedfordshire House of Lords ruling in 1995 (see above).

---

[37] *E and others v UK* (26 November 2002) ECtHR Application no 33218/96.

The Court heard that in 1977 the stepfather (WH) was convicted of indecently assaulting E and L (then aged 17 and 13) and sentenced to two years' probation. At the end of 1988, the stepfather was further convicted of sexual offences against E, L and T (who by then were in their twenties). It was only through these criminal proceedings that the (now adult) children learned that WH had been previously subject to criminal proceedings and been placed on probation. In 1992, the applicants brought negligence proceedings against the local authority: after the Bedfordshire ruling they withdrew the application, on counsel's advice.

The European Court held that there had been a breach of Articles 3 and 13. As regards Article 3, the Court judged that:

> . . . the pattern of lack of investigation, communication and co-operation by the relevant authorities disclosed in this case must be regarded as having had a significant influence on the course of events and that proper and effective management of their responsibilities might, judged reasonably, have been expected to avoid, or at least, minimise the risk or the damage suffered.

The Court accepted the Government's argument that an effective remedy may now be available in domestic courts, especially since the passing of the HRA and the power of the courts to rely directly on the provisions of the ECHR. However, it concluded that in 1996 such a remedy was not available. Three applicants were each awarded €16,000 and the fourth (T—the youngest applicant) awarded €32,000 in compensation.

This case underlines the Government's contention that the HRA brings new and sufficient protection for children. However, the question remains whether a case such as *E v UK* could be properly brought in a domestic court. The Government argued that the European Court must not find WH guilty of mistreatment beyond what had been decided in a criminal court, given that he was not party to the proceedings. The Court dismissed this, stating, 'Criminal law liability is distinct from international law responsibility under the Convention, this Court not being concerned with reaching any findings as to guilt or innocence under domestic law.' It considered the full extent of WH's horrific mistreatment of the children. This included WH deliberately standing on one of the children's naked feet in his shoes and punching her in the stomach; and making the children punch and hit each other with whips and chains—such actions were never considered by a criminal court. Could a domestic court considering ECHR breaches admit evidence not previously brought to a criminal court that potentially implicates one or more party, even if it is pertinent to the human rights claim?

The Human Rights Act

What of domestic courts using the HRA to consider the protection of children? We have already seen the myriad ways in which children's ECHR rights are compromised or breached—in the family, at school, in their neighbourhoods and in prison. A positive example of the use of the ECHR relates to the lifetime injunctions granted in 2001 'openly against the world' to protect Jon Venables and Robert Thompson from identification after their release.[38] The two 18-year-olds had spent the preceding eight years in secure units for the murder of James Bulger, and applied for the injunction to prevent reprisals and revenge attacks: their application was unsuccessfully opposed by three large news groups. The granting of the injunction largely rested on the provisions of the ECHR, principally Articles 2 and 3, the right to life and the right to protection from inhuman and degrading treatment or punishment. Dame Elizabeth Butler-Sloss concluded:

> It is a very strong possibility, if not, indeed, a probability, that on the release of these two young men, there will be great efforts to find where they will be living and, if that information becomes public they will be pursued. Among the pursuers may well be those intent on revenge. The requirement in the Convention that there can be no derogation from the rights under Article 2 and 3 provides exceptional support for the strong and pressing social need that their confidentiality be protected.

The scope of the information to be protected was broad, including any information on the identity or future whereabouts of either applicant. Information leading to the identity of the secure units where the boys were separately held was protected for a 12-month period following their release dates. Butler-Sloss LJ did not extend the injunction to cover information relating to the boys' time in the secure units, as personal information was already covered by professional confidentiality. She included in her understanding of health confidentiality 'art or any other form of therapy, and to all those taking part in group therapy, and not only the therapist'.

Another significant case was the judicial review brought in 2002 by the Howard League for Penal Reform on the application of the Children Act 1989 to Prison Service accommodation holding children.[39] The Prison Service Order 4950, pertaining to juveniles (under 18s), then included a statement that 'The Children Act does not apply to under 18-year-olds in prison establishments.' Mr Justice Munby declared this sentence to be 'wrong in law', and held that sections 17 and 47 of the Children Act do apply to children in prison—the local authority's duty to safeguard and promote the welfare of children in need in its area; and the duty on local authorities to make enquiries into children suffering from, or at risk of, significant harm—'subject to the necessary requirements of imprisonment.'

The judge declared Prison Service *written policy* in relation to juveniles as 'more than adequately' meeting its human rights obligations. However, he expressed strong concerns about the *implementation* of this policy:

---

[38] *Venables and Thompson v News Group Newspapers Limited and Others* [2001] EWHC QB 32 (8 January 2001).

[39] *The Howard League for Penal Reform v The Secretary of State for the Home Department and Department of Health* [2002] EWHC 2497 QB (Admin) (29 November 2002).

If it really be the case, as the Chief inspector of Prisons appears to think, that there are YOIs which are simply not matching up to what the Children Act 1989 would otherwise require, if it really be that case that children are still being subjected to the degrading, offensive and totally unacceptable treatment described and excoriated by the Chief Inspector . . . then it can only be a matter of time . . . before an action is brought under the Human Rights Act 1998 by or on behalf of a child detained in a YOI and in circumstances where, to judge from what the Chief Inspector is saying, such an action will very likely succeed.

Mr Justice Munby declined to give a judgment as regards local authorities undertaking child protection investigations in young offender institutions, because it raised a question of policy. He did, however, reiterate that individual claims could be brought in relation to breaches of statutory duty under the Children Act or the ECHR. In other words, the door is open for hundreds if not thousands of children to seek redress for horrendous experiences in prison, as catalogued by the Chief Inspector of Prisons. Compensation for some, if not all of the families of the 27 children that have died in custody since 1990, should be high on the agenda, given the state's duty to protect the right to life.

The Howard League case was needed as a 'push' to NGOs. It was a reminder that human rights advocacy is not just about persuading government to do better for children. Indeed, in the most problematic areas of policy such lobbying is proving increasingly ineffective. Mr Justice Munby on several occasions remarked that he was being asked to consider practice in the abstract; that the boundary of the case was ultimately drawn close because there was no applicant before him. If human rights are to be a force for change for children, some real children need to enter courtrooms.[40]

But, as this edited collection makes clear, the Human Rights Act was never simply about litigation. Jack Straw, the Home Secretary who steered the Bill through Parliament, delivered a speech at St Paul's Cathedral on the day the Act came into force:

> The ECHR is relevant to the UK today—and tomorrow—because the basic values at its heart are timeless. They are about the equal worth of all, and the belief in our responsibility to create a society that advances such equal worth and dignity.[41]

For children, it is the Convention on the Rights of the Child, not the ECHR or HRA, that holds most promise for increasing their status, and promoting their equal worth as human beings.

---

[40] The Howard League for Penal Reform has a new legal department that is systematically bringing cases challenging the treatment of children in prison.

[41] Speech by Jack Straw MP, *Human Rights and Personal Responsibility. New Citizenship for a New Millennium*. St Paul's Cathedral, London, 2 October 2000.

The Convention on the Rights of the Child

It was in 1979, during the International Year of the Child, that the Government of Poland recommended to the UN Human Rights Commission that a human rights treaty be developed to protect the world's children. The UN Declaration on the Rights of the Child had already existed since 1959—it included ten principles on how children should be treated: the preamble urged 'mankind owes to the child the best it has to give.' It explained that 'the child, by reason of his physical and mental immaturity, needs special safeguards and care, including appropriate legal protection, before as well as after birth.' This Declaration was based on the Geneva Declaration of the Rights of the Child 1924, and complemented the Universal Declaration of Human Rights 1948, which applied to all members of the human family.

Unlike declarations, which are not binding, treaties place obligations on states parties. The UK ratified the CRC in December 1991, with all-party support, and in doing so agreed to implement the full range of economic, social, cultural and civil and political rights of children. Since its adoption by the UN General Assembly in 1989, the Convention has become the most ratified of all international human rights treaties—accepted by 191 states—all except the US and Somalia. The Convention's detailed principles and standards are binding on states which have ratified it. The Vienna Convention on the Law of Treaties of 1969 underlines: 'Every treaty in force is binding upon the parties to it and must be performed by them in good faith.'

Upon ratifying the CRC, states parties have to submit an initial report on implementation after two years, and a periodic report every five years thereafter. On 19 September 2002, the Committee on the Rights of the Child carried out a six-hour examination of UK progress in meeting its human rights obligations to children. Althea Efunshile, then Director of the Children and Young People's Unit, led the UK delegation of civil servants. Her team included senior officials from the Department of Health, the Home Office and the Department for Education and Skills, and from the devolved administrations of Northern Ireland, Scotland and Wales.

The Government examination followed a pre sessional meeting with UK non-governmental organisations in June 2002. The England delegation was co-ordinated by the Children's Rights Alliance for England and included representatives from The Children's Society and Save the Children, as well as self-advocacy organisations Article 12 and the Young People's Rights Network. Each of the children's rights alliances from the four countries of the UK made verbal submissions to the Committee on the Rights of the Child: the remainder of the three-hour session was taken up with formal questions and answers. During the lunch break, members of the committee had a meeting with young people from across the UK.

Earlier in the year, on 18 May 2002, over 80 children and young people took part in an event in London organised by the Young People's Rights Network.

Jaap Doek, the chair of the Committee on the Rights of the Child, was guest of honour: the event was organised as a court hearing with the Prime Minister as defendant facing various charges of breaching children's human rights. A team of prosecution barristers, in wigs and gowns, called different groups of children and young people from across England to give evidence on, for example, children in custody, the rights of young children, young people in care, and the experiences of lesbian, gay, bisexual and transgender young people. Evidence was also presented on why children and young people in England need a Children's Rights Commissioner. At the end of the day, all the children and young people in the audience (the jury) were asked to give their verdict on whether the Prime Minister was guilty as charged.

The Committee on the Rights of the Child's 'concluding observations' were published on 4 October 2002.[42] The Children's Rights Alliance for England had widely circulated in advance a press notice explaining the monitoring process, with a summary of the key issues the committee was expected to raise. The media coverage of the concluding observations was huge. The committee's strong words on the reasonable chastisement defence—'a serious violation of the dignity of the child'—occupied most newspaper headlines and television broadcasts. The committee's criticisms of the rising numbers of children in custody, and its concerns about health, education and child protection in young offender institutions were also aired. So too was the Government's unequal treatment of asylum seekers—by October 2002, legislation had been passed to provide for asylum-seeking children to be educated separately from other children, in accommodation centres. The committee noted that the 'ongoing reform of the asylum and immigration system fails to address the particular needs and rights of asylum-seeking children.' As in 1995, when the committee first assessed the UK's progress on implementation of the CRC, the committee was 'extremely concerned' at the high proportion of children living in poverty and the effect this has on children's enjoyment of their rights.

CHILDREN AS RIGHTS HOLDERS: BIG VISION, LITTLE PROGRESS

In 1995, Peter Newell warned that far too little had changed in children's lives and status, since the ratification of the CRC in 1991. 'So far most of this is paper progress, words on paper.'[43] That same year, Thomas Hammarberg wrote:

> The changes caused by the Convention, important as they are, have not gone very deep. It is, in fact, important to remain humble about progress. The real situation of many children is not radically improved.[44]

[42] Download from www.unhchr.ch/tbs/doc.nsf/(Symbol)/CRC.C.15.Add.188.En?OpenDocument

[43] P Newell, 'Conclusion: Rights, Participation and Neighbourhoods' in in P Henderson (ed), *Children and Communities* (London, Pluto Press, 1995) 198.

[44] T Hammarberg, *Making Reality of the Rights of the Child. The UN Convention: What it says and how it can Change the Status of Children Worldwide* (Sweden, International Save the Children Alliance, 1995).

This has ultimately been the problem: a huge lack of government engagement with children as rights holders has relegated their human rights treaty to the in-tray of a few civil servants. There has been no systematic review of law, policy and practice; and no national plan for the implementation of this critical treaty. The gains in children's rights that have occurred over the last decade, particularly in the last five years, are almost incidental to the CRC. From John Major to Tony Blair, we have not heard a single member of the Westminster Cabinet publicly support the principles or detailed provisions of the CRC for children across the UK. Plenty of goodwill has been shown to children's human rights as a force for change internationally. But the significance of the CRC to improving children's lives here *in our own country* continues to elude most senior politicians.

In April 2001, during a House of Commons debate on Hilton Dawson's Private Member's Bill on a Children's Rights Commissioner for England, Eric Forth MP made the following statement:

> . . . we signed [the Convention on the Rights of the Child] because we did not want to look like the bad guys. Successive Governments sign up to all sorts of conventions without any thought as to their relevance to our society and our way of life . . . For goodness sake, what do people in the United Nations know about the problems that parents in Chislehurst, Rother Valley or any other constituency face? Absolutely nothing . . . Let us put aside United Nations and European Council conventions right from the outset. Let us accept that they have no relevance whatever to parents and children in the United Kingdom.[45]

I was sitting in the Stranger's Gallery with young people from various self-advocacy organisations—Article 12, the British Youth Council, the National Black Youth Forum and the UK Youth Parliament. The high level of cynicism appalled them.

This politician's reflections on the UK Government's ratification in 1991 of the Convention on the Rights of the Child could be dismissed as idiosyncratic. That children's human rights are still so openly dismissed and so blatantly ignored raises uncomfortable questions. Who else besides Eric Forth thinks the real reason for ratifying the CRC was to make the UK look good?

Expectations were raised with the establishment of the Children's and Young People's Unit in the Department for Education and Skills, but with cross-departmental responsibilities, in 2000. The unit took over responsibility for the CRC from the Department of Health. This alone was hugely symbolic—moving responsibility for the CRC from a single department raised hopes that the Government was at last seeing children's human rights as a matter for all children.

The unit developed a draft overarching strategy for children, which briefly mentioned the CRC. Nearly a year later, in October 2002, the then Minister for Children and Young People, John Denham, promised expansion:

---

[45] Debate on Children's Rights Commissioner Bill, *Hansard*, HC Col 625, 6 April 2001.

The overarching strategy will take the Convention on the Rights of the Child as part of its framework and use the Convention's principles to inform all our future work with children.[46]

By the time of the launch of the Children's Green Paper in September 2003, the CRC had been excluded altogether. More than one hundred pages are devoted to describing how the Government plans to better protect children and to maximise their potential. The word 'rights' is not mentioned once.

The document contains many statements about the Government's commitment to listen to and involve children in improving public services. This is one area in which there has been huge progress, in and outside government. However, this infectious 'listening culture' is not usually located within the context of respecting and upholding children's human rights. No doubt that is why there are so many research projects on the benefits of participation; and it explains the preoccupation with 'what works' in listening to children. Imagine hundreds of thousands of pounds being spent trying to prove that listening to women makes us more productive workers or less moody partners. How baffling it would seem if men repeatedly carried out investigations into the best ways of involving women in decision making: we would probably get the impression that they regarded us as a different species.

A human rights framework would transform participatory initiatives with children—listening to children would not be seen as a means to educate, socialise or rehabilitate them, it would simply be the first step in recognising them as fellow human beings. The Green Paper proposal that made all the headlines was the establishment of an independent commissioner for children. A rights framework is even missing from this post. The legislation establishing independent children's champions and watchdogs in Wales, Northern Ireland and Scotland places a duty on each commissioner to promote and safeguard children's rights; and they all work (or will work) within the framework of the Convention on the Rights of the Child.[47] What is *so* threatening about children's human rights in our country? Perhaps it is the fear of having to give up power to those people who currently have so little. As Mary John explains:

> The reason the idea of children's rights frightens so many adults, who mutter 'What about responsibilities' is based on a false view of the sort of power children are after. It is assumed they seek a form of power which involves unlicensed freedom. This is not

---

[46] Westminster Hall debate on UN Convention on the Rights of the Child, 24 October 2002.

[47] Peter Clarke, Children's Commissioner for Wales, took up office in April 2001; Nigel Williams, Northern Ireland Commissioner for Children and Young People, took up office in October 2003; and the Scottish Children's Commissioner, Kathleen Marshall, took up post in April 2004. The legislation establishing the commissioners: Wales—Part V Care Standards Act 2000; The Children's Commissioner for Wales (Appointment) regs 2000; The Children's Commissioner for Wales regs 2001; and Children's Commissioner for Wales Act 2001; Northern Ireland—The Commissioner for Children and Young People (Northern Ireland) Order 2003; Scotland— Commissioner for Children and Young People (Scotland) Act 2003.

the case. Children are not out to grab some of the action of invested power. What is involved in the exercise of children's rights is working towards changing the relationship between adults and children so that, through participation and voicing, each person works towards understanding and respecting each other's realities and point of view.[48]

Or perhaps it is as fundamental and as simple as this boy's comment during a discussion about adult attitudes towards children's rights: 'They don't treat us like humans. They treat us like babies who can't talk.'[49]

Babies are human beings with rights too, but in this context babyhood is used as shorthand for non-human. As non-speaking humans they are completely at the mercy of adult empathy. Babies and very young children barely figure in human rights discourse: we have not even set off on the journey to discover how their human rights can be protected. We are 15 years into the Convention on the Rights of the Child. That the *concept* of rights is still so vociferously dismissed and so quietly ignored for children who can articulate their thoughts and feelings in obvious and direct ways—right in the face of adults—shows just how far we have to travel.

---

[48] M John, *Children's Rights and Power. Charging Up for a New Century* (London, Jessica Kingsley Publishers, 2003), 269.

[49] C Willow, *It's not Fair. Young People's Reflections on Children's Rights* (London, The Children's Society, 1999), 32.

Index